Critical Legal Studies

Critical Legal Studies

A Guide to the Literature

Richard W. Bauman

WestviewPress

A Division of HarperCollins*Publishers*

10007198736

Copyright © 1996 by Westview Press, Inc., A Division of HarperCollins Publishers, Inc.

Published in 1996 in the United States of America by Westview Press, Inc., 5500 Central Avenue, Boulder, Colorado 80301-2877, and in the United Kingdom by Westview Press, 12 Hid's Copse Road, Cumnor Hill, Oxford OX2 9JJ

A CIP catalog record for this book is available from the Library of Congress.
ISBN 0-8133-8980-1 (HC)

The paper used in this publication meets the requirements of the American National Standard for Permanence of Paper for Printed Library Materials Z39.48-1984.

10   9   8   7   6   5   4   3   2   1

Contents

Preface

Work on this guide began several years ago when I prepared a prototype of it for a class I was offering on critical legal theory. To help my students navigate their way through the mass of literature, in both legal and other types of periodicals, that has flourished in and around the critical legal studies movement, I arranged citations to some of the more salient sources (accompanied by brief notes) under convenient headings. I have retained the same format in this published version.

This guide is not meant to be exhaustively taxonomic, nor does it contain every possible item that might have been included. The structure I have adopted is largely arbitrary. The same themes and literature could have been organized differently. There are several things this guide does not accomplish. First, it does not pretend to define critical legal studies with any degree of specificity. The comments at the beginning of each section should be considered merely suggestive, rather than definitive. They are primarily descriptive and often derive from some, but not necessarily all, of the published work listed under the relevant heading. There is little attempt to evaluate the contributions of any particular authors or of the movement as a whole. Although some writers are mentioned in the text of the remarks, this does not mean that the work of other writers not mentioned is in some way inferior or secondary.

Users of this bibliography should also be cautioned that the suggested themes or views are not necessarily consistent with every published piece of work that could justifiably be called radical critique. The descriptive contents of this bibliography are intended merely to help the inquisitive reader on first acquaintance with contemporary critical analysis of the law. That reader must sample and wrestle with the readings themselves before reaching an independent perspective about any particular values, arguments or insights that mark the movement. Third, there is nothing official about this guide. Considered as a whole, the contents of this guide should confound any idea that critical legal studies, which is nothing if not polyphonal, is unified by any narrow program or particular set of presuppositions. It would be a travesty to reduce it to a school of settled legal thinking.

The Conference on Critical Legal Studies functions without many of the formal trappings of other organizations. Members of the Conference might understandably quarrel with the choice of literature contained in the bibliographical parts of this guide and with the comments that begin each section. Some of the authors cited here may indeed be surprised that their names can be associated with critical legal studies. Therefore, another caveat is in order. When a piece has been chosen for citation in this guide, the main criterion is not that the author has subscribed to the Conference on Critical Legal Studies, but that the work in some fundamental sense provides a critique of established legal doctrine or legal theory. Moreover, if it is not necessarily radical, at least it it takes up, or is influenced by, problems or ideas that preoccupy critical legal studies. In addition, there are items included here that avowedly criticize the approach that critical legal writing has adopted. I have aimed at providing a rounded, comprehensive guide that directs the reader to areas of friction as well as agreement.

Readers seeking directions toward relevant literature should keep in mind that I have generally avoided repeated citations of work which cuts across several different headings. Certain pieces, such as Duncan Kennedy's work on the evolution of forms of legal consciousness, is so stimulating that it deserves consultation in regard to a myriad of possible topics. The same could be said of other critical legal scholars, including Roberto Unger, Mark Tushnet, and Robert Gordon, to name a few of the formative figures in the movment. Consequently, this guide will prove most useful to the researcher who, while eager to range freely throughout the sources listed, is alert to the chance that a theoretical piece under one heading can throw light on a doctrinal issue included under a different heading. Of course, I expect that, by attempting to bring this literature together, the results will present an irresistible target for deconstruction or for an analysis, *à la* Foucault, of the urge to collect and classify.

Mindful of the potential risks of misrepresenting the literature of the movement and misleading students or other scholars looking at the literature for the first time, I have pondered whether it would be inadvisable to publish this bibliography. After weighing the pros and cons, I decided to let its fate rest on a coin toss. I flipped a quarter into the air and let it fall on my desk. This did not solve the problem I faced, for the coin landed on its edge, wobbled a bit, then rested upright. So I knocked it over and got the result I wanted.

Richard W. Bauman

Acknowledgments

While circulating in underground form, the bibliographical aspect of this guide was referred to in print by Mark Tushnet and David Kairys, both of whom have provided sound advice about its continued development. For helpful assessments of earlier drafts, I am grateful also to James Boyle, Richard Devlin, Neil Duxbury, Robert Gordon, Donna Greschner, Karl Klare, and David Schneiderman. Responsibility for any errors or omissions remains, however, solely my own.

The crucial steps in bringing this project to a publishable state were accomplished while I was a visitor at Duke University School of Law in 1994-95. I am grateful to Dean Pamela Gann, Associate Dean Judith Horowitz, and the members of the Duke faculty, a number of whom were lavish with encouragement and suggestions. In particular, my thanks are due for the comments and camaraderie provided by Kate Bartlett, Herbert Bernstein, George Christie, James Cox, Deborah DeMott, Martin Golding, Paul Haagen, Clark Havighurst, Donald Horowitz, Benedict Kingsbury, Madeline Morris, Jeff Powell, Theresa Newman, Tom Rowe, Robert Schapiro, Laura Underkuffler, William Van Alstyne, and Jonathan Wiener. The staff of the law library, and particularly Dick Danner, Mark Bernstein and Janet Sinder, were remarkably gracious and always helpful in responding to my requests.

In putting the finishing touches on this guide, I relied on Ann Wynn's adeptness in dealing with macros, master documents, and my own frequent requests for remedial computer tutoring.

I could not imagine a more helpful group of editors, led by Spencer Carr, than those I have dealt with at Westview Press. Cindy Rinehart especially has been perceptive, instructive, and boundlessly enthusiastic.

Assembling this guide has been a quirky venture, but the quirkiness would, I hope, appeal to someone like, say, the late Arthur Leff, an inspirational figure for those who try to make legal scholarship less arcane and more accessible for lawyers and non-lawyers alike.

R.W.B.

Critical Legal Studies

1

Bibliographies of Critical Legal Studies

The major bibliography of critical legal studies published to date was compiled by Duncan Kennedy and Karl Klare. It was based on numerous successive drafts of an unpublished bibliography that had circulated for several years. The compilers listed 203 authors and more than 500 pieces of work, mostly articles, that, in their view, appeared either to be critical legal work or to show, "even obliquely, a CLS influence, however defined." They did not attempt a comprehensive definition of critical legal studies. Inclusion in the Kennedy and Klare bibliography was based partly on responses to an invitation to members of the Conference on Critical Legal Studies to identify which of their own work they wished to see listed. The earliest pieces included were published in 1963, and thus represent a kind of proto-critical analysis.

Hunt's bibliography is more selective and covers U.S. literature published between the mid-1970s and 1984. His list cites 113 pieces written by 44 authors. Again, there is no definition of critical legal studies or much by way of criteria given for selection. It specifically excludes any British work "in the critical tradition."

* * * *

HUNT, Alan, "Critical Legal Studies: A Bibliography" (1984) 47 Mod. L. Rev. 369-74

KENNEDY, Duncan, and KLARE, Karl, "A Bibliography of Critical Legal Studies" (1984) 94 Yale L. J. 461-90

2

Introduction to Critical Legal Studies

Writers in a critical legal mode repeatedly point out that there is no single manifesto that represents the main themes or arguments of critical legal thought. Readers who are curious about this perspective are required, therefore, to delve into the literature itself and to develop a sense about the different currents (and crosscurrents) that run through the many published pieces. One of the main features of critical legal studies is its fragmentation. There are no uniformly accepted views and no canonical texts. A certain pride is taken in the heterogeneity of the movement. Such loose affiliation as there is seems to derive from critical legal writers working with many of the following assumptions and techniques.

Critical legal writers tend to be methodologically unorthodox and politically dissident. They aim to cause uneasiness among their more mainstream or traditional colleagues, unsettling the conventional understanding of legal practices and disrupting the ordinary modes of legal discourse.

Critical legal scholarship has been characterized as a successor to such earlier radical intellectual movements of the 1920s and 1930s as U.S. legal realism and progressivism. The similarities between realism and critical legal studies include: objections to the "formalism" of previous legal and social thought; skepticism about the extent to which legal precedent uniquely determines subsequent legal outcomes; emphasis on the interplay of external factors or biases, such as economic interests, in the development of legal doctrine; fear of the reification of legal concepts as if they were natural and necessary; and recognition of the extent to which legal doctrine and legal institutions are contingent products in an evolutionary process of social change.

Critical legal writers distinguish themselves from realist predecessors by rejecting the earlier faith in the instrumental use of social science to find legal solutions. They also repudiate the general reformist bent and moderate liberalism of realist scholars. Critical legal writing is marked by its dedication to transforming legal practices to serve the values of equality and social solidarity. The critique of law, its theories, and its institutions is meant to break down hierarchies of gender, race, class, or so-called merit. By honing this political edge, the contemporary radical critique supplements and builds on realist insights and arguments. Critical legal studies goes beyond realism by claiming that legal reasoning is not only on occasion policy-oriented, but it is imbued with politics.

The main site of critical legal activity has tended to be law schools, mainly in the U.S., but also law schools scattered around the common law world. Much of the work of the movement has been, in the words of Peter Fitzpatrick, "curricular and institutional." The scholarship of the movement has been both theoretical and doctrinal. There is some tension between proponents of these different activities. At the level of theory, some critical legal writing has ambitiously sought to erect a complete social theory, of which law forms one dimension. By contrast, other articles produced from a critical legal perspective tend to be less grand, doctrinal analyses. Robert Gordon has argued that critical legal studies should not be viewed as offering a "global philosophy," but rather a "set of local critiques of local situations and discourses." Of course, writers such as Roberto Unger have both practiced theorizing on a grand scale, and also engaged in close doctrinal commentary and reconstruction.

While some writers within the movement have called for more practical strategies that would take the benefits of the critique outside the academic realm, there is also a strain of critical legal writing which resists the impulse to engage in everyday politics. At least one plausible way of beginning to overcome the "politics of stasis" is to start with the processes of law-making and legal training, to use "local strategies" to change our understanding, as well as the content, of the law.

Textual explication forms a major part of critical legal work. Through it, the radical critics have attempted to show the indeterminacy, incoherence, and contradictions contained in legal doctrine. At the time of the formation of critical legal studies, writers such as Duncan Kennedy used structuralist techniques to expose the assumptions underlying traditional legal discourse. In particular, abstract principles such as freedom of contract or the right of an individual to own and use property were examined for their ideological content. Other critical legal writers (such as Morton Horwitz) have studied the economic aspects of developed legal doctrine to try to explain the tilt exhibited by modern liberal-legal regimes. Since that first generation of critical legal scholarship, other techniques, often derived from disciplines outside law, have been used for critical purposes. These include semiotics, phenomenology, hermeneutics, and deconstruction. It is difficult to ascertain whether critical legal studies is so thoroughly a modernist approach to legal thinking that it cannot adapt to a postmodernist turn.

Overall, critical legal writing has challenged complacency and tried to reveal the contestable normative underpinnings of the law. It has censured traditional legal scholarship for its narrow dogmatism. In the words of Mark Tushnet, critical legal studies, if it has any particular program, is dedicated to the process of "interminable critique." Because the critique never rests, there is a general aversion to providing a utopian reconstruction of current liberal society.

* * * *

BOLIEK, Robert, Jr., "The Two Worlds of the Trashers and the Locust-Eaters: Flushing CLS From Out of the Bramble Bush" (1985) 37 Ala. L. Rev. 89-118

BOYLE, James (ed.), *Critical Legal Studies* (New York: New York University Press, 1994)

DUXBURY, Neil, *Patterns of American Jurisprudence* (Oxford: Clarendon Press, 1995) 420-509

FITZPATRICK, Peter, and **HUNT**, Alan (eds.), *Critical Legal Studies* (Oxford: Basil Blackwell, 1987)

FRASER, David, "What a Long, Strange Trip It's Been: Deconstructing Law From Legal Realism to Critical Legal Studies" (1988-89) 6 Austl. J. L. & Soc'y 35-43

FRUG, Gerald E., "A Critical Theory of Law" (1989) 1 Legal Educ. Rev. 43-57

GOODRICH, Peter, "Critical Legal Studies in England: Prospective Histories" (1992) 12 Oxford J. Legal Stud. 195-236

GORDON, Robert W., "Law and Ideology" (1988) 3(1) Tikkun 14-18, 83-86

GORDON, Robert W., "Unfreezing Legal Reality: Critical Approaches to Law" (1987) 15 Fla. St. U. L. Rev. 195-220

GRIGG-SPALL, Ian, and **IRELAND**, Paddy (eds.), *The Critical Lawyers' Handbook* (London: Pluto Press, 1992)

HAGER, Mark, "Against Liberal Ideology" [review of Mark Kelman, *A Guide to Critical Legal Studies*] (1988) 37 Am. U. L. Rev. 1051-76

HUTCHINSON, Allan C. (ed.), *Critical Legal Studies* (Totowa, N.J.: Rowman and Littlefield, 1989)

HUTCHINSON, Allan C., and **MONAHAN**, Patrick, "Law, Politics, and the Critical Legal Scholars: The Unfolding Drama of American Legal Thought" (1984) 36 Stan. L. Rev. 199-245

JABBARI, David, "Critical Legal Studies: A Revolution in Legal Thought?" in Zenon Bankowski (ed.), *Revolutions in Law and Legal Thought* (Aberdeen: Aberdeen University Press, 1991) 153-65

KAIRYS, David (ed.), *The Politics of Law: A Progressive Critique* (New York: Pantheon Books, 1982)

KAIRYS, David (ed.), *The Politics of Law: A Progressive Critique*, 2nd rev. ed. (New York: Pantheon Books, 1990)

KELMAN, Mark, *A Guide to Critical Legal Studies* (Cambridge, Mass.: Harvard University Press, 1987)

LEITER, Brian, "Current Debates: Critical Legal Studies" (1988) 3(5) Tikkun 87-91

MENAND, Louis, "Radicalism for Yuppies: What Is Critical Legal Studies?" (March 17, 1986) 194(11) New Republic 20-23

MEZEY, Naomi, "Legal Radicals in Madonna's Closet: The Influence of Identity Politics, Popular Culture, and a New Generation on Critical Legal Studies" (1994) 46 Stan. L. Rev. 1835-61

MINDA, Gary, "The Jurisprudential Movements of the 1980s" (1989) 50 Ohio St. L. J. 599-662

MINDA, Gary, *Postmodern Legal Movements* (New York: New York University Press, 1995) 106-27

NOTE, "CLS: A Pathfinder Into the Gospel of Radical Reformation" (1988) 8 Legal Ref. Serv. Q. 107-34

NOTE [Debra Livingston], "'Round and 'Round the Bramble Bush: From Legal Realism to Critical Legal Scholarship" (1982) 95 Harv. L. Rev. 1669-90

OETKEN, J. Paul, "Form and Substance in Critical Legal Studies" (1991) 100 Yale L. J. 2209-28

PRESSER, Stephen B., "Some Realism About Orphism or the Critical Legal Studies Movement and the New Great Chain of Being: An English Legal Academic's Guide to the Current State of American Law" (1984-85) 79 Nw. U. L. Rev. 869-99

SCHLEGEL, John Henry, "Critical Legal Studies for the Intelligent Lawyer" (Jan., 1988) 60 N.Y. St. Bar J. 10, 15, and 64

TUSHNET, Mark, "Critical Legal Studies: An Introduction to Its Origins and Underpinnings" (1986) 36 J. Legal Educ. 505-17

WHITE, G. Edward, "From Realism to Critical Legal Studies: A Truncated Intellectual History" (1986) 40 Sw. L. J. 819-43

3

The Special Role of
Roberto Unger

When the Conference on Critical Legal Studies was first organized, Roberto Mangabeira Unger, a Brazilian scholar teaching at Harvard Law School, had just published two texts about legal and social theory. In *Knowledge and Politics*, Unger claims to have identified the ideas central to a single style of thought that has profoundly gripped the modern mind. Together, these ideas form what Unger calls "liberalism." According to Unger, that system of ideology has epistemological, moral, psychological, as well as political elements. Unger's book offers a synthesized reconstruction of this dominant system of ideas. He subjects these liberal ideas to a "total critique." On his account, the principles underlying liberal conceptions of society, the self, human nature, and the kinds of relationship fostered by a liberal-legal regime, all founder because they lead to insoluble paradoxes. He concludes that there can be no satisfactory theory of society or law, so long as we continue to reside in the "prison-house" of modern liberalism. In bold and broad strokes, his writing is aimed at emancipating contemporary social and legal thought.

In *Law in Modern Society*, Unger engages in a complementary study. Where in *Knowledge and Politics* he was concerned to re-frame political philosophy, in *Law in Modern Society* he examines concepts of modernity and law (particularly the rule of law) as they have been treated by such thinkers as Durkheim, Marx, and Weber. After discussing the place of law in various selected societies (which typify tribal, aristocratic, and liberal social orders), he attempts to recast the aims, concepts, amd methodology of social theory itself. Unger concludes by favoring an "interpretive" method that avoids as much as possible the weaknesses and limitations of earlier social thought.

Unger's reformulation of the main tenets of liberalism proved very influential on critical legal writing in the late 1970s and throughout the 1980s. In particular, other scholars referred to Unger's critique of the distinctions between fact and subjective value, reason and desire, and self and community. A conception of social life relying on individualist and subjectivist assumptions make a defensible liberal theory impossible. Unger's view of the systematic failures of liberal political theory has been invoked repeatedly by subsequent radical critics of liberal legalism.

Though he has not positioned himself within any particular branch of critical legal studies, Unger responded to the growth of critical legal literature in *The Critical Legal Studies Movement*. In this essay, a shorter version of which was originally delivered as a lecture in 1982, Unger identified what he took to be the assumptions, purposes and achievements of critical legal work. He briefly mentions a couple of "tendencies" within the movement. He calls these the "structuralist" view, exemplified by Duncan Kennedy's analysis of Blackstone, and the functionalist/radical view, to be found in Morton Horwitz's history of nineteenth-century U.S. law. These two tendencies do not exhaust the range of critical legal literature: many pieces fall under neither description. Unger treats both these tendencies as essentially critical, rather than constructive. A large part of his essay is devoted to showing how doctrinal criticism can lead to the formulation of alternative institutional programs. To illustrate this, Unger discusses two examples of "deviationist doctrine," involving, first, the equal protection clause of the U.S. Constitution and, second, classical contract principles.

In his comprehensive trilogy, published in 1987 under the general title *Politics*, Unger offers a sweeping vision of modern social thought, programmatic proposals for setting up a genuinely democratic society, and background comparative studies on selected nations at various stages in their historical development. In the second of the three volumes, *False Necessity*, Unger entwines theoretical with programmatic discussion. He provides a vision of social reconstruction remarkable for its grandeur and optimism. Unger's program for a revolutionary democracy requires first of all the breaking up of "formative contexts," which include "entrenched social roles and hierarchies." His program is meant to surmount the routine sensibility that, on Unger's view, informs modern political debate. In place of established structures, Unger recommends revolutionizing governments, economies, and workplaces, all with the goal of furthering individual and collective empowerment.

His scheme involves reinventing social and political institutions on a massive scale. The process of experimentation would be endless. Creating an empowered democracy would require fundamentally altering personal relationships; mobilizing grassroots efforts to achieve governmental power; restructuring government to ensure that power is neither too centralized nor too diffuse; and fostering economic arrangements by guaranteeing a cluster of basic rights that Unger prescribes. These rights are supposed to preserve social plasticity, so that individuals are no longer confined within limiting social or institutional roles. Unger's vision significantly tries to avoid the implications of Weber's concept of the "iron cage" of bureaucracy and the economic consequences of modern rationality. In Unger's scheme, there is a great deal of emphasis on the power of imagination and the need to recharge politics with a post-liberal spirit. His prescribed society of civic participation and constant revision of organizations has appealed to critical legal writers who prize the pleasures of a robustly democratic polity.

Unger's role within critical legal studies is singular because he has tried (somewhat heroically) to portray liberalism from a world-historical framework. The scope of his work dwarves any other critical legal discussion of philosophical, historical, or sociological issues. In addition, Unger has been the architect of a post-liberal society, complete down to minute details. Despite his general approval of critical legal attempts to undermine the formative contexts perpetuated by law, Unger himself remains something of an interested bystander in relation to the movement. He shares with critical legal writers a sense of the political futility associated with contemporary liberalism, but he alone has articulated an imaginative alternative to modern states which would engender a widespread spiritual as much as a political revolution.

* * * *

Works by Unger:

UNGER, Roberto Mangabeira, *Knowledge and Politics* (New York: Free Press, 1975)

UNGER, Roberto Mangabeira, *Law in Modern Society* (New York: Free Press, 1976)

UNGER, Roberto Mangabeira, *Passion: An Essay on Personality* (New York: Free Press, 1984)

UNGER, Roberto Mangabeira, *The Critical Legal Studies Movement* (Cambridge, Mass.: Harvard University Press, 1986) [originally published in (1983) 96 Harv. L. Rev. 561-675]

UNGER, Roberto Mangabeira, *Politics: A Work in Constructive Social Theory*, three vols. (Cambridge: Cambridge University Press, 1987) including:

Vol. 1   *Social Theory: Its Situation and Its Task*;

Vol. 2   *False Necessity: Anti-Necessitarian Social Theory in the Service of Radical Democracy*; and

Vol. 3   *Plasticity into Power: Comparative-Historical Studies on the Institutional Conditions of Economic and Military Success.*

Works about Unger:

ALFORD, William P., "The Inscrutable Occidental? Implications of Roberto Unger's Uses and Abuses of the Chinese Past" (1986) 64 Tex. L. Rev. 915-72

ANDERSON, Perry, "A Dream of Change" [review of Roberto Unger, *Politics*] (Jan. 13-19, 1989) Times Lit. Supp. 37-38

ANDERSON, Perry, "Roberto Unger and the Politics of Empowerment" in *A Zone of Engagement* (London: Verso, 1992) 130-48

ASARO, Andrea, "The Public-Private Distinction in American Liberal Thought: Unger's Critique and Synthesis" (1983) 28 Am. J. Juris. 118-48

BALL, Milner, "The City of Unger" (1987) 81 Nw. U. L. Rev. 625-63

BOYLE, James, "Modernist Social Theory: Roberto Unger's *Passion*" (1985) 98 Harv. L. Rev. 1066-83

CHAFFIN, Deborah, "Passion and the Ethic of Empowerment" [review of Roberto Unger, *Passion*] (1985) 6 Cardozo L. Rev. 987-96

CLEARY, J. C. and **HIGONNET**, Patrice, "Plasticity Into Power: Two Crises in the History of France and China" (1987) 81 Nw. U. L. Rev. 664-92

COLLINS, Hugh, "Roberto Unger and the Critical Legal Studies Movement" (1987) 14 J. L. & Soc'y 387-410

CORNELL, Drucilla, "Beyond Tragedy and Complacency" (1987) 81 Nw. U. L. Rev. 693-717

DEVLIN, Richard F., "On the Road to Radical Reform: A Critical Review of Unger's *Politics*" (1990) 28 Osgoode Hall L. J. 641-721

DUNN, John, "Unger's *Politics* and the Appraisal of Political Possibility" (1987) 81 Nw. U. L. Rev. 732-50

DUXBURY, Neil, "Look Back in Unger: A Retrospective Appraisal of Law in Modern Society" (1986) 49 Mod. L. Rev. 658-79

EIDENMÜLLER, Horst, "Rights, Systems of Rights, and Unger's System of Rights" (1991) 10 L. & Phil. 1-28, 119-59

EWALD, William, "Unger's Philosophy: A Critical Legal Study" (1988) 97 Yale L. J. 665-756

FRASER, Andrew, "Reconstituting Enlightened Despotism" [review of Roberto Unger, *Politics*] (1988-89) 78 Telos 169-82

GALSTON, William A., "False Universality: Infinite Personality and Finite Existence in Unger's *Politics*" (1987) 81 Nw. U. L. Rev. 751-65

HARRIS, J. W., "Unger's Critique of Formalism in Legal Reasoning: Hero, Hercules, And Humdrum" (1989) 52 Mod. L. Rev. 42-63

HAWTHORN, Geoffrey, "Practical Reason and Social Democracy: Reflections on Unger's *Passion* and *Politics*" (1987) 81 Nw. U. L. Rev. 766-90

HERZOG, Don, "Rummaging Through the Emperor's Wardrobe" [review of Roberto Unger, *Politics*] (1988) 86 Mich. L. Rev. 1434-49

HOBSON, J. Allan, "Psychiatry as Scientific Humanism: A Program Inspired by Roberto Unger's *Passion*" (1987) 81 Nw. U. L. Rev. 791-816

HOLMES, Stephen, *The Anatomy of Antiliberalism* (Cambridge, Mass.: Harvard University Press, 1993) 141-75

HOLMES, Stephen, "The Professor of Smashing" [review of Roberto Unger, *Politics*] (Oct. 19, 1987) The New Republic 30-38

HUTCHINSON, Allan C., "A Poetic Champion Composes: Unger (Not) on Ecology and Women" [review of Roberto Unger, *Politics*] (1990) 40 U. Toronto L. J. 271-95

HUTCHINSON, Allan C. and **MONAHAN**, Patrick J., "The 'Rights' Stuff: Roberto Unger and Beyond" (1984) 62 Tex. L. Rev. 1477-1539

ISENBERGH, Joseph, "Why Law?" [review of Roberto Unger, *The Critical Legal Studies Movement*] (1987) 54 U. Chi. L. Rev. 1117-23

JUDT, Tony, "Radical Politics in a New Key?" (1987) 81 Nw. U. L. Rev. 817-31

KRONMAN, Anthony T., Review of Roberto Unger, *Knowledge and Politics* (1976) 61 Minn. L. Rev. 167-205

LEFF, Arthur Allen, "Memorandum" [review of Roberto Unger, *Knowledge and Politics*] (1977) 29 Stan. L. Rev. 879-89

LESSIG, Lawrence, "Plastics: Unger and Ackerman on Transformation" (1989) 98 Yale L. J. 1173-92

MILLER, Jeremy M., "A Critical Analysis of the Theories of Professor Unger" (1985) 12 W. St. U. L. Rev. 563-75

PANNIER, Russell, "Roberto Unger and the Critical Legal Studies Movement: An Examination and Evaluation" (1987) 13 Wm. Mitchell L. Rev. 647-83

PATEMAN, Carole, Review of Roberto Unger, *Passion* (1986) 96 Ethics 422-23

POWELL, H. Jefferson, "The Gospel According to Roberto: A Theological Polemic" [1988] Duke L. J. 1013-28

POWERS, Gerard F., "Critical Legal Bishops: Roberto Unger, the Catholic Bishops, and Distributive Justice" (1985) 2 Notre Dame J. L. Ethics & Pub. Pol'y 201-42

ROOS, John, "Unger and Aquinas on Universals and Particulars" (1993) 38 Am. J. Juris. 63-84

RORTY, Richard, "Unger, Castoriadis, and the Romance of a National Future" (1988) 82 Nw. U. L. Rev. 335-51 [reprinted in *Essays on Heidegger and Others: Philosophical Papers, Vol. 2* (Cambridge: Cambridge University Press, 1991) 177-92]

SIMON, William H., "Social Theory and Political Practice: Unger's Brazilian Journalism" (1987) 81 Nw. U. L. Rev. 832-68

SMOLIN, David M., "Roberto Unger's Theory of Personality, Law and Society: Critique and Proposal for a Revised Methodology" (1986) 55 U. Cin. L. Rev. 423-48

SNOWDEN, John Rockwell, "Miller on Unger: Another Story in Response" (1985) 13 West. St. U. L. Rev. 183-200

SPITZ, Derek, "Solidarity and Disaggregated Property Rights: Roberto Unger's Recasting of Democracy" (1991) 23 Colum. Hum. Rts. L. Rev. 43-92

SUNSTEIN, Cass R., "Routine and Revolution" (1987) 81 Nw. U. L. Rev. 869-93

TRUBEK, David M., "Radical Theory and Programmatic Thought" [review of Roberto Unger, *Politics*] (1989) 95 Am. J. Soc. 447-52

TURLEY, Jonathan, "The Hitchhiker's Guide to CLS, Unger, and Deep Thought" (1987) 81 Nw. U. L. Rev. 593-620

VAN DOREN, John W., "Understanding Unger" (1990) 16 Wm. Mitchell L. Rev. 57-105

VAN ZANDT, David E., "Commonsense Reasoning, Social Change, and the Law" (1987) 81 Nw. U. L. Rev. 894-940

WEINRIB, Ernest J., "Enduring Passion" [review of Roberto Unger, *Passion*] (1985) 94 Yale L. J. 1825-41

WEST, Cornel, "Between Dewey and Gramsci: Unger's Emancipatory Experimentalism" (1987) 81 Nw. U. L. Rev. 941-51

WEST, Cornel, "Critical Legal Studies and a Liberal Critic" (1988) 97 Yale L. J. 757-71 [reprinted in *Keeping Faith: Philosophy and Race in America* (New York: Routledge, 1993) 207-25]

WOODARD, Calvin, "Toward a 'Super Liberal State'" [review of Roberto Unger, *The Critical Legal Studies Movement*] (Nov. 23, 1986) N.Y. Times Bk. Rev. 27-29

YACK, Bernard, "Towards a Free Marketplace of Social Transformation" [review of Roberto Unger, *Politics*] (1988) 101 Harv. L. Rev. 1961-77

4

History of the Conference on Critical Legal Studies

Largely due to the efforts of David Trubek, Duncan Kennedy, and Mark Tushnet, the first meeting of the Conference on Critical Legal Studies was held in Madison, Wisconsin in the spring of 1977. Schlegel and Tushnet have each given an account of the initial attempts to organize the Conference, in which different views were registered about how formal should be the group's structure, as well as which legal academics should be invited. Although its first few meetings were for invitees only, the Conference quickly opened up to broader participation. Affiliation with critical legal studies now depends on self-identification. Such popular events as annual summer camps are attended by large numbers of scholars seeking a stimulating forum and a supportive environment. Although the Conference has by some accounts expanded into a movement (with connotations of political aims, strategizing and coalitions), Tushnet has more recently preferred to describe critical legal studies as a "political location," a metaphor of place signifying an area within which scholars associate with one another in research, mutual education, and a social network. Tushnet credits Duncan Kennedy in particular with realizing that critical legal studies should operate primarily to provide scholars with opportunities to exchange ideas about advanced and politically acute legal scholarship, rather than as an intellectual program that would embrace particular beliefs (either by prescription or by subscription).

Schlegel's account outlines in general terms what appeared to be the most important intellectual orientations of the original participants in the Conference. These range from a kind of orthodox Marxism (involving, for example, the historical determination of political and legal ideas and institutions by underlying social and economic relations), to a more critical Marxism (that denied any laws of historical change and emphasized instead historical contingency, human agency, and the totality of relations between legal ideas and material conditions of a society). A third significant perspective represented at the founding of the Conference derived from the social science movement in U.S. law schools. This latter kind of study was less interested in legal doctrine, and concentrated more on empirical studies of the relationship between "law on the books" and "law in action." These social scientists were less concerned than other members of the Conference about exposing and deconstructing the ideological content of liberal legalism.

Although this description might have captured the range of interests and methods represented in the initial discussions of a renewed leftist perspective in the legal academy, the subsequent history of critical legal studies has shown fragmentation of radical critiques into many more projects, some of them in tension with one another. Schlegel's account breaks off with a brief indication of how feminist studies might influence critical thinking. The more recent discussion by Tushnet analyzes what a difference to the critical agenda has been made by the growth of feminist legal scholarship (some of which, with greater or lesser degrees of sympathy, takes critical legal studies to task), minority scholarship, cultural radicalism, and postmodernism.

Tushnet emphasizes that leftist thinking in the law schools is not subtended completely by critical legal studies: other kinds of political commitments are still present. He also claims that critical thinking has undergone a process of assimilation. It has been "tolerated and contained" by the mainstream elements in the legal academy, notwithstanding a rightward shift in U.S. national politics. This general acceptance of critical legal studies as a novel "perspective" alongside, for example, feminism, has not precluded some instances of discrimination against practitioners of a radical critique. There are, in other words, limits to the acceptability of critical legal studies. In a "weakened form," mainstream legal scholarship has acknowledged some merit in the radical critique of law as a matter of politics (all the way down). In Tushnet's view, some of the potentially explosive effects of critical legal studies have been (to date, at least) defused.

* * * *

SCHLEGEL, John Henry, "Notes Toward an Intimate, Opinionated, and Affectionate History of the Conference on Critical Legal Studies" (1984) 36 Stan. L. Rev. 391-411

TUSHNET, Mark, "Critical Legal Studies: A Political History" (1991) 100 Yale L. J. 1515-44

5

Symposia on Critical Legal Studies

If the publication of a special issue devoted to a topic or perspective marks its coming of age, then critical legal studies can be said to have arrived with the appearance in 1984 of a symposium in the *Stanford Law Review*. That collection of essays included substantive contributions from several prominent members of the movement, reflecting the diverse strands of thinking that were growing under the rubric of radical critique. The symposium remains one of the most interesting attempts to bring together critical legal work and juxtapose it with both sympathetic and rather unfriendly appraisals.

In the interests of promoting balance, and also presumably to avoid confusing its readers, the *Cardozo Law Review* symposium divided contributions into several categories, including: histories of the movement, scholarship from inside the movement, and responsive scholarship from outside the movement. Note, however, that it, along with several other of the symposia listed below, failed to include any women among its contributors. Subsequent symposia in U.S. legal periodicals, particularly those addressing the relationship among progressive movements, such as feminism, critical legal studies, and race critique, embrace a broader range of authors.

Since 1990, *Law and Critique*, a journal devoted to publishing legal articles from a critical perspective, has been appearing semi-annually in the U.K.

* * * *

Critical Legal Studies Symposium (1984) 36 Stan. L. Rev. 1-674

Authors include: Peter Gabel and Duncan Kennedy; Robert W. Gordon; Thomas C. Heller; Allan C. Hutchinson and Patrick J. Monahan; Phillip E. Johnson; Mark G. Kelman; Lewis A. Kornhauser; John Henry Schlegel; Louis B. Schwartz; D. L. Shapiro; William H. Simon; Edward Sparer; David M. Trubek; Mark Tushnet; and G. Edward White.

Symposium: A Critique of Rights (1984) 62 Tex. L. Rev. 1363-417

Authors include: Mark Tushnet; Michael J. Perry; Staughton Lynd; Michael E. Tigar; Allan C. Hutchinson and Patrick J. Monahan; Anthony Chase; Peter Gabel; and Steve Bachmann.

Perspectives on Critical Legal Studies (1984) 52 Geo. Wash. L. Rev. 239-88

Authors include: Mark Tushnet; David Kairys; Peter Gabel; and Wythe Holt.

(1985) 6 Cardozo L. Rev. 693-1031

Authors include: Stephen Diamond; Arthur J. Jacobson; Jay M. Feinman; Kenneth M. Casebeer; William S. Blatt; Alan D. Freeman and John Henry Schlegel; Aviam Soifer; William W. Bratton, Jr.; Charles M. Yablon; Paul M. Shupack; and Anthony D'Amato.

A Symposium of Critical Legal Studies (1985) 34 Am. U. L. Rev. 929-1262

Authors include: James Boyle; Duncan Kennedy; Mary Joe Frug; K. C. Worden; John Moon; Donald R. C. Pongrace; Judith A. Harris; and Stephen Brainerd.

Professing Law: A Colloquy on Critical Legal Studies (1986) 31 St. Louis U. L. J. 1-109

This takes the form of a lecture by Sanford Levinson, followed by responses from John E. Dunsford; James R. Elkins; Jay M. Feinman; Gary Minda; Thomas L. Shaffer; Robert L. Stenger; and Joseph P. Tomaine.

(1987) 14 J. L. & Soc'y 1-197

Authors include: Peter Fitzpatrick; Alan Hunt; Paul Hirst and Phil Jones; Costas Douzinas and Ronnie Warrington; Anne Bottomley, Susie Gibson and Belinda Meteyard; Nikolas Rose; Roger Cotterrell; Hugh Collins; Devid Nelken; Joanne Conaghan and Louise Chudleigh; Paddy Ireland; Ian Grigg-Spall and Dave Kelly; Francis Snyder; and Alan Thomson.

6

Legal History

From a critical legal perspective, traditional legal historiography suffers from any number of serious faults. These tendencies may be more insidious than obvious. Among these is the tendency to present legal developments in a narrative fashion as if the law could be periodicized and rationally reconstructed without much reference to social, political or economic context. Also, critical legal literature has heavily criticized attempts to construct an objective or scientific methodology for legal history.

Another flaw arises out of what some critical legal writers have called a particular form of meta-narrative associated with "presentism," where the historical account assumes that past changes have represented steps in an inexorable march of progress. Developments are treated merely as as prologue to the present, in which, of course, legal achievements have reached their highest pitch.

A further problem arises when the legal historian treats an earlier period as marked by a particular set of ideas or ideologies. These can become blinders that do not permit the historian to recognize the dynamic interplay of different values and institutions in the development of an era.

Conventional legal historiography can also become prey to a simplistic conception of the relations between law, society, the economy, and political institutions and practices. For example, the view that law simply responds to external forces, and is determined largely by economic or social interests, has been rejected by many critical legal historians. This kind of analysis fails to capture the multifarious relations among different social constructs, whereby the economy, the government, what counts as property, and employment and personal affiliations are all constituted, defined, and sustained by law. There is a larger complex of forces that legal historians should identify.

Historical work from a critical legal perspective is often concerned with the following goals. The author might view historical writing as a creative and interpretive task, rather than an attempt to recount some objective truth about the past. Revising traditional historical accounts, frequently by reference to new perspectives, such as feminism, race, or the situation of an author outside the mainstream, is a common practice in critical legal histories. Instead of treating a historical period or subject as understandable through a few values or ideals, the critical legal historian might try to show how contested and contradictory were the values debated within that period or surrounding that subject. The object is to recreate specific details and render a textured account. To this end, critical legal historians rely on a wealth of sources besides simply case reports or other official legal materials. In the process, critical legal historians have shown they are prepared to deal in normative issues, to show how historical writing is itself fraught with political meaning.

Critical legal historians have developed a wide array of views on how best to explain the interrelationships of law, society, economics, and politics. Among the best known are the two volumes by Morton Horwitz tracing U.S. legal history, published fifteen years apart. Horwitz claims to show, first, how a general conception of law arose in the nineteenth century, which ultimately favored the interests of commercial firms. In his first volume, Horwitz charts a direct relationship between law, society and the expanding U.S. economy. Then, in his recent book, Horwitz shows how, in the current century, an orthodoxy arose among lawyers, judges, and scholars which served to protect the gains that commerce had made. In turn, this dominant form of legal thinking, called "classical legal thought," was challenged and replaced by "progressive legal thought." Horwitz's approach in his second volume reveals an increasingly complex sense of the relationship between law and other social constructs.

* * * *

BINDER, Guyora, "Angels and Infidels: Hierarchy and Historicism in Medieval Legal History" (1986) 35 Buffalo L. Rev. 527-99

DIAMOND, Stephen, "Not-So-Critical Legal Studies" (1985) 6 Cardozo L. Rev. 693-711

DUXBURY, Neil, "The Theory and History of American Law and Politics" (1993) 13 Oxford J. Legal Stud. 249-70

FEINMAN, Jay, "The Role of Ideas in Legal History" [review of G.

Edward White, *Patterns of American Legal Thought*] (1980) 78 Mich. L. Rev. 722-36

FRASER, Andrew, "Legal Amnesia: Modernism Versus the Republican Tradition in American Legal Thought" (1984) 60 Telos 15-52

GENOVESE, Eugene D., "Law and the Economy in Capitalist America: Questions for Mr. Hurst on the Occasion of His Curti Lectures" [1985] Am. Bar Fdn. Res. J. 113-22

GOODRICH, Peter, "Poor Illiterate Reason: History, Nationalism and the Common Law" (1992) 1 Social & Legal Stud. 7-28

GORDON, Robert W., "Critical Legal Histories" (1984) 36 Stan. L. Rev. 57-125

GORDON, Robert W., "The Elusive Transformation" [review of Morton J. Horwitz, *The Transformation of American Law, 1870-1960: The Crisis of Legal Orthodoxy*] (1994) 6 Yale J. L. & Hum. 137-62

GORDON, Robert W., "E. P. Thompson's Legacies" (1994) 82 Geo. L. J. 2005-11

GORDON, Robert W., "Historicism in Legal Scholarship" (1981) 90 Yale L. J. 1017-56

GORDON, Robert W., "The Ideal and the Actual in the Law: Fantasies and Practices of New York City Lawyers, 1870-1910" in Gerard W. Gawalt (ed.), *The New High Priests: Lawyers in Post Civil War America* (Westport: Greenwood Press, 1984) 51-74

GORDON, Robert W., "J. Willard Hurst and the Common Law Tradition in American Legal Historiography" (1975-76) 10 L. & Soc'y Rev. 9-55

GORDON, Robert W., *Lawyers as the American Aristocracy* (Cambridge, Mass: Harvard University Press, forthcoming)

GORDON, Robert W., "The Politics of Legal History and the Search for a Usable Past" (1990) 4 Benchmark 269-81

GORDON, Robert W., Review of Charles M. Cook, *The American Codification Movement, A Study of Antebellum Legal Reform* (1983) 36 Vand. L. Rev. 431-58

GORDON, Robert W., "Willard Hurst as a Colleague" [1980] Wis. L. Rev. 1123-33

GORDON, Robert W. and **NELSON**, William, "An Exchange on Critical Legal Studies between Robert W. Gordon and William Nelson" (1988) 6 L. & Hist. Rev. 139-86

HARRING, Sidney and **STRUTT**, Barry R., "Lumber, Law and Social Change: The Legal History of Willard Hurst" [1985] Am. Bar Fdn. Res. J. 123-37

HARTOG, Hendrik, *Law in the American Revolution and the Revolution in the Law: A Collection of Review Essays on American Legal History* (New York: New York University Press, 1981)

HARTOG, Hendrik, "Pigs and Positivism" [1985] Wis. L. Rev. 899-935

HARTOG, Hendrik, *Public Property and Private Power: The Corporation of the City of New York, 1730-1870* (Chapel Hill: University of North Carolina Press, 1983)

HAY, Douglas, "The Criminal Prosecution in England and Its Historians" (1984) 47 Mod. L. Rev. 1-29

HAY, Douglas and **SNYDER**, Francis (eds.), *Policing and Prosecution in Britain, 1750-1850* (Oxford: Clarendon Press, 1989)

HERGET, James E., "Unearthing the Origins of a Radical Idea: The Case of Legal Indeterminacy" (1995) 39 Am. J. Legal Hist. 59-70

HOLT, Wythe, "Morton Horwitz and the Transformation of American Legal History" (1982) 23 Wm. & Mary L. Rev. 663-723

HORWITZ, Morton J., "The Conservative Tradition in the Writing of American Legal History" [review of Gerald Dunne, *Justice Joseph Story and the Rise of the Supreme Court* and James McClellan, *Joseph Story and the American Constitution: A Study in Political and Legal Thought*] (1973) 17 Am. J. Legal Hist. 275-94

HORWITZ, Morton J., "The Historical Contingency of the Role of History" (1981) 90 Yale L. J. 1057-59

HORWITZ, Morton J., "History and Theory" (1987) 96 Yale L. J. 1825-35

HORWITZ, Morton J., Review of Grant Gilmore, *The Ages of American Law* (1978) 27 Buffalo L. Rev. 47-53

HORWITZ, Morton J., "The Rise of Legal Formalism" (1975) 19 Am. J. Legal Hist. 251-64

HORWITZ, Morton J., *The Transformation of American Law, 1780-1860* (Cambridge, Mass.: Harvard University Press, 1977)

HORWITZ, Morton J., *The Transformation of American Law, 1870-1960: The Crisis of Legal Orthodoxy* (New York: Oxford University Press, 1992)

KENNEDY, Duncan, "Toward an Historical Understanding of Legal Consciousness: The Case of Classical Legal Thought in America, 1850-1940" in Steven Spitzer (ed.), *Research in Law and Sociology*, vol. 3 (Greenwich: JAI Press, 1980) 3-24

KOFFLER, Judith, "Some Contributions of Edward I to the Capitalist Transformation of England" in Steven Spitzer (ed.), *Research in Law and Sociology*, vol. 3 (Greenwich, Conn.: JAI Press, 1980) 107-26

KONEFSKY, Alfred, "Introduction" to Alfred Konefsky and Andrew King (eds.), *The Papers of Daniel Webster (Vol. 1): Legal Papers, The New Hampshire Practice* (Hanover, N.H.: University Press of New England, 1974) xxxi-xxxix

KONEFSKY, Alfred S., "Of the Early History of Lower Federal Courts, Judges, and the Rule of Law" [review of Kermit Hall, *The Politics of Justice: Lower Federal Judicial Selection and the Second Party System, 1829-1861* and Marie K. B. Tachau, *Federal Courts in the Early Republic: Kentucky, 1789-1816*] (1981) 79 Mich. L. Rev. 645-52

KONEFSKY, Alfred, Review of Maxwell Bloomfield, *American Lawyers in a Changing Society, 1776-1876* (1977) 90 Harv. L. Rev. 829-35

LINDGREN, Janet, "Beyond Cases: Reconsidering Judicial Review" [1983] Wis. L. Rev. 583-638

LINEBAUGH, Peter, *The London Hanged: Crime and Civil Society in the Eighteenth Century* (Cambridge: Cambridge University Press, 1992)

LYND, Staughton, "In Memoriam: E. P. Thompson" (1994) 82 Geo. L. J. 2013-23

MAZOR, Lester, Review of Grant Gilmore, *The Ages of American Law* (1978) 46 Geo. Wash. L. Rev. 520-26

MAZOR, Lester, Review of Lawrence Friedman, *A History of American Law* (1975) 60 Minn. L. Rev. 147-61

MENSCH, Elizabeth, "The History of Mainstream Legal Thought" in David Kairys (ed.), *The Politics of Law: A Progressive Critique* (New York: Pantheon Books, 1982) 18-39

MENSCH, Elizabeth, "The History of Mainstream Legal Thought" in David Kairys (ed.), *The Politics of Law: A Progressive Critique*, 2nd rev. ed. (New York: Pantheon Books, 1990) 13-37

MOGLEN, Eben, "The Transformation of Morton Horwitz" [review of Morton J. Horwitz, *The Transformation of American Law, 1870-1960*] (1993) 93 Colum. L. Rev. 1042-59

PRESSER, Stephen B., "Revising the Conservative Tradition: Towards a New American Legal History" (1977) 52 N.Y.U. L. Rev. 700-25

PRESSER, Stephen B. and **HURLEY**, Becky Blair, "Saving God's Republic: The Jurisprudence of Samuel Chase" [1984] U. Ill. L. Rev. 771-822

REIFNER, Udo, "The Bar in the Third Reich: Anti-Semitism and the Decline of Liberal Advocacy" (1986) 32 McGill L. J. 96-124

RUBIN, G. R. and **SUGARMAN**, David, *Law, Economy and Society, 1750-1914: Essays in the History of English Law* (Abingdon: Professional Books, 1984)

SNYDER, Francis and **HAY**, Douglas (eds.), *Labourer, Law, and Crime: A Historical Perspective* (London: Tavistock, 1987)

STONE, Katharine V. W., "A Tribute to E. P. Thompson, Chronicler of the Dispossessed" (1994) 82 Geo. L. J. 2025-37

SUGARMAN, David, "'A Hatred of Disorder': Legal Science, Liberalism and Imperialism" in Peter Fitzpatrick (ed.), *Dangerous Supplements: Resistance and Renewal in Jurisprudence* (Durham: Duke University Press, 1991) 34-67

SUGARMAN, David, "Law, Economy and the State in England, 1750-1914: Some Major Issues" in David Sugarman (ed.), *Legality, Ideology, and the State* (London: Academic Press, 1983) 213-66

SUGARMAN, David, "Lawyers and Business in England, 1750-1950" in Carol Wilton (ed.), *Beyond the Law: Lawyers and Business in Canada, 1830-1930* (Toronto: The Osgoode Society, 1990) 437-79

SUGARMAN, David, "The Legal Boundaries of Liberty: Dicey, Liberalism, and Legal Science" (1983) 46 Mod. L. Rev. 102-11

SUGARMAN, David, Review of Morton Horwitz, *The Transformation of American Law, 1780-1860* (1980) 7 Brit. J. L. & Soc'y 297-310

SUGARMAN, David, "Theory and Practice in Law and History: A Prologue to the Study of the Relationship between Law and Economy from a Socio-Historical Perspective" in Bob Fryer *et al.* (eds.), *Law, State and Society* (London: Croom Helm, 1981) 70-106

SUGARMAN, David, "Writing 'Law and Society' Histories" [review of W. R. Cornish and G. de N. Clark, *Law and Society in England, 1750-1950*] (1992) 55 Mod. L. Rev. 292-308

TUSHNET, Mark V., *The American Law of Slavery, 1810-1860: Considerations of Humanity and Interest* (Princeton: Princeton University Press, 1981)

TUSHNET, Mark, "A Comment on Critical Method in Legal History" (1985) 6 Cardozo L. Rev. 997-1011

TUSHNET, Mark, "Perspectives on the Development of American Law: A Critical Review of Friedman's *A History of American Law*" [1977] Wis. L. Rev. 81-109

TUSHNET, Mark V., "The Warren Court as History: An Interpretation" in Mark V. Tushnet (ed.), *The Warren Court in Historical and Political Perspective* (Charlottesville: University of Virginia Press, 1993) 1-34

WHITE, Jefferson, "Representing Change in Early American Law: An Alternative to Horwitz's Approach" in William Pencak and Wythe W. Holt, Jr. (eds.), *The Law in America, 1607-1861* (New York: New York Historical Society, 1989) 238-68

7

Legal Theory

Among the most important motifs in critical legal theory has been its challenge to the view that law is composed primarily of determinative rules that are logically applied by neutral adjudicators to reach predictable, correct results. Critical legal authors have rejected, for example, H. L. A. Hart's explanation of law as essentially consisting in different types of rules whose legitimacy depends on their valid adoption by relevant authorities. Hart's theory had allowed for a limited zone of indeterminacy. It arises out of the "penumbra" surrounding the core meaning of general terms used in legal discourse. Radical theorists have grave doubts about the the essentialist conception of law as a system of primary or secondary rules, where the characteristic dispute is at an analytic or linguistic level.

Ronald Dworkin's attempt to show, in discussing Hart, that law is more than rules, that it consists also in background ethical principles which can be authoritatively introduced in legal reasoning, has fared no better than the simpler rule-centered approach. Critical legal authors have rejected Dworkin's conception of the political basis of adjudication. For Dworkin, law is related to politics, but not in the sense represented by the radical critique. While the Dworkinian judge, faced with a hard case, could as least notionally invoke abstract principles that belong to "the soundest theory of the settled law" (this is part of Dworkin's vision of law as integrity), critical legal authors deny that inconsistencies in legal doctrine can be resolved this way. This reference to higher-level principles simply displaces and deepens the controversy. In other words, another level of indeterminacy is introduced and no soundest theory of law can be constructed that will legitimate the outcome in the hard case.

Critical legal theorists also challenge the claim that law is amenable to neutral application. This brings into question one of the facets of the liberal conception of the rule of law. Many radical critics have reacted skeptically to the claim that either the textual inscription of a legal rule, or its interpretation by an allegedly non-partisan judge, are sufficient guarantees of the neutrality that is required by liberal political theory. From a critical perspective, the rule of law has been treated as an ideologically partisan concept in its own right. The radical critics have argued that the rule of law can be invoked to justify pernicious political regimes and practices. In all its manifestations, law remains the contingent result of ideological struggles among competing factions in which different visions of justice jostle for privileged recognition. Legal argument replicates political debates, and liberal legal attempts to impose constraints on the politics of judging are an illusion: judges cannot escape ideology when they construct their soundest theory of the settled law. Jack Balkin has criticized Dworkin for ignoring in his interpretive account of legal reasoning the "ideological, sociological, and psychological features of interpretation." Both Hart's and Dworkin's theories are incomplete because they are based solely on an "internal" perspective (that is, what a participant in the legal system might regard as law), while a critical persective combines internal with external points of reference.

Much critical writing of the 1970s and early 80s was decidedly "structuralist." These analyses were guided by a view of legal argument as a dialectical system that embraced various sets of opposed ideas. Work by Peter Gabel, Duncan Kennedy, and Gary Peller, and a host of critical discussions inspired by this method, saw binary structures reproduced in many areas of legal doctrine in more or less complex forms. These legal frameworks were taken to mirror structures that are present also in moral argument and epistemology. At the highest level, according to Peller, the most important dichotomous pair is "individualism" and "communalism." Around these binary structures, legal thinking is taught and practised.

Some radical critics have also called into question various conceptions of rationality that have guided conventional legal theories. With other types of post-Enlightenment thinkers, critical legal theorists have investigated whether law as a form of technocratic rationality has become problematic from a political perspective.

Critical legal theorists have doubted the extent to which legal reasoning can be used to reach certain, objective results. According to some accounts, legal doctrine is manipulable to such a degree that in many cases several outcomes are possible. From this point of view, law is a method for providing closure on social and political choices and too often is treated as validating that particular results are natural or necessary. Especially since the 1980s, and reflecting the new pragmatism that has emerged in contemporary philosophy, the radical critique has challenged traditional epistemological paradigms associated with modern liberal legal theories.

It has been claimed that critical legal writers can be roughly divided into two groups: first, those who, like Unger, seek to expose the incoherence of legal doctrine and the liberal principles that arguably underlie and determine that doctrine; and second, those writers who follow a radical indeterminacy approach. Writers in the latter mode view legal reasoning as unbounded by any constraints in the form of rules. In this latter, so-called "irrationalist" view, all legal reasoning and adjudication involves the creation of meaning, rather than the discovery of meanings already present in such materials as legislation, precedent, or general legal principles. There is some tension within critical legal theory about whether this denial of fixed meanings is nihilistic, in the sense that it involves a commitment to the illegitimacy of legal rules and principles. Some critics (such as Joseph Singer) apply the nihilistic label to themselves, while others (such as Jack Balkin) see in critical practice a relatively optimistic "affirmation of human possibilities that have been overlooked" that is not necessarily about the deligitimation of the existing system.

The irrationalist strand of critical legal studies has been compared with the practice of deconstruction in literary studies. As described by Balkin, critical legal work in this vein (which is one example of what has been called "trashing") purports to critique existing legal doctrine by showing that arguments used to support the adoption of a particular rule can also be used to support the opposite rule. Deconstruction also contributes to the critical enterprise of undermining standard interpretive conventions used in reading legal texts. Among the primary targets of deconstruction have been metaphors embedded in legal discourse. A metaphor can be deconstructed in the sense that the critic can reveal a latent "countervision" or "supplement." The deconstructive side to critical legal work has been, in David Hoy's term, "strangeness-maximizing."

Another common feature of critical legal writing, especially up to the mid-80s, was a general skepticism about the positive value of rights. Radical critics disparaged theories of law heavily dependent on rights to provide the moral content of particular doctrines. Rights-based theories tended to be viewed as inaccurate and politically regressive accounts of how the law does or should operate. From a critical perspective, rights become reified deposits in a false consciousness and they tend to shift into a legal forum questions that ought to be dealt with through democratic deliberation. In addition to the literature below, many items cited elsewhere in this bibliography under the heads of "Constitutional Law," "Feminism and Law," and "Racism, Minorities and Law" also deal with this issue.

* * * *

ALLAN, T. R. S., "Justice and Fairness in Law's Empire" (1993) 52 Cambridge L. J. 64-88

ALTMAN, Andrew, "Legal Realism, Critical Legal Studies, and Dworkin" (1986) 15 Phil. & Pub. Aff. 205-35

BAKER, C. Edwin, "Counting Preferences in Collective Choice Situations" (1978) 25 U.C.L.A. L. Rev. 381-416

BALKIN, J. M., "Being Just with Deconstruction" (1994) 3 Social & Legal Stud. 393-404

BALKIN, J. M., "The Crystalline Structure of Legal Thought" (1986) 39 Rutgers L. Rev. 1-110

BALKIN, J. M., "Deconstructive Practice and Legal Theory" (1987) 96 Yale L. J. 743-86

BALKIN, J. M., "The Hohfeldian Approach to Law and Semiotics" (1990) 44 U. Mia. L. Rev. 1119-42

BALKIN, J. M., "Ideological Drift and the Struggle Over Meaning" (1993) 25 Conn. L. Rev. 869-91

BALKIN, J. M., "(A) Just Rhetoric" [review of Costas Douzinas *et al.*, *Postmodern Jurisprudence: The Law of Text in the Texts of Law*] (1992) 55 Mod. L. Rev. 746-53

BALKIN, Jack M., "The Promise of Legal Semiotics" (1991) 69 Tex. L. Rev. 1831-52

BALKIN, J. M., "The Rhetoric of Responsibility" (1990) 76 Va. L. Rev. 197-263

BALKIN, J. M., "Taking Ideology Seriously: Ronald Dworkin and the CLS Critique" (1987) 55 U.M.K.C. L. Rev. 392-433

BALKIN, J. M., "Transcendental Deconstruction, Transcendant Justice" (1994) 92 Mich. L. Rev. 1131-86

BALKIN, J. M., "Understanding Legal Understanding: The Legal Subject and the Problem of Legal Culture" (1993) 103 Yale L. J. 105-76

BARRON, Anne, "Ronald Dworkin and the Challenge of Postmodernism" in Alan Hunt (ed.), *Reading Dworkin Critically* (New York: Berg, 1992) 141-55

BARTHOLEMEW, Amy and **HUNT**, Alan, "What's Wrong With Rights?" (1990) 9 L. & Inequality 1-58

BELLIOTTI, Raymond A., "The Rule of Law and the Critical Legal Studies Movement" (1986) 24 U. W. Ont. L. Rev. 67-78

BLATT, William S., "The History of Statutory Interpretation: A Study in Form and Substance" (1985) 6 Cardozo L. Rev. 799-845

BLOMLEY, Nicholas K. and **BAKAN**, Joel C., "Spacing Out: Towards a Critical Geography of Law" (1992) 30 Osgoode Hall L. J. 661-90

BLUM, Jeffrey M., "Critical Legal Studies and the Rule of Law" (1990) 38 Buffalo L. Rev. 59-155

BOLDT, Richard and **FELDMAN**, Marc, "The Faces of Law in Theory and Practice: Doctrine, Rhetoric, and Social Context" (1992) 43 Hast. L. J. 1111-45

BOYLE, James D. A., "Legal Fiction" (1987) 38 Hast. L. J. 1013-22

BOYLE, James, "Is Subjectivity Possible? The Post-Modern Subject in Legal Theory" (1991) 62 U. Colo. L. Rev. 489-524

BOYLE, James, "The Politics of Reason: Critical Legal Theory and Local Social Thought" (1985) 133 U. Pa. L. Rev. 685-785

BOYLE, James, "Thomas Hobbes and the Invented Tradition of Positivism: Reflections on Language, Power, and Essentialism" (1987) 135 U. Pa. L. Rev. 383-426

BRAINERD, Stephen, "The Groundless Assault: A Wittgensteinian Look at Language, Structuralism, and Critical Legal Theory" (1985) 34 Am. U. L. Rev. 1231-62

CAMPOS, Paul, "A Mirror for the Magistrate (Hypothetical Critical Legal Studies Jurisprudence)" (1992) 9 Const. Comm. 151-60

CARISON, David Gray, "Liberal Philosophy's Troubled Relation to the Rule of Law" (1993) 43 U. Toronto L. J. 257-88

CASEBEER, Kenneth M., "Escape From Liberalism: Fact and Value in Karl Llewellyn" [1977] Duke L. J. 671-703

CASEBEER, Kenneth, "The Judging Glass" (1978) 33 U. Mia. L. Rev. 59-124

CAUDILL, David Stanley, *Disclosing Tilt: Law, Belief and Criticism* (Amsterdam: Free University Press, 1989)

CHASE, Anthony, "Jerome Frank on American Psychoanalytic Jurisprudence" (1979) 2 Int'l J. L. & Psychiatry 29-54

CHASE, Anthony, "Law and Ideology Critique Under Spiritless Conditions: The Reagan Years" (1988) 17 Cap. U. L. Rev. 225-41

CHEVIGNY, Paul, "Why the Continental Disputes are Important: A Comment on Hoy and Garet" (1985) 58 S. Calif. L. Rev. 199-210

COLLINS, Hugh, "The Decline of Privacy in Private Law" in Peter Fitzpatrick and Alan Hunt (eds.), *Critical Legal Studies* (Oxford: Basil Blackwell, 1987) 91-103

COOK, Anthony E., "The Death of God in American Pragmatism and Realism: Resurrecting the Value of Love in Contemporary Jurisprudence" (1994) 82 Geo. L. J. 1431-517

COOK, Anthony E., "Reflections on Postmodernism" (1992) 26 New. Eng. L. Rev. 751-82

COOMBE, Rosemary, "'Same As It Ever Was': Rethinking the Politics of Legal Interpretation" (1989) 34 McGill L. J. 603-52

CORNELL, Drucilla, "Beyond Tragedy and Complacency" (1987) 81 Nw. U. L. Rev. 693-717

CORNELL, Drucilla, "Civil Disobedience and Deconstruction" (1991) 13 Cardozo L. Rev. 1309-15

CORNELL, Drucilla, "'Convention' and Critique" (1987) 7 Cardozo L. Rev. 679-91

CORNELL, Drucilla, "From the Lighthouse: The Province of Redemption and the Possibility of Legal Interpretation" (1990) 11 Cardozo L. Rev. 1687-914

CORNELL, Drucilla, "Institutionalization of Meaning, Recollective Imagination and the Potential for Transformative Legal Interpretation" (1988) 136 U. Pa. L. Rev. 1135-229

CORNELL, Drucilla, "In Union: A Critical Review of *Toward a Perfected State*" (1987) 135 U. Pa. L. Rev. 1089-121

CORNELL, Drucilla, *The Philosophy of the Limit* (London and New York: Routledge, 1992)

CORNELL, Drucilla, "The Poststructuralist Challenge to the Ideal of Community" (1987) 8 Cardozo L. Rev. 989-1022

CORNELL, Drucilla, "The Relevance of Time to the Relationship Between the Philosophy of the Limit and Systems Theory" (1992) 12 Cardozo L. Rev. 1579-603

CORNELL, Drucilla, "Taking Hegel Seriously: Reflections on Beyond Objectivism and Relativism" (1985) 7 Cardozo L. Rev. 139-84

CORNELL, Drucilla, "Toward a Modern/Postmodern Reconstruction of Ethics" (1985) 133 U. Pa. L. Rev. 291-380

CORNELL, Drucilla, "Two Lectures on the Normative Dimensions of Community in the Law" (1987) 54 Tenn. L. Rev. 347-63

CORNELL, Drucilla, "The Violence of the Masquerade: Law Dressed Up as Justice" (1990) 11 Cardozo L. Rev. 1047-64

DALTON, Clare, Review of David Kairys (ed.), *The Politics of Law: A Progressive Critique* (1983) 6 Harv. Wom. L. J. 229-48

D'AMICO, Robert, "What Theory? Whose Community?" [review of Maurizio Passerin d'Entrèves, *Modernity, Justice and Community*] (1990-91) 86 Telos 158-69

DANIELSEN, Dan and **ENGLE**, Karen (eds.), *After Identity: A Reader in Law and Culture* (New York: Routledge, 1995)

DAVIS, Michael, "Critical Jurisprudence: An Essay on the Legal Theory of Robert Burt's *Taking Care of Strangers*" [1981] Wis. L. Rev. 419-53

DELGADO, Richard, "Norms and Narratives: Can Judges Avoid Serious Moral Error?" (1991) 69 Tex. L. Rev. 1929-83

DELGADO, Richard, "Norms and Normal Science: Toward a Critique of Normativity in Legal Thought" (1991) 139 U. Pa. L. Rev. 933-62

DEVLIN, Richard F., "Doubting Donald: A Reply to Professor Donald Galloway's 'Critical Mistakes'" (1991) 11 Windsor Y.B. Acc. Just. 178-205

DEVLIN, Richard F., "Nomos and Thanatos (Part A). The Killing Fields: Modern Law and Legal Theory" (1989) 12 Dal. L. J. 298-348

DEVLIN, Richard F., "Nomos and Thanatos (Part B). Feminism as Jurisgenerative Transformation, or Resistance Through Partial Incorporation?" (1990) 13 Dal. L. J. 123-210

DOUZINAS, Costas; **GOODRICH**, Peter; and **HACHAMOVITCH**, Yifat, *Politics, Postmodernity, and Critical Legal Studies: The Legality of the Contingent* (London: Routledge, 1994)

DOUZINAS, Costas; **McVEIGH**, Shaun; and **WARRINGTON**, Ronnie, "Is Hermes Hercules' Twin? Hermeneutics and Legal Theory" in Alan Hunt (ed.), *Reading Dworkin Critically* (New York: Berg, 1992) 123-40

DOUZINAS, Costas and **WARRINGTON**, Ronnie, "The Face of Justice: A Jurisprudence of Alterity" (1994) 3 Social & Legal Stud. 405-25

DOUZINAS, Costas and **WARRINGTON**, Ronnie, with **McVEIGH**, Shaun, *Postmodern Jurisprudence: The Law of Text in the Texts of Law* (London: Routledge, 1991)

DRAHOS, Peter and **PARKER**, Stephen, "The Indeterminacy Paradox in Law" (1991) 21 U. West. Austl. L. Rev. 305-19

DUXBURY, Neil, "Deconstruction, History, and the Uses of Legal Theory" (1990) 41 N. Ir. Leg. Q. 167-75

DUXBURY, Neil, "Pragmatism Without Politics" [review of Richard A. Posner, *The Problems of Jurisprudence*] (1992) 55 Mod. L. Rev. 594-610

DUXBURY, Neil, "Robert Hale and the Economy of Legal Force" (1990) 53 Mod. L. Rev. 421-44

EASTMAN, Wayne, "Organization Life and Critical Legal Thought: A Psychopolitical Inquiry and Argument" (1992) 19 N.Y.U. Rev. L. & Soc. Ch. 721-96

EDMUNDSON, William A., "Transparency and Indeterminacy in the Liberal Critique of Critical Legal Studies" (1993) 24 Seton Hall L. J. 557-602

FELLAS, John, "Reconstructing Law's Empire" (1993) 73 B.U. L. Rev. 715-90

FITZPATRICK, Peter, "The Abstracts and Brief Chronicles of the Time: Supplementing Jurisprudence" in Peter Fitzpatrick (ed.), *Dangerous Supplements: Resistance and Renewal in Jurisprudence* (Durham: Duke University Press, 1991) 1-33

FRASER, David, "Estimated Prophet" [review of Duncan Kennedy, *Sexy Dressing Etc.*] (1995) 2 Rev. Const. Stud. 436-50

FRASER, David, "I Fought the Law and the Law Won" (1988-89) 5 Austl. J. L. & Soc'y 153-68

FRASER, David, "If I Had a Rocket Launcher: Critical Legal Studies as Moral Terrorism" (1990) 41 Hast. L. J. 777-804

FRASER, David, *The Man in White is Always Right: Cricket and the Law* (Sydney: Institute of Criminology, University of Sydney, 1993)

FRASER, David, "Truth and Hierarchy: Will the Circle Be Unbroken?" (1984) 33 Buffalo L. Rev. 729-75

FREEMAN, Alan D. and **MENSCH**, Elizabeth, "The Public-Private Distinction in American Law and Life" (1987) 36 Buffalo L. Rev. 237-57

FREEMAN, Alan D. and **SCHLEGEL**, John Henry, "Sex, Power and Silliness: An Essay on Ackerman's *Reconstructing American Law*" (1985) 6 Cardozo L. Rev. 847-64

GABEL, Peter, "Reification in Legal Reasoning" in Steven Spitzer (ed.), *Research in Law and Sociology,* vol. 3 (Greenwich, Conn.: JAI Press, 1980) 25-51

GABEL, Peter, Review of Ronald Dworkin, *Taking Rights Seriously* (1977) 91 Harv. L. Rev. 302-15

GABEL, Peter and **KENNEDY**, Duncan, "Roll Over Beethoven" (1984) 36 Stan. L. Rev. 1-55

GJERDINGEN, Donald H., "The Future of Legal Scholarship and the Search for a Modern Theory of Law" (1986) 35 Buffalo L. Rev. 381-477

GOETSCH, Charles C., "The Future of Legal Formalism" (1980) 24 Am. J. Legal Hist. 221-56

GOODRICH, Peter and **HACHAMOVITCH**, Yifat, "Time out of Mind: An Introduction to the Semiotics of Common Law" in Peter Fitzpatrick (ed.), *Dangerous Supplements: Resistance and Renewal in Jurisprudence* (Durham: Duke University Press, 1991) 159-81

GORDON, Robert W., "Holmes' Common Law as Legal and Social Science" (1982) 10 Hofstra L. Rev. 719-46

GORDON, Robert W., "New Developments in Legal Theory" in David Kairys (ed.), *The Politics of Law: A Progressive Critique* (New York: Pantheon Books, 1982) 281-93

GORDON, Robert W., "New Developments in Legal Theory" in David Kairys (ed.), *The Politics of Law: A Progressive Critique,* 2nd rev. ed. (New York: Pantheon Books, 1990) 413-25

GUDRIDGE, Patrick, "Legislation in Legal Imagination: Introductory Exercises" (1983) 37 U. Miami L. Rev. 493-572

GUDRIDGE, Patrick, "The Persistence of Classical Style" (1983) 131 U. Pa. L. Rev. 663-792

GÜNTHER, Klaus, *Hero-Politics in Modern Legal Times — Presuppositions of Critical Legal Studies and Their Critique* (Madison: Institute for Legal Studies, University of Wisconsin, 1990)

HALEWOOD, Peter, "Trends in American Critical Legal Thought" (1991) 25 U.B.C. L. Rev. 105-28

HARRIS, Judith A., "Recognizing Legal Tropes: Metonymy as Manipulative Mode" (1985) 34 Am. U. L. Rev. 1215-29

HARRISON, Jeffrey L. and **MASHBURN**, Amy R., "Jean-Luc Godard and Critical Legal Studies (Because We Need the Eggs)" (1989) 87 Mich. L. Rev. 1924-44

HELLER, Thomas, "Structuralism and Critique" (1984) 36 Stan. L. Rev. 127-98

HIRST, Paul and **JONES**, Phil, "The Critical Resources of Established Jurisprudence" in Peter Fitzpatrick and Alan Hunt (eds.), *Critical Legal Studies* (Oxford: Basil Blackwell, 1987) 21-32

HOLT, Wythe, "Tilt" (1984) 52 Geo. Wash. L. Rev. 281-88

HORWITZ, Morton J., "The History of the Public-Private Distinction" (1982) 130 U. Pa. L. Rev. 1423-28

HORWITZ, Morton J., "The Rise of Legal Formalism" (1975) 19 Am. J. Leg. Hist. 251-64

HORWITZ, Morton J., "The Rule of Law: An Unqualified Human Good?" [review of Douglas Hay *et al.*, *Albion's Fatal Tree* and E. P. Thompson, *Whigs and Hunters*] (1977) 86 Yale L. J. 561-66

HOY, David Couzens, "Dworkin's Constructive Optimism v. Deconstructive Legal Nihilism" (1987) 6 L. & Phil. 321-56

HOY, David Couzens, "Interpreting the Law: Hermeneutical and Poststructuralist Perspectives" (1985) 58 S. Cal. L. Rev. 35-76

HUNT, Alan, "The Big Fear: Law Confronts Postmodernism" (1990) 35 McGill L. J. 507-40

HUNT, Alan, "The Critique of Law: What is 'Critical' about Critical Legal Theory?" in Peter Fitzpatrick and Alan Hunt (eds.), *Critical Legal Studies* (Oxford: Basil Blackwell, 1987) 5-19

HUNT, Alan, *Explorations in Law and Society: Towards a Constitutive Theory of Law* (London: Routledge, 1993)

HUNT, Alan, "The Ideology of Law: Advances and Problems in Recent Applications of the Concept of Ideology to the Analysis of Law" (1985) 19 L. & Soc'y Rev. 11-37

HUNT, Alan, "Law's Empire or Legal Imperialism?" in Alan Hunt (ed.), *Reading Dworkin Critically* (New York: Berg, 1992) 9-43

HUNT, Alan, "Living Dangerously on the Deconstructive Edge" [review of Allan C. Hutchinson, *Dwelling on the Threshold*] (1988) 26 Osgoode Hall L. J. 867-95

HUSSON, Christine A. Desan, "Expanding the Legal Vocabulary: The Challenge Posed by the Deconstruction and Defence of Law" (1986) 95 Yale L. J. 969-91

HUTCHINSON, Allan C., "And Law (Or Further Adventures of the Jondo)" (1987) 36 Buffalo L. Rev. 285-99

HUTCHINSON, Allan C., "Crits and Cricket: A Deconstructive Spin (Or Was It a Googly?)" in Richard F. Devlin (ed.), *Canadian Perspectives on Legal Theory* (Toronto: Emond Montgomery, 1991) 181-205

HUTCHINSON, Allan C., *Dwelling on the Threshold: Critical Essays on Modern Legal Thought* (Toronto: Carswell, 1988)

HUTCHINSON, Allan C., "From Cultural Construction to Historical Deconstruction" [review of James Boyd White, *When Words Lose Their Meaning*] (1984) 94 Yale L. J. 209-38

HUTCHINSON, Allan C., "Identity Crisis: The Politics of Interpretation" (1992) 26 New Eng. L. Rev. 1173-219

HUTCHINSON, Allan C., ""Indiana Dworkin and Law's Empire" [review of Ronald Dworkin, *Law's Empire*] (1987) 96 Yale L. J. 637-65

HUTCHINSON, Allan C., "The Last Emperor?" in Alan Hunt (ed.), *Reading Dworkin Critically* (New York: Berg, 1992) 45-70

HUTCHINSON, Allan C., "Of Kings and Dirty Rascals: The Struggle for Democracy" (1984) 9 Queen's L. J. 273-92

HUTCHINSON, Allan C., "Part of an Essay on Power and Interpretation (With Suggestions on How to Make Bouillabaisse)" (1985) 60 N.Y.U. L. Rev. 850-86

HUTCHINSON, Allan C., "That's Just the Way It Is: Langille on Law" (1989) 34 McGill L. J. 145-59

HUTCHINSON, Allan C., "The Three 'R's': Reading/Rorty/Radically" (1989) 103 Harv. L. Rev. 555-85

HUTCHINSON, Allan C. and **WAKEFIELD**, John N., "A Hard Look at Hard Cases: The Nightmare of a Noble Dreamer" (1982) 2 Oxford J. Legal Stud. 86-110

HYDE, Alan, "Is Liberalism Possible?" [review of Bruce Ackerman, *Social Justice in the Liberal State*] (1982) 57 N.Y.U. L. Rev. 1031-58

JABBARI, David, "From Criticism to Construction in Modern Critical Legal Theory" (1992) 12 Oxford J. Leg. Stud. 507-42

JACOBSON, Arthur J., "Modern American Jurisprudence and the Problem of Power" (1985) 6 Cardozo L. Rev. 713-37

JAFF, Jennifer, "Radical Pluralism: A Proposed Theoretical Framework for the Conference on Critical Legal Studies" (1984) 72 Geo. L. J. 1143-54

JAFFEE, Leonard R., "Empathic Adjustment — An Alternative to Rules, Policies, and Politics" (1990) 58 U. Cin. L. Rev. 1161-230

KAIRYS, David, "Law and Politics" (1984) 52 Geo. Wash. L. Rev. 243-62

KAIRYS, David, "Legal Reasoning" in David Kairys (ed.), *The Politics of Law: A Progressive Critique* (New York: Pantheon Books, 1982) 11-17

KAIRYS, David, "Why Precedents Aren't Treated Equally" (June 9, 1980) Nat'l L. J. 15

KATZ, Al, "Studies in Boundary Theory: Three Essays in Adjudication and Politics" (1979) 28 Buffalo L. Rev. 383-435

KELLOGG, Frederic R., "Legal Scholarship in the Temple of Doom: Pragmatism's Response to Critical Legal Studies" (1990) 65 Tul. L. Rev. 15-56

KELMAN, Mark, "A Critique of Conservative Legal Thought" in David Kairys (ed.), *The Politics of Law: A Progressive Critique*, 2nd rev. ed. (New York: Pantheon Books, 1990) 436-52

KELMAN, Mark, "Emerging Centrist Liberalism" (1991) 43 Fla. L. Rev. 417-44

KENNEDY, David, "The Turn to Interpretation" (1985) 58 S. Cal. L. Rev. 251-75

KENNEDY, Duncan, "Freedom and Constraint in Adjudication: A Critical Phenomenology" (1986) 36 J. Legal Educ. 518-62

KENNEDY, Duncan, "Legal Formality" (1973) 2 J. Legal Stud. 351-98

KENNEDY, Duncan, "Psycho-Social CLS: A Comment on the Cardozo Symposium" (1985) 6 Cardozo L. Rev. 1013-31

KENNEDY, Duncan, "The Semiotics of Legal Argument" (1991) 42 Syracuse L. Rev. 75-116

KENNEDY, Duncan, "The Stages of the Decline of the Public-Private Distinction" (1982) 130 U. Pa. L. Rev. 1349-57

KENNEDY, Duncan, "The Structure of Blackstone's Commentaries" (1979) 28 Buffalo L. Rev. 205-382

KERRUISH, Valerie and **HUNT**, Alan, "Dworkin's Dutiful Daughter: Gender Discrimination in Law's Empire" in Alan Hunt (ed.), *Reading Dworkin Critically* (New York: Berg, 1992) 209-39

KLARE, Karl E., "Legal Theory and Democratic Reconstruction: Reflections on 1989" (1991) 25 U.B.C. L. Rev. 69-103

KRAMER, Matthew H., *Legal Theory, Political Theory, and Deconstruction: Against Rhadamanthus* (Bloomington: Indiana University Press, 1991)

LANDERS, Scott, "Wittgenstein, Realism, and CLS: Undermining Rule Scepticism" (1990) 9 L. & Phil. 177-203

LEHMAN, Warren, "The System and the Life World" (1989) 46 Wash. & Lee L. Rev. 411-24

LEVINSON, Sanford, "Escaping Liberalism: Easier Said Than Done" [review of David Kairys (ed.), *The Politics of Law: A Progressive Critique*] (1983) 96 Harv. L. Rev. 1466-88

LEVINSON, Sanford and **BALKIN**, Jack M., "Law, Music, and Other Performing Arts" (1991) 139 U. Pa. L. Rev. 1597-658

MALKAN, Jeffrey, "'Against Theory,' Pragmatism and Deconstruction" (1987) 71 Telos 129-54

MAZOR, Lester, "The Crisis of Liberal Legalism" [review of Eugene V. Rostow (ed.), *Is Law Dead?* and Robert Paul Wolff (ed.), *The Rule of Law*] (1972) 81 Yale L. J. 1032-53

MAZOR, Lester, "Disrespect for Law" in J. Roland Pennock and John Chapman (eds.), *Nomos XIX: Anarchism* (New York: New York University Press, 1978) 143-59

MINDA, Gary, "Jurisprudence at Century's End" (1993) 43 J. Legal Educ. 27-59

MINDA, Gary, *Postmodern Legal Movements: Law and Jurisprudence at Century's End* (New York: New York University Press, 1995)

MINOW, Martha, "Law Turning Outward" (1987) 76 Telos 65-92

MOON, John, "An Essay on Local Critique" (1986) 16 N.M. L. Rev. 513-34

MOORE, Terrence L., "Critical Legal Studies and Anglo-American Jurisprudence" (1990) 1 U.S. Air F. Acad. J. Legal Stud. 1-21

NASSER, Alan, "Legal Theory in Late Modernity" (1991) 42 Mercer L. Rev. 909-69

OLSEN, Frances, "Socrates on Legal Obligation: Legitimation Theory and Civil Disobedience" (1984) 18 Ga. L. Rev. 929-66

PAUL, Jeremy, "The Politics of Legal Semiotics" (1991) 69 Tex. L. Rev. 1779-829

PELLER, Gary, "The Metaphysics of American Law" (1985) 73 Cal. L. Rev. 1152-1290

PELLER, Gary, "The Politics of Reconstruction" [review of Bruce Ackerman, *Reconstructing American Law*] (1985) 98 Harv. L. Rev. 863-81

POWELL, Asa Mitchell, Jr., "Towards the Regeneration of Law and Ethics: Law as Process — A Response to Owen Fiss" (1988) 39 Mercer L. Rev. 591-640

SCHANCK, Peter C., "Understanding Postmodern Thought and Its Implications for Statutory Interpretation" (1992) 65 S. Cal. L. Rev. 2505-97

SCHLAG, Pierre, "The Brilliant, the Curious, and the Wrong" (1987) 39 Stan. L. Rev. 917-27

SCHLAG, Pierre, "Cannibal Moves: An Essay on the Metamorphoses of the Legal Distinction" (1988) 40 Stan. L. Rev. 929-72

SCHLAG, Pierre, "Contradiction and Denial" [review of Mark Kelman, *A Guide to Critical Legal Studies*] (1989) 87 Mich. L. Rev. 1216-24

SCHLAG, Pierre, "Fish v. Zapp: The Case of the Relatively Autonomous Self" (1987) 76 Geo. L. J. 37-58

SCHLAG, Pierre, "Foreword: Postmodernism and Law" (1991) 62 U. Colo. L. Rev. 439-53

SCHLAG, Pierre, "'Le hors du texte, c'est moi?': The Politics of Form and the Domestication of Deconstruction" (1990) 11 Cardozo L. Rev. 1631-74

SCHLAG, Pierre, "Missing Pieces: A Cognitive Approach to Law" (1989) 67 Tex. L. Rev. 1195-250

SCHLAG, Pierre, "Normative and Nowhere to Go" (1990) 43 Stan. L. Rev. 167-91

SCHLAG, Pierre, "Normativity and the Politics of Form" (1991) 139 139 U. Pa. L. Rev. 801-932

SCHLAG, Pierre, "The Problem of the Subject" (1991) 69 Tex. L. Rev. 1627-43

SEGALL, Eric J., "Justice Scalia, Critical Legal Studies, and the Rule of Law" (1994) 62 Geo. Wash. L. Rev. 991-1042

SELZNICK, Philip, "The Idea of a Communitarian Morality" (1987) 75 Calif. L. Rev. 445-63

SHERRY, Suzanna, "An Essay Concerning Toleration" (1987) 71 Minn. L. Rev. 963-89

SHIFFRIN, Steven, "Liberalism, Radicalism, and Legal Scholarship" (1983) 30 U.C.L.A. L. Rev. 1103-217 ⟵

SIMON, William H., "Homo Psychologicus: Notes on a New Legal Formalism" (1980) 32 Stan. L. Rev. 487-559

SINGER, Joseph William, "Catcher in the Rye Jurisprudence" (1983) 35 Rutgers L. Rev. 275-84

SINGER, Joseph William, "Legal Realism" [review of Laura Kalman, *Legal Realism at Yale, 1927-1960*] (1988) 76 Cal. L. Rev. 465-544

SINGER, Joseph William, "The Legal Rights Debate in Analytical Jurisprudence from Bentham to Hohfeld" [1982] Wis. L. Rev. 975-1059

SINGER, Joseph William, "The Player and the Cards: Nihilism and Legal Theory" (1984) 94 Yale L. J. 1-70

SINGER, Joseph William, "Radical Moderation" [review of Bruce Ackerman, *Reconstructing American Law*] [1985] Am. Bar Fdn. Res. J. 329-44

SOMEK, Alexander, "From Kennedy to Balkin: Introducing Critical Legal Studies From a Continental Perspective" (1994) 42 U. Kan. L. Rev. 759-83

STANDEN, Jeffrey A., "Critical Legal Studies as an Anti-Positivist Phenomenon" (1986) 72 Va. L. Rev. 983-98 ⟵

SUGARMAN, David, "Legal Theory, the Common Law Mind and the Making of Textbook Tradition" in William Twining (ed.), *Legal Theory and Common Law* (Oxford: Blackwell, 1986) 26-61

SWAN, Peter D., "Critical Legal Theory and the Politics of Pragmatism" (1989) 12 Dal. L. J. 349-76

THURSCHWELL, Adam, "On the Threshold of Ethics" (1994) 15 Cardozo L. Rev. 1607-55

TUSHNET, Mark, "The Left Critique of Normativity: A Comment" (1992) 90 Mich. L. Rev. 2325-47

TUSHNET, Mark, "The Possibilities of Interpretive Liberalism" (1991) 29 Alta. L. Rev. 276-92

TUSHNET, Mark, "Sex, Drugs and Rock 'n Roll: Some Conservative Reflections on Liberal Jurisprudence" (1982) 82 Colum. L. Rev. 1531-44

WARNER, Richard, "Why Pragmatism? The Puzzling Place of Pragmatism in Critical Theory" [1993] U. Ill. L. Rev. 535-63

WEST, Robin L., "Disciplines, Politics, and Law" in Austin Sarat and Thomas R. Kearns (eds.), *The Fate of Law* (Ann Arbor: University of Michigan Press, 1991) 119-57 [reprinted as "Disciplines, Subjectivity, and Law" in Robin L. West, *Narrative, Authority, and Law* (Ann Arbor: University of Michigan Press, 1991)] 265-98

WEST, Robin, "Law, Rights and Other Totemic Illusions: Legal Liberalism and Freud's Theory of the Rule of Law" (1986) 134 U. Pa. L. Rev. 817-82

WEST, Robin, "Liberalism Rediscovered: A Pragmatic Definition of the Liberal Vision" (1985) 46 U. Pitt. L. Rev. 673-738

WEST, Robin, "Relativism, Objectivity, and Law" (1990) 99 Yale L. J. 1473-502

WINTER, Steven L., "Contingency and Community in Normative Practice" (1991) 139 U. Pa. L. Rev. 963-1002

8

The Legal Profession

Critical legal literature has focused on the development of the profession generally and also on the roles and responsibilities of lawyers within the profession. Some critics, such as Richard Abel, have revised the standard accounts of how and to what ends lawyers in Western societies have achieved professional status. This goal has shaped the training, credentialing, functions, and supply of lawyers, as well as the market for legal services. In particular, the critical sociological perspective has challenged traditional methods for understanding the modern rise in demand for legal services and the degree to which the legal profession is self-regulating and is permitted to discipline its own members for misconduct. There has also been some scrutiny of the extent to which lawyers control the labor of subordinate employees.

Critical legal writers have also questioned the extent to which lawyers can serve as agents for social transformation. There is significant debate within the literature about whether a strong concept of agency best describes the situation of lawyers or whether structural restrictions imply limits to the scope for lawyers' progressive practice.

The critique has taken note of the changes in the membership of the profession, drawing lessons from the underrepresentation of women and minorities. The increased awareness of the importance of race, gender, class, and sexuality has inspired reevaluations of the relations between lawyers and clients, as well as among lawyers themselves.

A critique has also been levelled at various models of lawyering, including the advocacy model. There is much discussion about the relative positions of power for lawyers, clients, and the state. These analyses have had to take into account the extent to which traditional ideals of practice (such as lawyers' autonomy to choose their clients and the causes they represent, as well as to select strategy) continue to animate lawyers' work.

A favorite professional model stresses the autonomy of clients. Some critical legal authors have viewed legal discourse as impoverished so far as it potentially distorts or ignores the actual experiences of clients. Only those alleged "facts" necessary to satisfy established legal principles survive the sifting process that legal analysis involves.

Recent debates over the alleged demise of foundationalist ethics have worked their way into critical legal discussions. Many critical legal writers reject normative systems, such as codes of behavior adopted by governing bodies of the profession, in favor of more articulated, contextual modes of addressing ethical dilemmas. Critical legal literature in this area tends to resist the narrow, professional ideologies that have traditionally dominated discussion of legal ethics.

* * * *

ABEL, Richard L., *American Lawyers* (New York: Oxford University Press, 1989)

ABEL, Richard L., "Comparative Sociology of Legal Professions: An Exploratory Essay" [1985] Am. Bar Fdn. Res. J. 3-79

ABEL, Richard L., "The Decline of Professionalism?" (1986) 49 Mod. L. Rev. 1-41

ABEL, Richard L., "England and Wales: A Comparison of the Professional Projects of Barristers and Solicitors" in Richard L. Abel and Philip S. C. Lewis (eds.), *Lawyers and Society, Vol. 1: The Common Law World* (Berkeley: University of California Press, 1988) 23-122

ABEL, Richard L., *The Legal Profession in England and Wales* (Oxford: Basil Blackwell, 1988)

ABEL, Richard, "Socializing the Legal Profession: Can Redistributing Lawyers' Services Achieve Social Justice?" (1979) 1 L. & Pol'y Q. 5-51

ABEL, Richard L., "The Sociology of American Lawyers: A Bibliographic Guide" (1980) 2 L. & Pol'y Q. 335-91

ABEL, Richard, "Toward a Political Economy of Lawyers" [1981] Wis. L. Rev. 1117-87

ABEL, Richard, "The Transformation of the American Legal Profession" (1986) 20 L. & Soc'y Rev. 7-19

ABEL, Richard L., "United States: The Contradictions of Professionalism" in Richard L. Abel and Philip S. C. Lewis (eds.), *Lawyers and Society, Vol. 1: The Common Law World* (Berkeley: University of California Press, 1988) 186-243

ABEL, Richard, "Why Does the A.B.A. Promulgate Ethical Rules?" (1981) 59 Tex. L. Rev. 639-88

ABEL, Richard L. and **LEWIS**, Philip S. C., "Putting Law Back into the Sociology of Lawyers" in Richard L. Abel and Philip S. C. Lewis (eds.), *Lawyers and Society, Vol. 3: Comparative Theories* (Berkeley: University of California Press, 1989) 478-526

ALFIERI, Anthony V., "Impoverished Practices" (1993) 81 Geo. L. J. 2567-663

ASHE, Marie, "'Bad Mothers,' 'Good Mothers,' and 'Legal Ethics'" (1993) 81 Geo. L. J. 2533-66

AUERBACH, Jerold S., *Unequal Justice: Lawyers and Social Change in America* (New York: Oxford University Press, 1976)

BAMBERGER, E. Clinton, "Of Lawyers, Law Firms, and Law Practice for People: Ideas for New Lawyers" (1980) 12 Colum. Hum. Rts. L. Rev. 57-63

BEZDEK, Barbara, "Reconstructing a Pedagogy of Responsibility" (1992) 43 Hast. L. J. 1159-74

CAHN, Naomi R., "Inconsistent Stories" (1993) 81 Geo. L. J. 2475-531

CAIN, Maureen, "Necessarily Out of Touch: Thoughts on the Social Organisation of the English Bar" in Pat Carlen (ed.), *The Sociology of Law: Sociological Review Monograph No. 23* (Keele: University of Keele, 1976) 226-50

CAIN, Maureen and **HARRINGTON**, Christine B. (eds.), *Lawyers in a Postmodern World: Translation and Transgression* (Buckingham: Open University Press, 1994)

CHASE, Anthony, "Lawyers and Popular Culture: A Review of Mass Media Portrayals of American Attorneys" [1986] Am. Bar Fdn. Res. J. 281-300

CHASE, Anthony, "Toward a Legal Theory of Popular Culture" [1986] Wis. L. Rev. 527-69

CHAYES, Abram and **CHAYES**, Antonia, "Corporate Counsel and the Elite Law Firm" (1985) 37 Stan. L. Rev. 277-300

CHESTER, Ronald, *Unequal Access: Women Lawyers in a Changing America* (South Hadley, Mass.: Bergin & Garvey Publishers, 1985)

CHESTER, Ronald, "Women Lawyers in the Urban Bar: An Oral History" (1982-83) 18 New Eng. L. Rev. 521-76

COOK, Anthony E., "Towards a Postmodern Ethic of Service" (1993) 81 Geo. L. J. 2457-74

ELLMANN, Stephen, "The Ethic of Care as an Ethic for Lawyers" (1993) 84 Geo. L. J. 2665-726

FEINMAN, Jay and **HOLT**, Wythe, Review of Dennis R. Nolan (ed.), *Readings in the History of the American Legal Profession* (1982) 7 J. Legal Prof. 233-46

FREEMAN, Alan D., "A Critical Legal Look at Corporate Practice" (1987) 37 J. Legal Educ. 315-26

FRUG, Jerry, "Argument as Character" (1988) 40 Stan. L. Rev. 869-927

GABEL, Peter and **HARRIS**, Paul, "Building Power and Breaking Images: Critical Legal Theory and the Practice of Law" (1982-83) 11 N.Y.U. Rev. L. & Soc. Ch. 369-411

GALANTER, Marc, *Tournament of Lawyers: The Growth and Transformation of the Big Law Firm* (Chicago: University of Chicago Press, 1991)

GLASBEEK, Harry J., "Some Strategies for an Unlikely Task: The Progressive Use of Law" (1989) 21 Ottawa L. Rev. 387-418

GLENNON, Theresa, "Lawyers and Caring: Building an Ethic of Care into Professional Responsibility" (1992) 43 Hast. L. J. 1175-86

GORDON, Robert W., "The Devil and Daniel Webster" [review of A. S. Konefsky and A. J. King (eds.), *The Papers of Daniel Webster*, 2 vols.] (1984) 94 Yale L. J. 445-60

GORDON, Robert W., "Lawyers as the 'American Aristocracy': A Nineteenth Century Ideal That May Still be Relevant" (1985) 20 Stanford Law. 2(10)

GORDON, Robert W., "Legal Thought and Legal Practice in the Age of American Enterprise, 1870-1920" in Gerald L. Geison (ed.), *Professions and Professional Ideologies in America* (Chapel Hill: University of North Carolina Press, 1983) 70-139

GORDON, Robert W. and **SIMON**, William H., "The Redemption of Professionalism" in Robert L. Nelson, David M. Trubek, and Rayman L. Solomon (eds.), *Lawyers' Ideals/Lawyers' Practices: Transformations in the American Legal Profession* (Ithaca, N.Y.: Cornell University Press, 1992) 230-57

HARRINGTON, Christine B., "Outlining a Theory of Legal Practice" in Maureen Cain and Christine B. Harrington (eds.), *Lawyers in a Postmodern World: Translation and Transgression* (Buckingham: Open University Press, 1994) 49-69

JAFF, Jennifer, "Law and Lawyer in Pop Music: A Reason for Self-Reflection" (1986) 40 U. Mia. L. Rev. 659-69

JOHNSON, Alex M., Jr., "Think Like a Lawyer, Work Like a Machine: The Dissonance Between Law School and Law Practice" (1991) 64 S. Cal. L. Rev. 1231-60

KENNEDY, Duncan, "Rebels From Principle: Changing the Corporate Law Firm From Within" (Fall, 1981) Harv. L. Sch. Bull. 36-40

KENNEDY, Duncan, "The Responsibility of Lawyers for the Justice of Their Causes" (1987) 18 Tex. Tech L. Rev. 1157-63

KENYATTA, Muhammad, "Community Organizing, Client Involvement and Poverty Law" (Oct., 1983) 35 Monthly Rev. 18-27

LAW, Sylvia A., "Personal and Professional Roles in Their Economic and Sexual Contexts" (1978) 53 N.Y.U. L. Rev. 628-35

LESNICK, Howard; **DVORKIN**, Elizabeth; and **HIMMELSTEIN**, Jack, *Becoming a Lawyer: A Humanistic Perspective on Legal Education and Professionalism* (St. Paul, Minn.: West, 1981)

LÓPEZ, Gerald P., "Lay Lawyering" (1984) 32 U.C.L.A. L. Rev. 1-60

LÓPEZ, Gerald P., *Rebellious Lawyering: One Chicano's Vision of Progressive Law Practice* (Boulder, Co.: Westview Press, 1992)

MACAULAY, Stewart, "Law Schools and the World Outside Their Doors: Notes on the Margins of 'Professional Training in the Public Interest'" (1968) 54 Va. L. Rev. 617-36

MACAULAY, Stewart, "Law Schools and the World Outside Their Doors II: Some Notes on Two Recent Studies of the Chicago Bar" (1982) 32 J. Legal Educ. 506-42

MENKEL-MEADOW, Carrie, "Culture Clash in the Quality of Life in the Law: Changes in the Economics, Diversification and Organization of Lawyering" (1994) 44 Case West. L. Rev. 621-63

MENKEL-MEADOW, Carrie, "Feminization of the Legal Profession: The Comparative Sociology of Lawyers" in Richard Abel and Philip S. C. Lewis (eds.), *Lawyers and Society, Vol. 3: Comparative Theories* (Berkeley: University of California Press, 1989) 196-255

NELSON, Robert and **MACAULAY**, Stewart, "Ideology, Practice, and Professional Autonomy: Social Values and Client Relationships in the Large Law Firm" (1985) 37 Stan. L. Rev. 503-64

NELSON, Robert L. and **TRUBEK**, David M., "Arenas of Professionalism: The Professional Ideologies of Lawyers in Context" in Robert L. Nelson, David M. Trubek, and Rayman L. Solomon (eds.), *Lawyers' Ideas/Lawyers' Practices: Transformations in the American Legal Profession* (Ithaca, N.Y.: Cornell University Press, 1992) 177-214

OLIVAS, Michael A., "Breaking the Law on Principle: An Essay on Lawyers' Dilemmas, Unpopular Causes, and Legal Regimes" (1991) 52 U. Pitt. L. Rev. 815-57

POWELL, Asa Mitchell, Jr., "Towards the Regeneration of Law and Ethics: Law as Process — A Response to Owen Fiss" (1988) 39 Mercer L. Rev. 591-640

RABINOWITZ, Victor, "The Radical Tradition in the Law" in David Kairys (ed.), *The Politics of Law: A Progressive Critique* (New York: Pantheon Books, 1982) 310-18

REIFNER, Udo, "The Bar in the Third Reich: Anti-Semitism and the Decline of Liberal Advocacy" (1986) 32 McGill L. J. 96-124

RHODE, Deborah, "Moral Character as a Professional Credential" (1985) 94 Yale L. J. 491-603

RHODE, Deborah, "Past Tension: Uneven Certification Standards Make One Lawyer's Character Another's Disrespect for the Law" (1985) 14 Student Law. 46-47

RHODE, Deborah, "The Rhetoric of Professional Reform" (1986) 45 Md. L. Rev. 274-97

RHODE, Deborah, "Solicitation" (1986) 36 J. Legal Educ. 317-30

RHODE, Deborah, "Why the ABA Bothers: A Functional Perspective on Professional Codes" (1981) 59 Tex. L. Rev. 689-721

RHODE, Deborah L. and **SCHWARTZ**, Murray L., "Ethical Perspectives on Legal Practice" (1985) 37 Stan. L. Rev. 589-659

SCHEINGOLD, Stuart, "The Contradictions of Radical Law Practice" in Maureen Cain and Christine B. Harrington (eds.), *Lawyers in a Postmodern World: Translation and Transgression* (Buckingham: Open University Press, 1994) 265-85

SERON, Carroll, "Managing Entrepreneurial Legal Services: The Transformation of Small-Firm Practice" in Robert L. Nelson, David M. Trubek, and Rayman L. Solomon (eds.), *Lawyers' Ideals/Lawyers' Practices: Transformations in the American Legal Profession* (Ithaca, N.Y.: Cornell University Press, 1992) 63-92

SIMON, William H., "Babbitt v. Brandeis: The Decline of the Professional Ideal" (1985) 37 Stan. L. Rev. 565-87

SIMON, William H., "Ethical Discretion in Lawyering" (1988) 101 Harv. L. Rev. 1083-145

SIMON, William H., "The Ideology of Advocacy: Procedural Justice and Professional Ethics" [1978] Wis. L. Rev. 29-144

SIMON, William H., "Judicial Clerkships and Elite Professional Culture" (1986) 36 J. Legal Educ. 129-37

SIMON, William H., "Visions of Practice in Legal Thought" (1984) 36 Stan. L. Rev. 469-507

SOIFER, Aviam, "Lawyers and Loyalty" [review of Peter Irons, *Justice at War: The Story of the Japanese Internment Cases*] (1984) 12 Revs. Am. Hist. 575-82

SUGARMAN, David, "Blurred Boundaries: The Overlapping Worlds of Law, Business and Politics" in Maureen Cain and Christine B. Harrington (eds.), *Lawyers in a Postmodern World: Translation and Transgression* (Buckingham: Open University Press, 1994) 105-123

SZELÉNYI, Ivan and **MARTIN**, Bill, "The Legal Profession and the Rise and Fall of the New Class" in Richard L. Abel and Philip S. C. Lewis (eds.), *Lawyers and Society, Vol. 3: Comparative Theories* (Berkeley: University of California Press, 1989) 256-88

WHITMAN, Douglas, "Advertising by American Lawyers" (1993) 13 Bridgeport L. Rev. 813-55

WILKINS, David B., "Legal Realism for Lawyers" (1990) 104 Harv. L. Rev. 468-524

9

Contract Law

Critical legal treatments of contract law have often revisited descriptions of the rise of classical contract law in the nineteenth century and the subsequent assault on it by legal realists. From a critical point of view, the rejection of many of the assumptions and norms of classical contract doctrine was not complete: traces of the legacy of Langdell, Holmes, Williston and the first *Restatement of Contracts* remain. Although realists left their mark on this field of private law ordering, the ultimate result was the construction of a "neoclassical" model of contract doctrine. This model retains its dominant influence over contemporary contract theorists.

Neoclassicism exhibits the following characteristics and assumptions. Contractual liability is still predicated on notions of autonomous and competent parties' reciprocal promises or some other basis for actual or notional agreement. This is the primary mode for contract formation. Enforcement of bargains still hinges generally on the presence of consideration, though forms of detrimental reliance have been incorporated also into the body of neoclassical doctrine. Courts are not supposed to review the merits or substance of the bargains over which disputes have arisen. Only in limited circumstances is it permissible for judges to inquire into the fairness of those bargains. When contractual obligations have been breached, the standard remedies, including the award of damages to compensate unfulfilled expectations, still reflect classical norms about the purposes of contract law in the capitalist economic order.

Critical legal approaches to contract law have challenged the reconstruction of contract doctrine in this neoclassical image. Critical legal theorists have examined the roots of contract law in the eighteenth century, in order to unearth the assumptions that prevailed before the advent of classical contract law. These studies purport to show that in pre-classical times, contractual obligation was not so distinctive from other forms of obligation, such as tort. Liability for commercial dealings did not hinge primarily on the ideal of a consensual bargain between self-interested parties. There was present in the law a sense that contractual obligations might arise out of evidence of reliance, and adjudication (by both judges and juries) could take into account community standards in reviewing the substance of bargains.

The abstract, formal doctrines developed by both classical and neoclassical theorists have been subjected to analysis by critical legal writers. These critiques, especially those employing the methods of deconstruction, argue that the goals of contract law are contradictory and in continuous tension. They include protection of both self-reliant individualism and aspirations to a smoothly functioning, interdependent commercial world. In addition, the rules and principles of conventional contract law are indeterminate. Some of them valorize a regime of minimal judicial or legislative invasion into the marketplace, while others endorse an interventionist legal approach in order to maximize the security of the parties' expectations. Even the neoclassical model allows for judicial activism, where it is necessary to uphold the sanctity of agreements.

Critical legal theorists have assessed contemporary alternatives to neoclassical contract doctrine. For example, the "relational" theory of contract associated with Ian Macneil and the writing on "empirical" contract law have offered useful insights into the background values and actual operation of contract doctrine. Nevertheless, these alternatives are inadequate. From a critical perspective, the alternative theories fail to grasp the political setting in which contract law is shaped and applied. On the critical account, the primary functions of contract doctrine are to sustain, legitimate, and stabilize the prevailing economic system. This is not to say that critical legal writing in this area adheres to some crude form of determinism. Contract doctrine does not invariably develop in response to the needs of the economically dominant litigant, but over time that doctrine favors the maintenance of existing social and economic relations.

Once the student of law understands the ideological function of contract doctrine, it is possible to conceive of contract law as a vehicle for social transformation. Critical legal theorists have emphasized the creative re-fashioning of contract doctrine to promote an egalitarian social order. Among the recommendations is that contractual analysis should describe factual settings by reference to the parties "entire lives," and not just their economic interests (see the work by Feinman). Also, a critical approach to contract doctrine would explicitly take into account the political consequences of particular doctrines and the theories which favor them.

* * * *

BRATTON, William W., Jr., "Manners, Metaprinciples, Metapolitics and Kennedy's *Form and Substance*" (1985) 6 Cardozo L. Rev. 871-915

BRIETZKE, Paul H., "Public Policy: Contract, Abortion, and the CIA" (1984) 18 Val. U. L. Rev. 741-940

COLLINS, Hugh, "Contract and Legal Theory" in William Twining (ed.), *Legal Theory and Common Law* (Oxford: Blackwell, 1986) 136-54

COLLINS, Hugh, "Distributive Justice Through Contracts" [1992] Curr. Legal Probs. 49-67

COLLINS, Hugh, *The Law of Contract*, 2nd ed. (London: Weidenfeld & Nicolson, 1993)

COLLINS, Hugh, "The Transformation Thesis and the Ascription of Contractual Responsibility" in Thomas Wilhelmsson (ed.), *Perspectives of Critical Contract Law* (Aldershot, Hants: Dartmouth Pub. Co., 1993) 293-310

DALTON, Clare, "An Essay in the Deconstruction of Contract Doctrine" (1985) 94 Yale L. J. 999-1114

FEINMAN, Jay M., "A Case Study in Critical Contract Law" [1988] Ann. Surv. Am. L. 272-92

FEINMAN, Jay M., "Critical Approaches to Contract Law" (1983) 30 U.C.L.A. L. Rev. 829-60

FEINMAN, Jay M., "The Jurisprudence of Classification" (1989) 41 Stan. L. Rev. 661-717

FEINMAN, Jay M., "The Meaning of Reliance: A Historical Perspective" [1984] Wis. L. Rev. 1373-89

FEINMAN, Jay M., "Promissory Estoppel and Judicial Method" (1984) 97 Harv. L. Rev. 678-718

FEINMAN, Jay M., "Relational Contract and Default Rules" (1993) 3 S. Cal. Interdis. L. J. 43-58

FEINMAN, Jay M., "The Significance of Contract Theory" (1990) 58 U. Cin. L. Rev. 1283-318

FEINMAN, Jay M. and **GABEL**, Peter, "Contract Law as Ideology" in David Kairys (ed.), *The Politics of Law: A Progressive Critique* (New York: Pantheon Books, 1982) 172-84

FEINMAN, Jay M. and **GABEL**, Peter, "Contract Law as Ideology" in David Kairys (ed.), *The Politics of Law: A Progressive Critique*, 2nd rev. ed. (New York: Pantheon Books, 1990) 373-86

FRUG, Mary Joe, "Re-Reading Contracts: A Feminist Analysis of a Contracts Casebook" (1985) 34 Am. U. L. Rev. 1065-140

GABEL, Peter, "Intention and Structure in Contractual Conditions: Outline of a Method for Critical Legal Theory" (1977) 61 Minn. L. Rev. 601-43

GOODRICH, Peter, "Contractions: Rousseau in the Year Two Thousand" in Anthony Carty (ed.), *Post-Modern Law* (Edinburgh: Edinburgh University Press, 1990) 40-70

GORDON, Robert W., "Macaulay, Macneil, and the Discovery of Solidarity and Power in Contract Law" [1985] Wis. L. Rev. 565-79

GORDON, Robert W., Review of Grant Gilmore, *The Death of Contract* [1974] Wis. L. Rev. 1216-39

GORDON, Robert W., "Unfreezing Legal Reality: Critical Approaches to Law" (1987) 15 Fla. St. U. L. Rev. 195-220

HOLT, Wythe, "Recovery by the Worker Who Quits: A Comparison of the Mainstream, Legal Realist, and Critical Legal Studies Approaches to a Problem of Nineteenth Century Contract Law" [1986] Wis. L. Rev. 677-732

HORWITZ, Morton J., "The Historical Foundations of Modern Contract Law" (1974) 87 Harv. L. Rev. 917-56

HORWITZ, Morton J., Review of Grant Gilmore, *The Death of Contract* (1975) 42 U. Chi. L. Rev. 787-97

KENNEDY, Duncan, "Distributive and Paternalist Motives in Contract and Tort Law, With Special Reference to Compulsory Terms and Unequal Bargaining Power" (1982) 41 Md. L. Rev. 563-658

KENNEDY, Duncan, "Form and Substance in Private Law Adjudication" (1976) 89 Harv. L. Rev. 1685-1778

KLARE, Karl, "Contracts Jurisprudence and the First-Year Casebook" [review of Charles L. Knapp, *Problems in Contract Law: Cases and Materials*] (1979) 54 N.Y.U. L. Rev. 876-99

KONEFSKY, Alfred; **MENSCH**, Elizabeth; and **SCHLEGEL**, John Henry, "In Memoriam: The Intellectual Legacy of Lon Fuller" [review of Lon L. Fuller and Melvin A. Eisenberg, *Basic Contract Law*, 4th ed.] (1981) 30 Buffalo L. Rev. 263-64

MACAULAY, Stewart, "Elegant Models, Empirical Pictures, and the Complexities of Contract" (1977) 11 L. & Soc'y Rev. 507-28

MACAULAY, Stewart, "An Empirical View of Contract" [1985] Wis. L. Rev. 465-82

MACAULAY, Stewart, "Non-Contractual Relations in Business: A Preliminary Study" (1963) 28 Am. Soc. Rev. 55-67

MACAULAY, Stewart, "Private Legislation and the Duty to Read — Business Run by IBM Machine, the Law of Contracts and Credit Cards" (1966) 19 Vand. L. Rev. 1051-1121

MACAULAY, Stewart, "The 'Reliance Interest' and the World Outside the Law Schools' Doors" [1991] Wis. L. Rev. 247-91

MACNEIL, Ian R., "Relational Contract: What We Do and Do Not Know" [1985] Wis. L. Rev. 483-525

MACURDY, Allan H., "Classical Nostalgia: Racism, Contract Ideology, and Formalist Legal Reasoning in *Patterson* v. *McLean Credit Union*" (1990-91) 18 N.Y.U. Rev. L. & Soc. Ch. 987-1025

MENSCH, Elizabeth, "Freedom of Contract as Ideology" [review of P. S. Atiyah, *The Rise and Fall of Freedom of Contract*] (1981) 33 Stan. L. Rev. 753-72

NOCKLEBY, John, "Tortious Interference with Contractual Relations in the Nineteenth Century: The Transformation of Property, Contract, and Tort" (1980) 93 Harv. L. Rev. 1510-39

SOIFER, Aviam, "Status Contract, and Promises Unkept" (1987) 96 Yale L. J. 1916-59

SPANN, Girardeau A., "A Critical Legal Studies Perspective on Contract Law and Practice" [1988] Ann. Surv. Am. L. 223-57

WHITFORD, William C., "Ian Macneil's Contributions to Contract Scholarship" [1985] Wis. L. Rev. 545-64

WILHELMSSON, Thomas, "Questions for a Critical Contract Law — and a Contradictory Answer: Contract as Social Cooperation" in Thomas Wilhelmsson (ed.), *Perspectives of Critical Contract Law* (Aldershot, Hants: Dartmouth Pub. Co., 1993) 9-52

10

Tort Law

Critical legal literature has reexamined the modern foundations of tort law. Writers have criticized the standard historical paradigms by which the law regarding civil redress for personal injuries changed from an ethically-based system, which involved intentional harms, into one centered on the tortfeasor's negligence. In particular, these accounts are criticized for making the shift in legal assumptions appear as a progressive social imperative. Historians such as Morton Horwitz have traced the extent to which legal doctrines were adopted in order to stave off the potential use of tort law as a device to redistribute economic wealth or to re-engineer society. Instead, tort law, by limiting an enterprise's responsiblity for many negative externalities of its activities, became an important device for encouraging the growth and success of capitalist ventures.

These aims were served by doctrines which required, for example, proof that the defendant's alleged cause of an injury was the "proximate" cause, rather than a "remote" cause, and there was no "intervening" cause. Such doctrines helped courts determine whether there was a single responsible defendant in each case, whose conduct was sufficiently faulty that legal responsiblity should be assigned. These orthodox approaches of the nineteenth century were challenged even before legal realists criticized traditional causation doctrines. Later attempts to develop liability rules framed in terms of "foreseeability" and what the "reasonable" potential tortfeasor should have been able to calculate as the risks of injury, were just additional means for courts to determine outcomes under the guise of applying a set of objective criteria. These rules simply concealed the extent to which the common law development of tort doctrine allowed courts to make highly political decisions about which parties should typically bear the costs of injuries.

From the perspective of its radical critics, modern tort law is problematic, but not because there is a "liability crisis." Whether too many or too few claims are actually brought concerns critical legal writers less than the issue of whether the purported aims of tort law are especially well-served by the current system. Under contemporary tort law, individual plaintiffs seek monetary awards from courts to compensate them for injuries caused by the activities of defendants. Like other legal fields, tort law depends on liberal legal assumptions in which doctrine is developed as a matter of abstract, apparently neutral principle (for example, a fundamental respect for individuals' autonomous choices in relation to work conditions and consumer goods and services). Following these principles, courts are supposed to reach coherent results in particular cases. In fact, from a critical legal perspective, tort law reflects typically capitalist relations of production and the commodification of human satisfaction and experience.

Critical legal writers have doubted whether tort law regimes do much to deter injurious behavior and to promote safety precautions. The empirical evidence is thin regarding whether liability rules actually do make a difference to parties whose activities might be harmful. Also, under current rules, potential tortfeasors may rationally conclude (with respect to some potential victims such as employees or consumers) that the cost of precautions is more than the costs likely to arise from litigation down the road. Even if there is an identifiable hazard, because of the existence of liability insurance and also because executive decision-makers are protected by the doctrine of *respondeat superior*, no personal liability may be visited on the persons most directly responsible for an injury.

The workings of the tort system do not guarantee that all tortfeasors will be held liable for all injuries caused to victims, so a firm might choose to ignore many of the legal risks associated with its operations. In the words of Richard Abel, the judicial decision to compensate a plaintiff is "inescapably political and unprincipled." The system is inefficient: many victims go uncompensated; some are undercompensated; and a few receive extremely generous awards. Critical legal writers would agree that, to this extent, success in a tort action is equivalent to striking it rich in a "lottery."

In addition, contemporary tort law still heavily concentrates on the claims of individual victims. Only by overcoming extraordinary legal obstacles can groups injured by the same alleged tortfeasor bring an action that will reflect the overall damage caused.

Another deficiency with current tort law, from not only a critical legal point of view, but one identified by other reformers of this area of law, is the extent to which injuries resulting from accidents are treated as compensable, while other causes of disability are excluded from a tort regime. Critical legal writers have joined other critics who claim that tort law rests on inconsistent and arguably outmoded moral and epistemological foundations. In this regard, other critiques of the tort system, such as those deriving from feminism, have also provoked questions about the standards and rules contained in tort doctrine. For instance, questions have been asked about whether the standards used ot determine the "normal" response to distressing incidents have not been predominantly male. Also, these critiques point out the historical, political, and gender-biased roots of tort doctrines such as the one providing immunity for wrongs when the injured party is the tortfeasor's spouse.

Some critical legal authors have imagined a legal regime that would replace tort law. The measures include a centralized compensation agency, probably administered by government, that would offer universal coverage against disabling injuries, whether caused by accident or illness. The decision to compensate would not be based on the fault of a wrongdoer and would not require adjudication in the courts. Some writers (such as Abel) have doubted whether compensation for intangible harms, like pain and suffering or emotional distress, ought to continue to be compensable under a new regime. The system would be comprehensive and force all potential wrongdoers to internalize or insure against the costs of all accidents. Legal doctrines that turn on the comparative negligence of claimants and alleged wrongdoers would no longer apply: all victims would be eligible for compensation regardless of their own behavior. The amount of compensation would not necessarily reflect the existing levels of wealth or income enjoyed by claimants. Under the current tort system, non-earning activities (such as housework) have been devalued. Under a revamped system, compensation should be available for all victims, even if this means that wealthy victims would receive less than they would under the current system.

* * * *

ABEL, Richard L., "Blaming Victims" [review of Mary Douglas and Aaron Wildavsky, *Risk and Culture: An Essay on the Selection of Technological and Environmental Dangers*] [1985] Am. Bar Fdn. Res. J. 401-17

ABEL, Richard L., "A Critique of American Tort Law" (1981) 8 Brit. J. L. & Soc'y 199-231

ABEL, Richard L., "A Critique of Torts" (1990) 37 U.C.L.A. L. Rev. 785-831

ABEL, Richard L., "£'s of Cure, Ounces of Prevention" [review of Donald Harris *et al.*, *Compensation and Support for Illnes and Injury*] (1985) 73 Calif. L. Rev. 1003-23

ABEL, Richard L., "The Real Tort Crisis — Too Few Claims" (1987) 48 Ohio St. L. J. 443-67

ABEL, Richard L., "Risk as an Arena of Struggle" (1985) 83 Mich. L. Rev. 772-812

ABEL, Richard L., "Should Tort Law Protect Property Against Accidental Loss?" (1986) 23 San Diego L. Rev. 79-123, reprinted in Michael Furmston (ed.), *The Law of Tort: Policies and Trends in Liability for Damage to Property and Economic Loss* (London: Duckworth, 1986) 155-90

ABEL, Richard L., "A Socialist Approach to Risk" (1982) 41 Md. L. Rev. 695-754

ABEL, Richard, "Torts" in David Kairys (ed.), *The Politics of Law: A Progressive Critique* (New York: Pantheon Books, 1982) 185-200

ABEL, Richard L., "Torts" in David Kairys (ed.), *The Politics of Law: A Progressive Critique*, 2nd rev. ed. (New York: Pantheon Books, 1990) 326-49

BANKS, Taunya Lovell, "Teaching Laws With Flaws: Adopting a Pluralistic Approach to Torts" (1992) 57 Mo. L. Rev. 443-54

BELL, Peter A., "Analyzing Tort Law: The Flawed Promise of Neocontract" (1990) 74 Minn. L. Rev. 1177-249

BENDER, Leslie, "Changing the Values in Tort Law" (1990) 25 Tulsa L. Rev. 759-73

BENDER, Leslie, "Feminist (Re)Torts: Thoughts on the Liability Crisis, Mass Torts, Power, and Responsiblities" [1990] Duke L. J. 848-912

BENDER, Leslie, "A Lawyer's Primer on Feminist Theory and Tort" (1988) 38 J. Legal Educ. 3-37

BENDER, Leslie, "An Overview of Feminist Torts Scholarship" (1993) 78 Cornell L. Rev. 575-96

BENDER, Leslie and **LAWRENCE**, Perrette, "Is Tort Law Male? Foreseeability Analysis and Property Managers' Liability for Third Party Rapes of Residents" (1993) 69 Chi.-Kent L. Rev. 313-43

BOYLE, James, "The Anatomy of a Torts Class" (1985) 34 Am. U. L. Rev. 1003-63

BUSH, Robert A. Baruch, "Between Two Worlds: The Shift from Individual to Group Responsibility in the Law of Causation of Injury" (1987) 34 U.C.L.A. L. Rev. 1473-563

CAHN, Naomi R., "The Looseness of Legal Language: The Reasonable Woman Standard in Theory and in Practice" (1992) 77 Cornell L. Rev. 1398-446

CONAGHAN, Joanne and **MANSELL**, Wade, *The Wrongs of Torts* (London: Pluto Press, 1993)

DELGADO, Richard and **LESKOVAC**, Helen, "Informed Consent in Human Experimentation: Bridging the Gap Between Ethical Thought and Current Practice" (1986) 34 U.C.L.A. L. Rev. 67-130

DOUGHERTY, Jude P., "Accountability Without Causality: Tort Litigation Reaches Fairy Tale Levels" (1991) 41 Cath. U. L. Rev. 1-18

FELDTHUSEN, Bruce, "Discriminatory Damage Qualification in Civil Actions for Sexual Battery" (1994) 44 U. Toronto L. J. 133-67

FINLEY, Lucinda M., "A Break in the Silence: Including Women's Issues in a Torts Course" (1989) 1 Yale J. L. & Fem. 41-73

GOODZEIT, Carolyn A., "Rethinking Emotional Distress Law: Prenatal Malpractice and Feminist Theory" (1994) 63 Fordham L. Rev. 175-214

GORDON, Robert W., Review of G. E. White, *Tort Law in America* (1981) 94 Harv. L. Rev. 903-18

HORWITZ, Morton J., "The Doctrine of Objective Causation" in David Kairys (ed.), *The Politics of Law: A Progressive Critique* (New York: Pantheon Books, 1982) 201-13

HORWITZ, Morton J., "The Doctrine of Objective Causation" in David Kairys (ed.), *The Politics of Law: A Progressive Critique*, 2nd rev. ed. (New York: Pantheon Books, 1990) 360-72

HOWE, Adrian, *The Problem of Privatized Injuries: Feminist Strategies for Litigation* (Madison: Institute for Legal Studies, University of Wisconsin, 1989)

HUTCHINSON, Allan C., "Beyond No-Fault" (1985) 73 Calif. L. Rev. 755-71

HUTCHINSON, Allan C. and **MORGAN**, Derek, "The Canengusian Connection: The Kaleidoscope of Tort Theory" (1984) 22 Osgoode Hall L. J. 69-113

KELMAN, Mark, "The Necessary Myth of Objective Causation Judgments in Liberal Political Theory" (1987) 63 Chi.-Kent L. Rev. 579-637

LAW, Sylvia A., "A Consumer Perspective on Medical Malpractice" (1986) 49 L. & Contemp. Probs. 305-20

LEE, Randy, "A Look at God, Feminism, and Tort Law" (1992) 75 Marq. L. Rev. 369-408

LINDGREN, Janet S., "Judges and Statutes: Essays on Agent Orange" (1984) 6 L. & Pol'y 189-202

LINDGREN, Janet S., "Social Theory and Judicial Choice: Damages and Federal Statutes" (1979) 28 Buffalo L. Rev. 711-63

MARTIN, Robyn, "A Feminist View of the Reasonable Man: An Alternative Approach to Liability in Negligence for Personal Injury" (1994) 23 Anglo-Am. L. Rev. 334-74

McCONNELL, Joyce E., "Beyond Metaphor: Battered Women, Involuntary Servitude and the Thirteenth Amendment" (1992) 4 Yale J. L. & Fem. 207-53

McCONNELL, Joyce E., "Incest as Conundrum: Judicial Discourse on Private Wrong and Public Harm" (1992) 1 Tex. J. Wom. & L. 143-72

MUNGER, Frank W., "Social Change and Tort Litigation: Industrialization, Accidents, and Trial Courts in Southern West Virginia, 1872 to 1940" (1987) 36 Buffalo L. Rev. 75-118

SCHWARTZ, Gary T., "Tort Law and the Economy in Nineteenth-Century America: A Reinterpretation" (1981) 90 Yale L. J. 1717-75

TOBIAS, Carl, "Gender Issues and the Prosser, Wade, and Schwartz Torts Casebook" (1988) 18 Golden Gate U. L. Rev. 495-527

TOBIAS, Carl, "Interspousal Tort Immunity in America" (1989) 23 Ga. L. Rev. 359-478

WILDMAN, Stephanie M., "Enlightened Social Insurance in a World Made Safer" [review of Stephen D. Sugarman, *Doing Away With Personal Injury Law*] (1990) 44 U. Mia. L. Rev. 877-92

WILDMAN, Stephanie M., "Review Essay: The Power of Women" [review of Catharine MacKinnon, *Toward a Feminist Theory of the State*] (1990) 2 Yale J. L. & Fem. 435-52

11

Constitutional Law

A great deal of critical legal writing in constitutional law has been on controversies arising out of the courts' power to review measures adopted by the other, co-ordinate branches of government, including the legislature and the executive. As it has for contemporary constitutional theory generally, the most vexed problem for radical critics has been explaining and justifying the role of judges in interpreting basic constitutional documents and applying them to specific disputes. This is not to say that critical legal writing ignores other important questions in constitutional law, such as the structure of government, the evolution of constitutional doctrine, or the use of a constitutional framework to build a progressive society. Such issues as first amendment protection, reproductive rights, the constitutionalization of economic and property rights, and antidiscrimination law have all been addressed in critical legal literature.

When critical legal writing appeared in the 1970s, the crucial debates in U.S. constitutional law circles concerned the legitimacy of judicial review. Writers such as Mark Tushnet joined those debates which he characterized as having a distinctly liberal flavor. In his view, constitutional theory has been "essentially a concomitant of liberalism." Each position already staked out shares certain assumptions about the need to constrain judges, in practising constitutional review, from giving effect to their subjective preferences. The source of this danger is the undoubted fluidity of meaning in the text of the U.S. constitution and in the precedents that have been decided by reference to that document. What stops judges from simply imposing their own partisan political views? Critical legal authors have examined the various conventional perspectives on the question and identified the weaknesses of each.

Among the positions rejected by critical legal writers have been the following. They have repudiated the "interpretivist" or "original intent" approach, according to which constitutional cases should be decided in a manner consistent with the intent of the framers. The radical critique has also disposed of the appeal to "neutral principles" as a constraint on judicial discretion. This approach presupposes an illusory consensus about which principles underlie judicial reasoning. Critical legal authors have also criticized the division of issues into "expedient" matters that should be left to the ordinary political process, and issues of "principle" that should engage the courts. Finally, the radical critics have rejected attempts by writers such as John Hart Ely to construct a normative theory of constitutional adjudication, in which certain types of political malfunctions are treated as justifying judicial intervention and correction. Courts are supposed to keep surveillance on the means by which lawmakers arrive at political choices, rather than inquire into the substance or merits of the resulting measures. From a critical legal perspective, such "process-oriented" theories are flawed, for they simply confirm the *status quo*. They rely on problematic assumptions that liberal democratic government, especially its representative institutions, functions for the most part well, if not perfectly.

Critical legal writers have reevaluated U.S. constitutional history to show the extent to which constitutional doctrine can be employed for conservative purposes. From a radical critic's perspective, the two eras noted for progressive lawmaking, the New Deal in the 1930s and the civil rights struggle of the 1950s and 60s, were brief interludes in what has otherwise been a consistently conservative pattern of U.S. Supreme Court constitutional decisionmaking. Even these so-called progressive periods invite reexamination to determine how the orientation of the court reflected the views held by certain segments of the national political elite.

Realizing that the invocation of constitutionally protected rights has been a strategy available to conservative and liberal proponents alike, radical critics have hesitated to recommend rights-based advocacy as a form of progressive practice. The critique has refused to place implicit faith in the use of rights. Rights lack an epistemological warrant, they are unstable over time, and they create the illusion that constitutional analysis can lead to correct and determinate results.

On the other hand, critical legal writing has also acknowledged that appeals to rights (either as entrenched rights or as arguable extensions to established rights) can sometimes be effective and defensible, especially where those rights have already been won (for example, in relation to the reproductive rights of women). These appeals can be useful both inside the courtroom and in general political forums. They can form one part of the overall structure of argument, but, realistically, the rhetoric of rights can be used just as readily against progressive reforms as in their favor.

Some critical legal writers have been skeptical about the value of rights discourse because of the attention this diverts away from ordinary political action by progressive movements. By locating the struggle in constitutional litigation, groups can find their organization is somewhat demobilized while lawyers take over job of articulating the views of the cause. The issues then become framed in a constitutional mode, as if the matter could not be resolved better through democratic deliberation.

In prescribing a post-liberal constitutional scholarship and practice, critical legal writers have dealt mostly in generalities. Tushnet has invoked a "communal" vision in which citizens join a genuinely political conversation in which they share an understanding of the importance of dialogue. Constitutional discourse would then be participatory and amount to something broader than debates within Congress or within a courtroom. Other writers have sought to revive a "civic republican" ideal, with its elements of equality, an active citizenry, and an accent on civic virtue (as opposed to individual self-interest). This attempt to resuscitate republicanism and shape constitutional theory around it has itself been sharply criticized from other quarters within the movement.

This guide does not contain a separate, free-standing section on critical research in administrative law. An indication of the critique in this area can be found in a couple of articles, by Allan Hutchinson and David Jabbari, listed below.

* * * *

BAKAN, Joel C., "Constitutional Arguments: Interpretation and Legitimation in Canadian Constitutional Thought" (1989) 27 Osgoode Hall L. J. 123-93

BAKAN, Joel C., "Constitutional Interpretation and Social Change: You Can't Always Get What You Want (Nor What You Need)" (1991) 70 Can. Bar Rev. 307-28

BAKAN, Joel C., "Strange Expectations: A Review of Two Theories of Judicial Review" (1990) 35 McGill L. J. 439-88

BAKAN, Joel, "What's Wrong With Social Rights?" in Joel Bakan and David Schneiderman (eds.), Social Justice and the Constitution: Perspectives on a Social Union for Canada (Ottawa: Carleton University Press, 1992) 85-99

BAKER, C. Edwin, *Advertising and a Democratic Process* (Princeton: Princeton University Press, 1994)

BAKER, C. Edwin, "Commercial Speech: A Problem in the Theory of Freedom" (1976) 62 Iowa L. Rev. 1-56

BAKER, C. Edwin, *Human Liberty and Freedom of Speech* (New York: Oxford University Press, 1989)

BAKER, C. Edwin, "Neutrality, Process, and Rationality: Flawed Interpretations of Equal Protection" (1980) 58 Tex. L. Rev. 1029-96

BAKER, C. Edwin, "Outcome Equality or Equality of Respect: The Substantive Content of Equal Protection" (1983) 131 U. Pa. L. Rev. 933-98

BAKER, C. Edwin, "The Process of Change and the Liberty Theory of the First Amendment" (1981) 55 S. Cal. L. Rev. 293-344

BAKER, C. Edwin, "Property and Its Relation to Constitutionally Protected Liberty" (1986) 134 U. Pa. L. Rev. 741-816

BAKER, C. Edwin, "Rediscovering Economic Liberties" (1989) 41 Rutgers L. Rev. 753-84

BAKER, C. Edwin, "Scope of the First Amendment Freedom of Speech" (1978) 25 U.C.L.A. L. Rev. 964-1040

BAKER, C. Edwin, "Unreasoned Reasonableness: Mandatory Parade Permits and Time, Place, and Manner Regulations" (1983) 78 Nw. U. L. Rev. 937-1024

BAKER, C. Edwin, "Utility and Rights: Two Justifications for State Action Increasing Equality" (1974) 84 Yale L. J. 39-59

BALKIN, J. M., "Federalism and the Conservative Ideology" (1987) 19 Urb. Law. 459-92

BALKIN, J. M., "Ideology and Counter-Ideology from Lochner to Garcia" (1986) 54 U.M.K.C. L. Rev. 175-214

BALKIN, J. M., "Some Realism About Pluralism: Legal Realist Approaches to the First Amendment" [1990] Duke L. J. 375-430

BALKIN, J. M., "What is a Postmodern Constitutionalism?" (1992) 90 Mich. L. Rev. 1966-90

BLUM, Jeffrey, "The Divisible First Amendment: A Critical Functionalist Approach to Freedom of Speech and Electoral Campaign Spending" (1983) 58 N.Y.U. L. Rev. 1273-382

BOYLE, James, "A Process of Denial: Bork and Post-Modern Conservatism" (1991) 3 Yale L. & Hum. 263-314

BRAVEMAN, Daan and **BENDER**, Leslie, *Power, Privilege and Law: A Civil Rights Reader* (St. Paul, Minn.: West Pub. Co., 1995)

BREST, Paul, "Affirmative Action and the Constitution: Three Theories" (1987) 72 Iowa L. Rev. 281-85

BREST, Paul, "Congress as Constitutional Decisionmaker and Its Power to Counter Judicial Doctrine" (1986) 21 Ga. L. Rev. 57-105

BREST, Paul, "Constitutional Citizenship" (1986) 34 Cleve. St. L. Rev. 175-97

BREST, Paul, "The Fundamental Rights Controversy: The Essential Contradictions of Normative Constitutional Scholarship" (1981) 90 Yale L. J. 1063-1109

BREST, Paul, "Further Beyond the Republican Revival: Toward Radical Republicanism" (1988) 97 Yale L. J. 1623-31

BREST, Paul, "Interpretation and Interest" (1982) 34 Stan. L. Rev. 765-73

BREST, Paul, "State Action and Liberal Theory: A Casenote on *Flagg Bros.* v. *Brooks*" (1982) 130 U. Pa. L. Rev. 1296-1330

BREST, Paul, "The Substance of Process" (1981) 42 Ohio St. L. J. 131-42

BREST, Paul, "Who Decides?" (1985) 58 S. Calif. L. Rev. 661-71

BREST, Paul and **VANDENBERG**, Ann, "Politics, Feminism, and the Constitution: The Anti-Pornography Movement in Minneapolis" (1987) 39 Stan. L. Rev. 607-61

BRIGHAM, John, *Constitutional Language: An Interpretation of Judicial Decision* (Westport, Conn.: Greenwood Press, 1978)

BRIGHAM, John, *The Cult of the Court* (Philadelphia: Temple University Press, 1987)

CAMPOS, Paul, "Against Constitutional Theory" (1992) 4 Yale J. L. & Hum. 279-310

CARTY, Anthony, "English Constitutional Law from a Postmodernist Perspective" in Peter Fitzpatrick (ed.), *Dangerous Supplements: Resistance and Renewal in Jurisprudence* (Durham: Duke University Press, 1991) 182-206

CASEBEER, Kenneth M., "Toward a Critical Jurisprudence — A First Step By Way of the Public-Private Distinction in Constitutional Law" (1983) 37 U. Miami L. Rev. 379-431

CHASE, Anthony, "The Left on Rights: An Introduction" (1984) 62 Tex. L. Rev. 1541-61

CHASE, Anthony, "A Note on the Aporias of Critical Constitutionalism" (1987) 36 Buffalo L. Rev. 403-19

CHEVIGNY, Paul G., "Philosophy of Language and Free Expression" (1980) 55 N.Y.U. L. Rev. 157-94

COLE, David and **ESKRIDGE**, William N., Jr., "From Hand-Holding to Sodomy: First Amendment Protection of Homosexual (Expressive) Conduct" (1994) 29 Harv. C.R.-C.L. L. Rev. 319-51

CONKLIN, William E., *Images of a Constitution* (Toronto: University of Toronto Press, 1989)

COOK, Anthony E., "The Temptation and Fall of Original Understanding" [review of Robert Bork, *The Tempting of America*] [1990] Duke L. J. 1163-206

COTTROL, Robert J. and **DIAMOND**, Raymond T., "The Second Amendment: Toward an Afro-Americanist Reconsideration" (1991) 80 Geo. L. J. 309-61

DELGADO, Richard, "Campus Antiracism Rules: Constitutional Narratives in Collision" (1991) 85 Nw. U. L. Rev. 343-87

DENVIR, John, "Justice Brennan, Justice Rehnquist, and Free Speech" (1985) 80 Nw. U. L. Rev. 285-320

DENVIR, John, "Justice Rehnquist and Constitutional Interpretation" (1983) 34 Hast. L. J. 1011-53

DENVIR, John, "Liberal Justice?" [review of G. E. White, *Earl Warren: A Public Life*] (1983) 5 Cardozo L. Rev. 239-47

DENVIR, John, "The New Constitutional Law" [review of Michael J. Perry, *The Constitution, the Courts and Human Rights*] (1983) 44 Ohio St. L. J. 139-45

DONOVAN, Dolores, "Informers Revisited: Government Surveillance of Domestic Political Organizations and the Fourth and Fifth Amendments" (1984) 33 Buffalo L. Rev. 333-88

FELDMAN, Stephen M., "The Persistence of Power and the Struggle for Dialogic Standards in Postmodern Constitutional Jurisprudence: Michelman, Habermas, and Civic Republicanism" (1993) 81 Geo. L. J. 2243-90

FLAGG, Barbara J., "Enduring Principle: On Race, Process, and Constitutional Law" (1994) 82 Cal. L. Rev. 935-80

FRASER, Andrew, "Beyond the Charter Debate: Republicanism, Rights and Civic Virtue in the Civil Constitution of Canadian Society" (1993) 1 Rev. Const. Stud. 27-74

FRASER, Andrew, "Neo-Conservative Constitutionalism" [review of Suri Ratnapala, *Welfare State or Constitutional State?*] (1992) 14 Syd. L. Rev. 385-88

FRASER, Andrew, "The Partial Republic" [review of Cass R. Sunstein, *The Partial Constitution*] (1995) 2 Rev. Const. Stud. 396-435

FRASER, Andrew, "Populism and Republican Justice" (1991) 88 Telos 95-119

FRASER, Andrew, "Slaying the Republican Dragon: Reply to David Fraser" (1990) 85 Telos 79-88

FRASER, Andrew, *The Spirit of the Laws: Civic Federalism and the Unfinished Project of Republican Modernity* (Toronto: University of Toronto Press, 1990)

FRASER, David, "Fraser vs. Fraser" [review of Andrew Fraser, *The Spirit of the Laws*] (1990) 84 Telos 185-92

FRASER, David, "Righting the Constitution" [review of Stephen Macedo, *The New Right v. The Constitution*] (1987-88) 74 Telos 188-90

FRASER, David and **FREEMAN**, Alan, "What's Hockey Got to Do With It Anyway? Comparative Canadian-American Perspectives on Constitutional Law and Rights" (1987) 36 Buffalo L. Rev. 259-84

FREEMAN, Alan and **MENSCH**, Elizabeth, "The Public-Private Distinction in American Law and Life" (1987) 36 Buffalo L. Rev. 237-57

FRUG, Jerry, "Administrative Democracy" (1990) 40 U. Toronto L. J. 559-86

FRUG, Gerald, "The City as a Legal Concept" (1980) 93 Harv. L. Rev. 1057-1154

FRUG, Gerald E., "Empowering Cities in a Federal System" (1987) 19 Urb. Law. 553-68

GABEL, Peter, "Founding Father Knows Best: A Reponse to Tushnet" (1987) 36 Buffalo L. Rev. 227-35

GABEL, Peter, "The Mass Psychology of the New Federalism: How the Burger Court's Political Imagery Legitimizes the Privatization of Everyday Life" (1984) 52 Geo. Wash. L. Rev. 263-71

GABEL, Peter, "The Phenomenology of Rights-Consciousness and the Pact of the Withdrawn Selves" (1984) 62 Tex. L. Rev. 1563-99

GLASBEEK, Harry J., "From Constitutional Rights to 'Real' Rights — R-I-G-HTS FO-OR-WA-ARD HO'" (1990) 10 Windsor Y.B. Acc. Just. 468-95

GLASBEEK, Harry J., "A No-Frills Look at the Charter of Rights and Freedoms or How Politicians and Lawyers Hide Reality" (1990) 9 Windsor Y.B. Acc. Just. 293-352

GLASBEEK, Harry J., "The Politics of Rights: A Politics With Little Class" (1992) 1 Soc. & Legal Stud. 45-70

GLASBEEK, Harry, "The Social Charter: Poor Politics for the Poor" in Joel Bakan and David Schneiderman (eds.), *Social Justice and the Constitution: Perspectives on a Social Union for Canada* (Ottawa: Carleton University Press, 1992) 115-23

GLASBEEK, Harry J. and **MANDEL**, Michael, "The Legalization of Politics in Advanced Capitalism: The Canadian Charter of Rights and Freedoms" (1983) 2 Socialist Stud. 84-124

GRANO, Joseph D., "Deconstructing the Constitution" (1988-89) 2(1) Academic Questions 10-21

HARRIS, Ladonna, "Constitutional and Tribal Governance" in A. E. Dick Howard (ed.), *The United States Constitution: Roots, Rights, and Responsibilities* (Washington, D.C.: Smithsonian Institution Press, 1992) 115-27

HARTOG, Hendrik, "Imposing Constitutional Traditions" (1987) 29 Wm. & Mary L. Rev. 75-82

HODGKISS, Anita, "Petitioning and the Empowerment Theory of Practice" (1987) 96 Yale L. J. 569-92

HORWITZ, Morton J., "The Bork Nomination and American Constitutional History" (1988) 39 Syracuse L. Rev. 1029-39

HORWITZ, Morton J., "Republicanism and Liberalism in American Constitutional Thought" (1987) 29 Wm. & Mary L. Rev. 57-74

HORWITZ, Morton J., "Rights" (1988) 23 Harv. C.R.-C.L. L. Rev. 393-406

HUTCHINSON, Allan C., "Alien Thoughts: A Comment on Constitutional Scholarship" (1985) 58 S. Cal. L. Rev. 701-13

HUTCHINSON, Allan C., "Mice Under a Chair: Democracy, Courts, and the Administrative State" (1990) 40 U. Toronto L. J. 374-404

HUTCHINSON, Allan C., "Tribal Noises" [review of Laurence Tribe, *Constitutional Choices*] [1986] Am. Bar Fdn. Res. J. 79-103

HUTCHINSON, Allan C., "The Rise and Ruse of Administrative Law and Scholarship" (1985) 48 Mod. L. Rev. 293-324

HUTCHINSON, Allan C., *Waiting for Coraf: A Critique of Law and Rights* (Toronto: University of Toronto Press, 1995)

HUTCHINSON, Allan C. and **PETTER**, Andrew J., "Private Rights/Public Wrongs: The Liberal Lie of the Charter" (1988) 38 U. Toronto L. J. 278-97

JABBARI, David, "Critical Theory in Administrative Law" (1994) 14 Oxford J. Legal Stud. 189-215

JACKMAN, Martha, "Constitutional Rhetoric and Social Justice: Reflections on the Justiciability Debate" in Joel Bakan and David Schneiderman (eds.), *Social Justice and the Constitution: Perspectives on a Social Union for Canada* (Ottawa: Carleton University Press, 1992) 17-28

JAFF, Jennifer, "Hiding Behind the Constitution: The Supreme Court and Procedural Due Process in Cleveland Board of Education v. Loudermill" (1985) Akron L. Rev. 631-48

KAINEN, James, "Nineteenth Century Interpretations of the Federal Contract Clause: The Transformation From Vested to Substantive Rights Against the State" (1982) 31 Buffalo L. Rev. 381-480

KAIRYS, David, "Freedom of Speech" in David Kairys (ed.), *The Politics of Law: A Progressive Critique* (New York: Pantheon Books, 1982) 140-71

KAIRYS, David, "Freedom of Speech" in David Kairys (ed.), *The Politics of Law: A Progressive Critique*, 2nd rev. ed. (New York: Pantheon Books, 1990) 237-72

KAIRYS, David, *With Liberty and Justice for Some: A Critique of the Conservative Supreme Court* (New York: Free Press, 1993)

KATZ, Al and **TEITELBAUM**, Lee, "PINS Jurisdiction, the Vagueness Doctrine, and the Rule of Law" (1977-78) 53 Ind. L. J. 1-34

KELMAN, Mark, "On Democracy-Bashing: A Skeptical Look at the Theoretical and 'Empirical' Practice of the Public Choice Movement" (1988) 74 Va. L. Rev. 199-273

KENNEDY, Duncan, "American Constitutionalism as Civil Religion: Notes of an Atheist" (1995) 19 Nova L. Rev. 909-21

KENYATTA, Muhammad, "From Lochner to Roe: Community Consciousness as Constitutional Consciousness" (1987) 11 Legal Stud. F. 29-40

KENYATTA, Muhammad, "'We, Black Believers': Momma's Doubts About the E.R.A." (1984) 2 Law & Inequality 327-33

KOFFLER, Judith, "Constitutional Catarrh" [review of John Hart Ely, *Democracy and Distrust*] (1981) 1 Pace L. Rev. 403-20

KONEFSKY, Alfred S., "Men of Great and Little Faith: Generations of Constitutional Scholarship" (1981) 30 Buffalo L. Rev. 365-84

LaRUE, Lewis H., "Constitutional Law and Constitutional History" (1987) 36 Buffalo L. Rev. 373-401

LaRUE, Lewis H., "The Continuing Presence of Dred Scott" (1985) 42 Wash. & Lee L. Rev. 57-63

LaRUE, L. H., *Political Discourse: A Case Study of the Watergate Affair* (Athens: University of Georgia Press, 1988)

LaRUE, Lewis, "Politics and the Constitution" (1977) 86 Yale L. J. 1011-14

LaRUE, Lewis, "The Rhetoric of Powell's *Bakke*" (1981) 38 Wash. & Lee L. Rev. 43-61

LaRUE, Lewis, "What is the Text in Constitutional Law? Does It Include Thoreau?" (1986) 20 Ga. L. Rev. 135-47

LAW, Sylvia A., "The Founders on Families" in A. E. Dick Howard (ed.), *The United States Constitution: Roots, Rights, and Responsibilities* (Washington, D.C.: Smithsonian Institution Press, 1992) 213-39

LAW, Sylvia A., "Rethinking Sex and the Constitution" (1984) 132 U. Pa. L. Rev. 955-1040

LEEDES, Gary C., "Why the Reagan Administration Resists Radical Transformation of the Constitution" (1987-88) 10 U. Ark. Little Rock L. J. 275-316

LESSARD, Hester, "Creation Stories: Social Rights and Canada's Social Contract" in Joel Bakan and David Schneiderman (eds.), *Social Justice and the Constitution: Perspectives on a Social Union for Canada* (Ottawa: Carleton University Press, 1992) 101-14

LEUBSDORF, John, "Deconstructing the Constitution" (1987) 40 Stan. L. Rev. 181-201

LEVINSON, Sanford, "Constituting Communities Through Words That Bind: Reflections on Loyalty Oaths" (1986) 84 Mich. L. Rev. 1440-70

LEVINSON, Sanford, "Could Meese be Right This Time?" (1987) 61 Tul. L. Rev. 1071-78

LEVINSON, Sanford, "Gerrymandering and the Brooding Omnipresence of Proportional Representation: Why Won't It Go Away?" (1985) 33 U.C.L.A. L. Rev. 257-81

LOBEL, Jules, "Foreign Affairs and the Constitution: The Transformation of the Original Understanding" in David Kairys (ed.), *The Politics of Law: A Progressive Critique*, 2nd rev. ed. (New York: Pantheon Books, 1990) 273-93

LOBEL, Jules, "The Limits of Constitutional Power: Conflicts Between Foreign Policy and International Law" (1985) 71 Va. L. Rev. 1071-180

LÓPEZ, Gerald P., "Reconceiving Civil Rights Practice: Seven Weeks in the Life of a Rebellious Collaboration" (1989) 77 Geo. L. J. 1603-717

LYND, Staughton, "Communal Rights" (1984) 62 Tex. L. Rev. 1417-41

MANDEL, Michael, *The Charter of Rights and the Legalization of Politics in Canada*, 2nd rev. ed. (Toronto: Thompson Educational Publishing, 1994)

MAZOR, Lester J., "Constitutional Law: Cases, Comments, and Questions" [review of William B. Lockhart, Yale Kamisar, and Jesse H. Choper, *Cases and Materials on Constitutional Rights and Liberties*] (1965) 49 Minn. L. Rev. 1202-11

MAZOR, Lester J., "The Exhaustion of the Ideals of Freedom and Equality in the United States" in Gray Dorsey (ed.), *Equality and Freedom: International and Comparative Jurisprudence*, Vol. 1 (New York: Oceana Publications, 1977) 175-82

McCAHERY, Joseph, "Modernist and Postmodernist Perspectives on Public Law in British Critical Legal Studies" (1993) 2 Social & Legal Stud. 397-421

MENSCH, Elizabeth and **FREEMAN**, Alan, *The Politics of Virtue: Is Abortion Possible?* (Durham, N.C.: Duke University Press, 1993)

MENSCH, Elizabeth and **FREEMAN**, Alan, "A Republican Agenda for Hobbesian America" (1989) 41 Fla. L. Rev. 581-622

MERRITT, Adrian, "The Nature and Function of Law: A Criticism of E. P. Thompson's *Whigs and Hunters*" (1980) 7 Brit. J. L. & Soc'y 194-214

MINOW, Martha, "Interpreting Rights: An Essay for Robert Cover" (1987) 96 Yale L. J. 1860-915

MINOW, Martha, "When Difference Has Its Home: Group Homes for the Mentally Retarded, Equal Protection, and Legal Treatment of Difference" (1987) 22 Harv. C.R.-C.L. L. Rev. 111-89

MONAHAN, Patrick J., "At Doctrine's Twilight: The Structure of Canadian Federalism" (1984) 34 U. Toronto L. J. 47-99

MONAHAN, Patrick J., "Judicial Review and Democracy: A Theory of Judicial Review" (1987) 21 U.B.C. L. Rev. 87-164

MOON, John, "The Freedom of Information Act: A Fundamental Contradiction" (1985) 34 Am. U. L. Rev. 1157-89

NEDELSKY, Jennifer, "Reconceiving Rights as Relationship" (1993) 1 Rev. Const. Stud. 1-26

NEDELSKY, Jennifer and **SCOTT**, Craig, "Constitutional Dialogue" in Joel Bakan and David Schneiderman (eds.), *Social Justice and the Constitution: Perspectives on a Social Union for Canada* (Ottawa: Carleton University Press, 1992) 59-83

NERKEN, Ira, "A New Deal for the Protection of Fourteenth Amendment Rights: Challenging the Doctrinal Bases of the Civil Rights Cases and State Action Theory" (1977) 12 Harv. C.R.-C.L. L. Rev. 297-366

PARKER, Richard D., "'Here, the People Rule': A Constitutional Populist Manifesto" (1993) 27 Valparaiso U. L. Rev. 531-84

PARKER, Richard D., "Issues of Community and Liberty" (1985) 8 Harv. J. L. & Pub. Pol'y 287-97

PARKER, Richard, "The Past of Constitutional Theory — And Its Future" (1981) 42 Ohio St. L. J. 223-59

PELLER, Gary, "The Discourse of Constitutional Degradation" (1992) 81 Geo. L. J. 313-41

PONGRACE, Donald R. C., "Stereotypification of the Fourth Amendment's Public/Private Distinction: An Opportunity for Clarity" (1985) 34 Am. U. L. Rev. 1191-214

POST, Robert C., *Constitutional Domains: Democracy, Community, Management* (Cambridge, Mass.: Harvard University Press, 1995)

PROSSER, Tony, "Towards a Critical Public Law" (1982) 9 J. L. & Soc'y 1-19

REGAN, Milton C., Jr., "Community and Justice in Constitutional Theory" [1985] Wis. L. Rev. 1073-1133

REIFNER, Udo, *The Law of the Illegal State: Labor Law and Constitutional Law in German Fascism* (New York: Campus, 1981)

REYNOLDS, Hayward D., "Deconstructing State Action: The Politics of State Action" (1994) 20 Ohio U. L. J. 874-929

RHODE, Deborah L., "Equal Rights in Retrospect" (1983) 1 L. & Inequality 1-72

SCALES-TRENT, Judy, "Black Women and the Constitution: Finding Our Place, Asserting Our Rights" (1989) 24 Harv. C.R.-C.L. L. Rev. 9-44

SCHNEIDERMAN, David, "The Constitutional Politics of Poverty" in Joel Bakan and David Schneiderman (eds.), *Social Justice and the Constitution:*

Perspectives on a Social Union for Canada (Ottawa: Carleton University Press, 1992) 125-38

SHEPPARD, Colleen, "The 'I' and the 'It': Reflections on a Feminist Approach to Constitutional Theory" in Richard F. Devlin (ed.), *Canadian Perspectives on Legal Theory* (Toronto: Emond Montgomery, 1991) 415-31

SHERRY, Suzanna, "Civic Virtue and the Feminine Voice in Constitutional Adjudication" (1986) 72 Va. L. Rev. 543-616

SHERRY, Suzanna, "An Essay Concerning Toleration" (1987) 71 Minn. L. Rev. 963-89

SOIFER, Aviam, "Complacency and Constitutional Law" (1981) 42 Ohio St. L. J. 383-409

SOIFER, Aviam, *Law and the Company We Keep* (Cambrdige, Mass.: Harvard University Press, 1995)

SOIFER, Aviam, "Moral Ambition, Formalism, and the 'Free World' of *DeShaney*" (1989) 57 Geo. Wash. L. Rev. 1513-32

SOIFER, Aviam, "Protecting Civil Rights: A Critique of Raoul Berger's History" (1979) 54 N.Y.U. L. Rev. 651-706

SOIFER, Aviam, "Status, Contract, and Promises Unkept" (1987) 96 Yale L. J. 1916-59

SOIFER, Aviam, "Truisms That Will Never Be True: The Tenth Amendment and the Spending Power" (1986) 57 U. Colo. L. Rev. 793-833

SPANN, Girardeau, "Deconstructing the Legislative Veto" (1984) 68 Minn. L. Rev. 473-544

SPANN, Girardeau A., *Race Against the Court: Supreme Court and Minorities in Contemporary America* (New York: New York University Press, 1994)

STREETER, Thomas, "Beyond Freedom of Speech and the Public Interest: The Relevance of Critical Legal Studies to Communication Policy" (1990) 40(2) J. Communication 43-63

TIGAR, Michael E., "Whose Rights? What Danger?" [review of Norman Dorsen (ed.), *Our Endangered Rights: The ACLU Report on Civil Liberties Today*] (1985) 94 Yale L. J. 970-95

TUSHNET, Mark, "Anti-Formalism in Recent Constitutional Theory" (1985) 83 Mich. L. Rev. 1502-44

TUSHNET, Mark, "Boundaries and Balancing in Constitutional History" [review of Harold M. Hyman and William M. Wiecek, *Equal Justice Under Law: Constitutional Development, 1835-1875*] [1983] Am. Bar Fdn. Res. J. 440-50

TUSHNET, Mark V., *Central America and the Law: The Constitution, Civil Liberties, and the Courts* (Boston: South End Press, 1988)

TUSHNET, Mark, "Civil Rights and Social Rights: The Future of the Reconstruction Amendments" (1992) 25 Loy. L.A. L. Rev. 1207-19

TUSHNET, Mark, "Community and Fairness in Democratic Theory" (1987) 15 Fla. St. U. L. Rev. 417-29

TUSHNET, Mark, "The Concept of Tradition in Constitutional Historiography" (1987) 29 Wm. & Mary L. Rev. 93-99

TUSHNET, Mark, "Conservative Constitutional Theory" (1985) 59 Tul. L. Rev. 910-27

TUSHNET, Mark, "A Conservative Defense of Liberal Constitutional Law" [review of Rogers M. Smith, *Liberalism and American Constitutional Law*] (1986) 100 Harv. L. Rev. 423-34

TUSHNET, Mark, "The Constitution as an Economic Document: Beard Revisited" (1987) 56 Geo. Wash. L. Rev. 106-13

TUSHNET, Mark, "The Constitution of Religion" (1986) 18 Conn. L. Rev. 701-38

TUSHNET, Mark, "Constitutional Interpretation, Character, and Experience" (1992) 72 B.U. L. Rev. 747-63

TUSHNET, Mark, "Critical Legal Studies and Constitutional Law: An Essay in Deconstruction" (1984) 36 Stan. L. Rev. 623-47

TUSHNET, Mark V., "The Critique of Rights" (1993) 47 S.M.U. L. Rev. 23-34

TUSHNET, Mark, "The Culture(s) of Free Expression" (1991) 76 Cornell L. Rev. 1106-16

TUSHNET, Mark, "Darkness on the Edge of Town: The Contribution of John Hart Ely to Constitutional Theory" (1980) 89 Yale L. J. 1037-62

TUSHNET, Mark V., *The Death Penalty* (New York: Facts on File, 1994)

TUSHNET, Mark, "The Degradation of Constitutional Discourse" (1992) 31 Geo. L. J. 251-311

TUSHNET, Mark, "Dia-Tribe" [review of Laurence Tribe, *American Constitutional Law*] (1980) 78 Mich. L. Rev. 694-710

TUSHNET, Mark, "The Dilemmas of Liberal Constitutionalism" (1981) 42 Ohio St. L. J. 411-26

TUSHNET, Mark V., "Disaggregating Church and Culture" (1992) 42 DePaul L. Rev. 235-51

TUSHNET, Mark, "An Essay on Rights" (1984) 62 Tex. L. Rev. 1363-403

TUSHNET, Mark, "Federalism and the Traditions of American Political Theory" (1985) 19 Ga. L. Rev. 981-97

TUSHNET, Mark, "The Flag-Burning Episode: An Essay on the Constitution" (1990) 61 U. Colo. L. Rev. 39-53

TUSHNET, Mark, "Following the Rules Laid Down: A Critique of Interpretivism and Neutral Principles" (1983) 96 Harv. L. Rev. 781-827

TUSHNET, Mark, "Judges and Constitutional Theory: A View From History" (1992) 63 U. Colo. L. Rev. 425-39

TUSHNET, Mark, "Law and Group Rights: Federalism as a Model" in Allan C. Hutchinson and Leslie J. M. Green (eds.), *Law and the Community: The End of Indivividualism?* (Toronto: Carswell, 1989) 277-97

TUSHNET, Mark, "Legal Realism, Structural Review, and Prophecy" (1983) 8 U. Dayton L. Rev. 809-31

TUSHNET, Mark V., *Making Civil Rights Law: Thurgood Marshall and the Supreme Court, 1936-1961* (New York: Oxford University Press, 1994)

TUSHNET, Mark, "Metaprocedure?" (1989) 63 S. Cal. L. Rev. 161-79

TUSHNET, Mark, "A Note on the Revival of Textualism in Constitutional Theory" (1985) 58 S. Cal. L. Rev. 683-700

TUSHNET, Mark, "The Politics of Constitutional Law" in David Kairys (ed.), *The Politics of Law: A Progressive Critique*, 2nd rev. ed. (New York: Pantheon Books, 1990) 219-36

TUSHNET, Mark, "The Possibilities of Interpretive Liberalism" (1991) 29 Alta. L. Rev. 276-92

TUSHNET, Mark, "Principles, Politics, and Constitutional Law" (1989) 88 Mich. L. Rev. 49-81

TUSHNET, Mark, "Public and Private Education: Is There a Constitutional Difference?" [1991] U. Chi. Legal F. 43-74

TUSHNET, Mark, *Red, White, and Blue: A Critical Analysis of Constitutional Law* (Cambridge, Mass.: Harvard University Press, 1988)

TUSHNET, Mark, "Reflections on the Role of Purpose in the Jurisprudence of the Religion Clauses" (1985-86) 27 Wm. & Mary L. Rev. 997-1009

TUSHNET, Mark, "Religion and Theories of Constitutional Interpretation" (1987) 33 Loyola L. Rev. 221-40

TUSHNET, Mark, "Rights: An Essay in Informal Political Theory" (1989) 17 Pol. & Soc'y 403-51

TUSHNET, Mark V., "Scalia and the Dormant Commerce Clause: A Foolish Formalism" (1991) 12 Cardozo L. Rev. 1717-43

TUSHNET, Mark, "Sloppiness in the Supreme Court, O.T. 1935 - O.T. 1944" (1986) 3 Const. Comm. 73-89

TUSHNET, Mark, "The Supreme Court and Its First Amendment Constitutency" (1993) 44 Hast. L. J. 881-99

TUSHNET, Mark, "The Supreme Court as Communicator: Carter's *Contemporary Constitutional Lawmaking*" [1987] Am. Bar Fdn. Res. J. 225-31

TUSHNET, Mark, "The Supreme Court, the Supreme Law of the Land, and Attorney General Meese: A Comment" (1987) 61 Tul. L. Rev. 1017-25

TUSHNET, Mark, "Thurgood Marshall and the Brethren" (1992) 80 Geo. L. J. 2109-30

TUSHNET, Mark, "Truth, Justice and the American Way: An Interpretation of Public Law Scholarship in the Seventies" (1979) 57 Tex. L. Rev. 1307-59

TUSHNET, Mark, "The U.S. Constitution and the Intent of the Framers" (1987) 36 Buffalo L. Rev. 217-26

TUSHNET, Mark and **JAFF**, Jennifer, "Why the Debate of Congress' Power to Restrict the Jurisdiction of the Federal Courts is Unending" (1984) 72 Geo. L. J. 1311-31

TUSHNET, Markand **LEZIN**, Katya, "What Really Happened in *Brown* v. *Board of Education*" (1991) 91 Colum. L. Rev. 1867-930

VILLMOARE, Adelaide H., "The Left's Problems With Rights" (1985) 9 Legal Stud. F. 39-46

WECHSLER, Burton, "Federal Courts, State Criminal Law and the First Amendment" (1974) 49 N.Y.U. L. Rev. 740-906

WECHSLER, Burton, "*Younger* v. *Harris*, Federalism and Fairytales" in The Equal Justice Foundation, *Taking Ideals Seriously, The Case for a Lawyers' Public Interest Movement* (Washington, D.C.: Equal Justice Foundation, 1981) 56-67

WEST, Robin, "The Aspirational Constitution" (1993) 88 Nw. U. L. Rev. 241-68

WEST, Robin, "Constitutional Scepticism" (1992) 72 B.U. L. Rev. 765-99

WEST, Robin, "Equality Theory, Marital Rape, and the Promise of the Fourteenth Amendment" (1990) 42 Fla. L. Rev. 45-79

WEST, Robin, "The Meaning of Equality and the Interpretive Turn" (1990) 66 Chi-Kent L. Rev. 451-80

WEST, Robin, "Progressive and Conservative Constitutionalism" (1990) 88 Mich. L. Rev. 641-721

WEST, Robin, *Progressive Constitutionalism* (Durham: Duke University Press, 1994)

WEST, Robin, "Taking Freedom Seriously" (1990) 104 Harv. L. Rev. 43-106

WILLIAMS, Patricia J., "Commercial Rights and Constitutional Wrongs" (1990) 49 Md. L. Rev. 293-313

WILLIAMS, Robert A., Jr., "Linking Arms Together: Multicultural Constitutionalism in a North American Indigenous Vision of Law and Peace" (1994) 82 Cal. L. Rev. 981-1049

WILLIAMS, Susan H., "Feminist Jurisprudence and Free Speech Theory" (1994) 68 Tul. L. Rev. 1563-81

WINTER, Steven L., "Indeterminacy and Incommensurability in Constitutional Law" (1990) 78 Calif. L. Rev. 1441-541

WINTER, Steven L., "An Upside/Down View of the Countermajoritarian Difficulty" (1991) 69 Tex. L. Rev. 1881-927

WISOTSKY, Steven, "Crackdown: The Emerging 'Drug Exception' to the Bill of Rights" (1987) 38 Hast. L. J. 889-926

12

Criminal Law and Criminology

Critical legal literature has sought to illuminate the processes by which crimes are created, defined and prosecuted. It has also tried to determine why legal reponses to rising rates of violent crime in the U.S. have generally failed.

From theoretical and historical perspectives, radical critics have tried to explain the development of criminal law according to models more useful than those traditionally offered. Critical legal writers reject explanations of the adoption of criminal laws as somehow reflective of shared values, societal needs, moral indignation, or the increasing rationality of the legal system. Instead, critical legal authors have examined the adoption and definition of criminal offences in their entire social and political context. For example, laws regarding theft have been studied against the background of changes in political and economic structures of the sixteenth and seventeenth centuries. Some kinds of wrongs that formerly gave rise merely to civil actions became criminal offences. This transformation took place when the general economy was moving from a feudal to a mercantile and then to a fully capitalist mode of organization. The enforcement of particularly harsh laws in the seventeenth century, which prescribed the death penalty for such offences as poaching and wood-stealing, has been analyzed with a view to understanding why conviction under these laws did not result in the hanging of more offenders. Critical legal writers have also discussed changes to criminal laws as one product of nineteenth-century industrialization, particularly in respect of workers' mobility and control over the means of production and over the relative safety and security of their workplaces.

Radical critics have studied the increased incidence of violent crime in the U.S. during the 1980s. They have exposed and evaluated the assumptions of both liberal mainstream criminology and also conservative responses. In the 1960s, liberal criminologists tended to view criminal behavior as a result of persistent social and economic inequalities. Programs to ameliorate unemployment, poverty, and poor education were developed to address the causes of crime. The conservative emphasis was not on the social origins of crime. Instead, from the 1970s forward, conservative policy-makers and legislators have called for more law enforcement personnel, more prisons, and more courts. The conservative approach favors deterrence as the primary goal, rather than rehabilitation of offenders. In contrast with the allegedly lenient policies of liberal criminologists, conservatives have successfully pressed for mandatory sentencing guidelines that ensure longer prison terms. Despite the increased incarceration rate, the incidence of violent crime has not been reduced.

Critical legal authors have stressed the need to investigate and respond to the structural features of crime, including the complex relationships between race, economic and social class, family background, availability of health and mental health services, community integration, and levels of education. Unlike the proponents of liberal social programs of the 1960s, critical legal writers have recommended an aggressive and intensive approach to tackling the problems of crime, especially in inner-city neighborhoods where violence and drugs are endemic. Measures to increase public safety and individual security should be taken, but it is not a proper response to make it legal to protect property with deadly force. In addition to training and employing more police, civilians should also be trained to patrol their neighborhoods and give the community a greater chance to help control its own problems. Instead of relying on harsh sentencing, legislators should devote more resources to treatment and prevention, through programs both inside correctional institutions and when an offender is on parole or probation. There should also be a serious effort to fund and administer family support programs and early childhood education in the inner cities.

* * * *

ALEXANDER, Elizabeth, "The New Prison Administrators and the Court: New Directions in Prison Law" (1978) 56 Tex. L. Rev. 963-1008

ARENELLA, Peter, "Rethinking the Functions of Criminal Procedure: The Warren and Burger Courts' Competing Ideologies" (1983) 72 Geo. L. J. 185-248

AUSTIN, Regina, "'The Black Community,' Its Lawbreakers, and a Politics of Identification" (1992) 65 S. Cal. L. Rev. 1769-817

BARKAN, Steven E., *Protestors on Trial: Justice in the Southern Civil Rights and Vietnam Antiwar Movements* (Camden, N.J.: Rutgers University Press, 1985)

CARDARELLI, Albert P. and **HICKS**, Stephen C., "Radicalism in Law and Criminology: A Retrospective View of Critical Legal Studies and Radical Criminology" (1993) 84 J. Crim. L. & Criminology 502-53

CHAMBLISS, William J., "The Creation of Criminal Law and Crime Control in Britain and America" in William J. Chambliss and Marjorie S. Zatz (eds.), *Making Law: The State, the Law, and Structural Contradictions* (Bloomington: Indiana University Press, 1993) 36-64

CHAMBLISS, William J., "Markets, Profits, Labor and Smack" (1977) 1 Contemp. Crises 53-76

CHAMBLISS, William J., "The Political Economy of Smack: Opiates, Capitalism and Law" in Rita J. Simon (ed.), *Research in Law and Sociology*, vol. 1 (Greenwich, Conn.: JAI Press, 1978) 115-41

CHAMBLISS, William, "A Sociological Analysis of the Law of Vagrancy" (1964) 12 Soc. Probs. 46-67

CHAMBLISS, William J., "Toward a Radical Criminology" in David Kairys (ed.), *The Politics of Law: A Progressive Critique* (New York: Pantheon Books, 1982) 230-41

CHAMBLISS, William J., "Types of Deviance and the Effectiveness of Legal Sanctions" [1967] Wis. L. Rev. 703-19

CHAMBLISS, William J. and **SEIDMAN**, Robert, *Law, Order and Power*, 2nd ed. (Reading, Mass.: Addison-Wesley, 1982)

CHASE, Anthony, "Aspects of Extraterritorial Criminal Jurisdiction in Anglo-American Practice" (1977) 11 Int'l Law. 555-65

CURRIE, Elliott, *Confronting Crime: An American Challenge* (New York: Pantheon Books, 1985)

CURRIE, Elliott, "Crime, Justice, and the Social Environment" in David Kairys (ed.), *The Politics of Law: A Progressive Critique*, 2nd rev. ed. (New York: Pantheon Books, 1990) 294-313

DELGADO, Richard, "'Rotten Social Background' — Should the Criminal Law Recognize a Defense of Severe Environmental Deprivation?" (1985) 3 L. & Inequality 9-90

DONNERSTEIN, Edward; **CHAMPION**, Cheryl A.; **SUNSTEIN**, Cass R.; and **MacKINNON**, Catharine A., "Pornography: Social Science, Legal and Clinical Perspectives" (1986) 4 L. & Inequality 17-49

DONOVAN, Dolores and **WILDMAN**, Stephanie, "Is the Reasonable Man Obsolete? A Critical Perspective on Self-Defense and Provocation" (1981) 14 Loy. L.A. L. Rev. 435-68

FRASER, David, "The Shame File" [review of John Braithwaite, *Crime, Shame and Reintegration*] (1992) 8 Austl. J. L. & Soc'y 106-11

GERSHMAN, Bennett, "The Gate is Open but the Door is Locked — Habeas Corpus and Harmless Error" (1994) 51 Wash. & Lee L. Rev. 115-33

GERSHMAN, Bennett, "Why Prosecutors Misbehave" (March/April, 1986) 22 Crim. L. Bull. 131-43

GREENBERG, David F.; **KESSLER**, R. C.; and **LOFTIN**, Colin, "Social Inequality and Crime Control" (1985) 76 J. Crim. L. & Criminology 684-704

GRIFFITHS, John, "Ideology in Criminal Procedure or a Third 'Model' of the Criminal Process" (1970) 79 Yale L. J. 359-417

HARRING, Sidney L., *Policing a Class Society: The Experience of American Cities, 1865-1915* (New Brunswick, N.J.: Rutgers University Press, 1983)

HAY, Douglas, "The Criminal Prosecution in England and Its Historians" (1984) 47 Mod. L. Rev. 1-29

HAY, Douglas; **LINEBAUGH**, Peter; **RULE**, John; **THOMPSON**, E. P.; and **WINSLOW**, Cal, *Albion's Fatal Tree: Crime and Society in Eighteenth-Century England* (New York: Pantheon Books, 1975)

JOHNSON, Sheri Lynn, "Confessions, Criminals, and Community" (1991) 26 Harv. C.R.-C.L. L. Rev. 327-411

JOHNSON, Sheri Lynn, "The Language and Culture (Not to Say Race) of Peremptory Challenges" (1993) 35 Wm. & Mary L. Rev. 21-92

JOHNSON, Sheri Lynn, "Racial Imagery in Criminal Cases" (1993) 67 Tul. L. Rev. 1739-805

JOHNSON, Sheri Lynn, "Unconscious Racism and the Criminal Law" (1988) 73 Cornell L. Rev. 1016-37

KELMAN, Mark, "Interpretive Construction in the Substantive Criminal Law" (1981) 33 Stan. L. Rev. 591-673

KELMAN, Mark, "The Origins of Crime and Criminal Violence" in David Kairys (ed.), *The Politics of Law: A Progressive Critique* (New York: Pantheon Books, 1982) 214-29

KENNEDY, Duncan, "Sexual Abuse, Sexy Dressing, and the Eroticization of Domination" (1992) 26 New Eng. L. Rev. 1309-93

KOFFLER, Judith and GERSHMAN, Bennett, "The New Seditious Libel" (1984) 69 Cornell L. Rev. 816-82

LACEY, Nicola, "A Clear Conception of Intention: Elusive or Illusory?" (1993) 56 Mod. L. Rev. 621-42

LACEY, Nicola, *State Punishment, Political Principles, and Community Values* (London: Routledge, 1988)

LACEY, Nicola; WELLS, Celia; and MEURE, Dirk, *Reconstructing Criminal Law* (London: Weidenfeld and Nicolson, 1990)

LINEBAUGH, Peter, *The London Hanged: Crime and Civil Society in the Eighteenth Century* (Cambridge: Cambridge Universty Press, 1992)

MATHIESEN, Thomas, *Prison on Trial: A Critical Assessment* (London: Sage Pubications, 1990)

McCONVILLE, Michael and MIRSKY, Chester, "Looking Through the Guilty Plea Glass: The Structural Framework of English and American Courts" (1993) 2 Social & Legal Stud. 173-93

McCONVILLE, Michael and MIRSKY, Chester, "The State, the Legal Profession and the Defense of the Poor" (1988) 15 J. L. & Soc'y 342-60

NELKEN, David, "Critical Criminal Law" in Peter Fitzpatrick and Alan Hunt (eds.), *Critical Legal Studies* (Oxford: Basil Blackwell, 1987) 105-17

NICOLSON, Donald, "Truth, Reason and Justice: Epistemology and Politics in Evidence Discourse" (1994) 57 Mod. L. Rev. 726-44

NORRIE, Alan, *Crime, Reason and History* (London: Weidenfeld and Nicolson, 1993)

NORRIE, Alan, "A Critique of Criminal Causation" (1991) 54 Mod. L. Rev. 685-701

NORRIE, Alan, *Law, Ideology and Punishment* (Dordrecht: Kluwer, 1990)

NORRIE, Alan, Review of Nicola Lacey, *State Punishment, Political Principles, and Community Values* (1990) 18 Int'l J. Soc. L. 112-22

NORRIE, Alan, "Subjectivism, Objectivism and the Limits of Criminal Recklessness" (1992) 12 Oxford J. Legal Stud. 45-58

NOTE, "A Communitarian Defense of Group Libel Laws" (1988) 101 Harv. L. Rev. 682-701

NOWLIN, Christopher, "Critics, Nietzsche, and the Criminal Law" (1992) 5 Can. J. L. & Juris. 275-98

PAPKE, David Ray, *Framing the Criminal: Crime, Cultural Work, and the Loss of Critical Perspective, 1830-1900* (Hamden, Conn.: Archon Books, 1987)

PELLER, Gary, "Criminal Law, Race, and the Ideology of Bias: Transcending the Critical Tools of the Sixties" (1993) 67 Tul. L. Rev. 2231-52

RAFTER, Nicole H., *Partial Justice: Women, Prison, and Social Control* (New Brunswick, N.J.: Transaction Publishers, 1990)

ROBERTS, Dorothy E., "Crime, Race, and Reproduction" (1993) 67 Tul. L. Rev. 1945-77

ROBERTS, Dorothy E., "Motherhood and Crime" (1993) 79 Iowa L. Rev. 95-141

ROBERTS, Dorothy E., "Punishing Drug Addicts Who Have Babies: Women of Color, Equality, and the Right of Privacy" (1991) 104 Harv. L. Rev. 1419-82

RUDOVSKY, David, "The Criminal Justice System and the Role of the Police" in David Kairys (ed.), *The Politics of Law: A Progressive Critique* (New York: Pantheon Books, 1982) 242-52

RUDOVSKY, David, "The Criminal Justice System and the Role of the Police" in David Kairys (ed.), *The Politics of Law: A Progressive Critique*, 2nd rev. ed. (New York: Pantheon Books, 1990) 314-25

RUSSELL, Katheryn K., "A Critical View From the Inside: An Application of Critical Legal Studies to Criminal Law" (1994) 85 J. Crim. & Criminology 222-40

SARAT, Austin and **BERKOWITZ**, Roger, "Disorderly Differences: Recognition, Accomodation, and American Law" (1994) 6 Yale J. L. & Hum. 285-316

SAUNDERS, R. P. and **HASTINGS**, Ross, "Ideology in the Work of the Law Reform Commission of Canada: The Case of the Working Paper on the General Part" (1983) 25 Crim. L. Q. 206-22

SCHNABLY, Stephen, "Normative Judgment, Social Change and Legal Reasoning in the Context of Abortion and Privacy" (1984-85) 13 N.Y.U. Rev. L. & Soc. Change 715-910

SCHNEIDER, Elizabeth M., "The Violence of Privacy" (1991) 23 Colum. L. Rev. 973-99

SNIDER, Laureen, "Feminism, Punishment and the Potential of Empowerment" (1991) 9(1) Can. J. L. & Soc'y 75-104

SNIDER, Laureen, "The Regulatory Dance: Understanding Reform Processes in Corporate Crime" (1991) 19 Int'l J. Soc. L. 209-36

SUGARMAN, David, "A 'Legal History' or a 'Social History' of Crime: What's in a Name?" [review of J. A. Sharpe, *Crime in Seventeenth-Century England: A County History*] [1986] Am. Bar Fdn. Res. J. 359-63

TENNENBAUM, Abraham N., "The Crisis in Criminology" (1992) 92 Telos 51-62

TIGAR, Michael E., "New Frontiers: The Expansion of International Criminal Law" (1987) 22 Tex. Int'l L. J. 411-17

TUSHNET, Mark and **JAFF**, Jennifer, "Critical Legal Studies and Criminal Procedure" (1986) 35 Cath. U. L. Rev. 361-84

TUSHNET, Mark and **SEIDMAN**, Louis Michael, "A Comment on Tooley's *Abortion and Infanticide*" (1986) 96 Ethics 350-55

WEST, Robin L., "Narrative, Responsibility and Death: A Comment on the Death Penalty Cases From the 1989 Term" (1990) 1 Md. J. Contemp. Legal Issues 161-77

WISOTSKY, Steven, "Crackdown: The Emerging 'Drug Exception' to the Bill of Rights" (1987) 38 Hast. L. J. 889-926

WISOTSKY, Steven, "Exposing the War on Cocaine: The Futility and Destructiveness of Prohibition" [1983] Wis. L. Rev. 1305-1426

WISOTSKY, Steven, "The Ideology of Drug Testing" (1987) 11 Nova L. J. 763-78

13

Labor Law

In their work analyzing modern labor law, especially the legal framework for collective bargaining in Western democracies, critical legal authors have noted the extent to which labor law is saturated with liberal values. Foremost among these is the freedom of contract that modern collective bargaining legislation, such as that adopted in the 1930s in the U.S., was meant to enshrine. This legislative structure for unionized labor was arguably a great improvement on the previous common law rules, under which, it has been claimed, industrial strife was guaranteed. The major policies of modern statutory frameworks have been to preserve industrial peace (that is, avoid individual work stoppages and overall class war) and to contain labor disputes within an administrative process that lets both management and unions plead their respective cases before neutral arbitrators. The important assumptions here are that the statutory rules are relatively determinate, the disputes are essentially economic in nature, and there is little scope or need for adjudicators to rely on political values or factors to resolve labor differences.

Critical legal writers have attempted to explain the development of modern institutions for collective bargaining and the legal doctrines that arose first at common law and then under the statutory guidelines. This work has uncovered tensions within the basic principles and assumptions of contemporary labor law. This writing has also assessed the ways in which collective bargaining and the representation of labor unions in public policy formation have led to significant gains in promoting workplace satisfaction. Because of enactments that provide minimum wage laws, maximum limits on hours of work, occupational health and safety rules, and prohibitions against discrimination based on race, gender, age, and sexuality, it is evidently too crude to explain the evolution of modern labor law according to some radical functionalist or class interest perspective. Labor law has not been thoroughly instrumentalist in terms of protecting the interest of various class elites. Explanations grounded in the "needs" or "imperatives" of capitalism do not satisfactorily explain contemporary labor law doctrine.

One problem that critical legal authors have had with modern labor law doctrine is the vaunted claim to neutrality on the part of system. From a radical point of view, it is unclear that courts and the police actually perform as neutrals in the event of strikes or lockouts. The use of the labor injunction issued by a court continues to be an important part of the management's arsenal. A union's or its leaders' disobedience of such orders can have civil and even criminal consequences. Also, in many collective bargaining disputes, the police can be used as a security force for management, on the grounds that some of the activities of unions (such as secondary boycotts and secondary picketing) are unreasonably disruptive.

Radical critics have noted the extent to which rules for collective bargaining in the U.S. in particular have failed to provide real opportunities for employees to participate in the governance or administration of their workplaces. Management continues to enjoy a host of exclusive rights to direct the enterprise, while workers' interests have been consistently conceived as limited to basic economic terms and conditions of work. Neither collective bargaining legislation nor other statutes determining the distribution of power within an enterprise give employees significant opportunities to have a voice, let alone a vote. When the matter in issue involves adopting business policies or causing the enterprise to enter into major transactions (such as the sale of the enterprise or the closing or relocation of the firm or the plant), power remains exclusively in the domain of corporate executives. Labor law, along with other bodies of legal doctrine, assumes that the only stakeholders whose views count in this process are shareholders and, on occasion, creditors. Employees are treated as being either uninterested or unqualified, even though the ultimate decision will have great impact on their lives.

In the critical legal view, the enactment of modern labor law regimes has not reduced the vast inequalities between workers and the enterprises which employ them. As the proportion of unionized workers in the U.S. continues to decline, it becomes even less likely that economic and social disparities will gradually disappear. Radical critics have doubted, however, whether it would be preferable to have all working conditions administered through a centralized bureaucracy. Karl Klare, for example, has pointed out the benefits of maintaining some kind of adversarial bargaining mechanism that results in a collective contract. His recommendations for deeply reforming the current system envision labor lawyers using their skills as advocates, negotiators and as public policy framers. They are in a position to use collective bargaining law, as much as the system will tolerate, to redistribute power and remove the forms of hierarchy that currently permeate the system. Critical legal writing has ambitiously addressed the meaning of "work" in people's lives, trying to understand the satisfaction that might derive from employee participation in a genuinely democratic workplace. With the specter of privatization of various government services and the consequent growth of non-unionized labor, critical labor theorists have to concentrate further on understanding the greater imbalance in power that the law will help shape and sustain.

* * * *

ANSLEY, Frances Lee, "Standing Rusty and Rolling Empty: Law, Poverty, and America's Eroding Industrial Base" (1993) 81 Geo. L. J. 1757-896

ATLESON, James, "The Circle of Boys Market: A Comment on Judicial Inventiveness" (1985) 7 Indus. Rel. L. J. 88-108

ATLESON, James B., *Collective Bargaining in Private Employment*, 2nd ed. (Washington, D.C.: Bureau of National Affairs, 1984)

ATLESON, James, "The Implicit Assumptions of Labor Law Scholarship: Making Sense of the Last Fifty Boycott Decisions, or How I Spent My Summer Vacation" (1985) 35 J. Legal Educ. 395-413

ATLESON, James, "Management Prerogatives, Plant Closings, and the N.L.R.A." (1982-83) 11 N.Y.U. Rev. L. & Soc. Change 83-117

ATLESON, James, "Obscenities in the Workplace: A Comment on Fair and Foul Expression and Status Relationships" (1985) 34 Buffalo L. Rev. 693-723

ATLESON, James, "Reflections on Labor, Power, and Society" (1985) 44 Md. L. Rev. 841-72

ATLESON, James, "Threats to Health and Safety: Employee Self-Help Under the N.L.R.A." (1975) 59 Minn. L. Rev. 647-713

ATLESON, James, *Values and Assumptions in American Labor Law* (Amherst: University of Massachusetts Press, 1983)

ATLESON, James, "Work Group Behavior and Wildcat Strikes: The Causes and Functions of Industrial Civil Disobedience" (1973) 34 Ohio St. L. J. 750-814

AUSTIN, Regina, "Employer Abuse, Worker Resistance, and the Tort of Intentional Infliction of Emotional Distress" (1988) 41 Stan. L. Rev. 1-59

AUSTIN, Regina and **DIETRICH**, Sharon, "Employer Abuse of Low-Status Workers: The Possibility of Uncommon Relief From the Common Law" in David Kairys (ed.), *The Politics of Law: A Progressive Critique*, 2nd rev. ed. (New York: Pantheon Books, 1990) 350-59

BARTOSIC, Florian and **MINDA**, Gary, "The Labor Law Legacy of the Burger Court's Last Term: A Failure of Imagination and Vision" (1986) 28 Ariz. L. Rev. 533-94

BARTOSIC, Florian and **MINDA**, Gary, "Labor Law Myth in the Supreme Court, 1981 Term: A Plea for Realistic and Coherent Theory" (1982) 30 U.C.L.A. L. Rev. 271-326

BECKER, Craig, "Property in the Workplace: Labor, Capital, and Crime in the Eighteeenth-Century British Woolen and Worsted Industry" (1983) 69 Va. L. Rev. 1487-1515

BEERMANN, Jack M. and **SINGER**, Joseph William, "Baseline Questions in Legal Reasoning: The Example of Property in Jobs" (1989) 23 Ga. L. Rev. 911-95

BRODIN, Mark S., "Costs, Profits, and Equal Employment Opportunity" (1987) 62 Notre Dame L. Rev. 318-65

BRODIN, Mark, "The Role of Fault and Motive in Defining Discrimination: The Seniority Question Under Title VII" (1984) 62 N.C. L. Rev. 943-97

BRODIN, Mark, "The Standard of Causation in the Mixed-Motive Title VII Action: A Social Policy Perspective" (1982) 82 Colum. L. Rev. 292-326

CASEBEER, Kenneth M., "Teaching an Old Dog Old Tricks: *Coppage* v. *Kansas* and At-Will Employment Revisited" (1985) 6 Cardozo L. Rev. 765-97

CHASE, Anthony, "A Challenge to Workers' Rights" (1984) 8 Nova L. J. 671-85

CLARK, Leroy and **PARKER**, Gwendolyn, "The Labor Law Problems of the Prisoner" (1975) 28 Rutgers L. Rev. 840-60

CLOKE, Kenneth, "Mandatory Political Contributions and Union Democracy" (1981) 4 Ind. Rel. L. J. 527-86

CLOKE, Kenneth, "Political Loyalty, Labor Democracy and the Constitution" (1976) 5 U. San Fern. V. L. Rev. 159-226

CLUNE, William, III and **HYDE**, Patrick, "Final Offer Interest Arbitration in Wisconsin: Legislative History, Participant Attitudes, Future Trends" (1981) 64 Marq. L. Rev. 455-505

CONAGHAN, Joanne, "Critical Labour Law: The American Contribution" (1987) 14 J. L. & Soc'y 334-52

COTTROL, Robert J., "Law, Labor, and Liberal Ideology: Explorations on the History of a Two-Edged Sword" (1993) 67 Tul. L. Rev. 1531-59

CRAIN, Marion, "Between Feminism and Unionism: Working Class Women, Sex Equality, and Labor Speech" (1994) 82 Geo. L. J. 1903-2001

CRAIN, Marion, "Feminism, Labor, and Power" (1992) 65 S. Cal. L. Rev. 1819-86

DANIELSEN, Dan, "Representing Identities: Legal Treatment of Pregnancy and Homosexuality" (1992) 26 New Eng. L. Rev. 1453-508

FEINMAN, Jay, "The Development of the Employment at Will Rule" (1976) 20 Am. J. Legal Hist. 118-35

FINKIN, Matthew W., "Does Karl Klare Protest Too Much?" (1985) 44 Md. L. Rev. 1100-10

FISCHL, Richard Michael, "Self, Others, and Section 7: Mutualism and Protected Protest Activities Under the National Labor Relations Act" (1989) 89 Colum. L. Rev. 789-865

FORBATH, William, "The Ambiguities of Free Labor: Labor and the Law in the Gilded Age" [1985] Wis. L. Rev. 767-817

FOSTER, Jim, "Health and Safety versus Profits in the Coal Industry: The *Gateway* Case and Class Struggle" (1983-84) 11 Appalachian J. 122-41

FRUG, Mary Joe, "Securing Job Equality for Women: Labor Market Hostility to Working Mothers" (1979) 59 Boston U. L. Rev. 55-103

FUDGE, Judy, "Reconceiving Employment Standards Legislation: Labour Law's Little Sister and the Feminization of Labour" (1991) 7 J. L. & Soc. Pol'y 73-89

FUDGE, Judy and **GLASBEEK,** Harry, "The Politics of Rights: A Politics With Little Class" (1992) 1 Social & Legal Stud. 45-70

GEOHAGEN, Thomas, *Which Side Are You On? Trying to be for Labor When It's Flat on Its Back* (New York: Farrar, Straus and Giroux, 1991)

GLASBEEK, Harry J., "Agenda for Canadian Labour Law Reform: A Little Liberal Law, Much More Democratic Socialist Politics" (1993) 31 Osgoode Hall L. J. 233-63

GLASBEEK, Harry J., "Contempt for Workers" (1990) 28 Osgoode Hall L. J. 1-52

GLASBEEK, Harry J., "Labour Relations Policy and Law as Mechanisms of Adjustment" (1987) 25 Osgoode Hall L. J. 179-237

GLASBEEK, Harry J., "The New Fordism in Canada: Capital's Offensive, Labour's Opportunity" (1989) 27 Osgoode Hall L. J. 517-60

GLASBEEK, Harry J., "Privatizing Discipline: The Case of Mandatory Drug Testing" (1990) 9 Windsor Y.B. Acc. Just. 30-62

GOLDBERG, Michael, "Affirmative Action in Union Government: The Landrum-Griffin Act Implications" (1983) 44 Ohio St. L. J. 649-89

GOLDBERG, Michael J., "The Duty of Fair Representation: What the Courts Do in Fact" (1985) 34 Buffalo L. Rev. 89-171

GOLDSMITH, Andrew, "Process, Power and 'Consent': Some Notes Towards a Critical Theory of Collective Bargaining" (1987) 7 Windsor Y.B. Acc. Just. 21-45

GRIFFIN, Kevin and **KAY**, Leslie, "Plant Closures: Assessing the Victims' Remedies" (1983) 19 Willamette L. J. 199-27

HARRING, Sidney L., "Car Wars: Strikes, Arbitration, and Class Struggle in the Making of Labor Law" (1986) 14 N.Y.U. Rev. L. & Soc. Ch. 849-72

HOLT, Wythe, "Labor Conspiracy Cases in the United States, 1805-1842: Bias and Legitimation in Common Law Adjudication" (1984) 22 Osgoode Hall L. J. 591-663

HOLT, Wythe, "Recovery by the Worker Who Quits: A Comparison of the Mainstream, Legal Realist, and Critical Legal Studies Approaches to a Problem of Nineteenth Century Contract Law" [1986] Wis. L. Rev. 677-732

HYDE, Alan, "Beyond Collective Bargaining: The Politicization of Labor Relations Under Government Contract" [1982] Wis. L. Rev. 1-41

HYDE, Alan, "Can Judges Identify Fair Bargaining Procedures? A Comment on Freed, Polsby and Spitzer, *Unions, Fairness, and the Conundrums of Collective Choice*" (1984) 57 S. Calif. L. Rev. 415-24

HYDE, Alan, "Democracy in Collective Bargaining" (1984) 93 Yale L. J. 793-856

HYDE, Alan, "Economic Labor Law v. Political Labor Relations: Dilemmas for Liberal Legalism" (1981) 60 Tex. L. Rev. 1-68

HYDE, Alan, "Rights for Canadian Members of International Unions Under the (U.S.) Labor-Management Reporting and Disclosure Act" (1986) 61 Wash. L. Rev. 1007-39

JOHNSON, Bruce, "Taking Care of Labor: The Police in American Politics" (1976) 3 Theory & Soc'y 89-117

KARSTEN, Peter, "'Bottomed on Justice': A Reappraisal of Critical Legal Studies Concerning Breaches of Labor Contracts by Quitting or Firing in Britain and the U.S., 1630-1880" (1990) 34 Am. J. Legal Hist. 213-61

KELMAN, Ellen M., "American Labor Law and Legal Formalism: How 'Legal Logic' Shaped and Vitiated the Rights of American Workers" (1983) 58 St. John's L. Rev. 1-68

KENNEDY, Duncan, "Critical Labor Law Theory: A Comment" (1981) 4 Indust. Rel. L. J. 503-6

KLARE, Karl, "The Bitter and the Sweet: Reflections on the Supreme Court's *Yeshiva* Decision" (1983) 71 Socialist Rev. 99-129

KLARE, Karl E., "Critical Theory and Labor Relations Law" in David Kairys (ed.), *The Politics of Law: A Progressive Critique* (New York: Pantheon Books, 1982) 65-88

KLARE, Karl E., "Critical Theory and Labor Relations Law" in David Kairys (ed.), *The Politics of Law: A Progressive Critique*, 2nd rev. ed. (New York: Pantheon Books, 1990) 61-89

KLARE, Karl, "Judicial Deradicalization of the Wagner Act and the Origins of Modern Legal Consciousness, 1937-1941" (1978) 62 Minn. L. Rev. 265-339

KLARE, Karl, "Labor Law and the Liberal Political Imagination" (1982) 62 Socialist Review 45-71

KLARE, Karl, "Labor Law as Ideology: Toward a New Historiography of Collective Bargaining Law" (1981) 4 Ind. Rel. L. J. 450-82

KLARE, Karl E., "The Labor-Management Cooperation Debate: A Workplace Democracy Perspective" (1988) 23 Harv. C.R.-C.L. L. Rev. 39-83

KLARE, Karl E., "Lost Opportunity: Concluding Thoughts on the Finkin Critique" (1985) 44 Md. L. Rev. 111-23

KLARE, Karl, "Management Prerogatives, Plant Closings, and the N.L.R.A.: A Response" (1982-83) 11 N.Y.U. Rev. L. & Soc. Ch. 118-21

KLARE, Karl, "Power/Dressing: Regulation of Employee Appearance" (1992) 26 New Eng. L. Rev. 1395-451

KLARE, Karl, "The Public-Private Distinction in Labor Law" (1982) 130 U. Pa. L. Rev. 1358-1422

KLARE, Karl, "Traditional Labor Law Scholarship and the Crisis of Collective Bargaining Law: A Reply to Professor Finkin" (1985) 44 Md. L. Rev. 731-840

KRAAMWINKEL, Margriet, "Women's Work and the Law: New Perspectives on the Labor Market Strategy" (1992) 26 New Eng. L. Rev. 823-42

LESNICK, Howard, "The Consciousness of Work and the Values of American Labor Law" [review of James Atleson, *Values and Assumptions in American Labor Law*] (1983) 32 Buffalo L. Rev. 833-57

LESNICK, Howard, "The Structure of Post-War Labor Relations: Response" (1982-83) 11 N.Y.U. Rev. L. & Soc. Ch. 142-46

LYND, Staughton, *The Fight Against Shutdowns: Youngstown's Steel Mill Closings* (San Pedro, Ca.: Single Jack Books, 1982)

LYND, Staughton, "Government Without Rights: The Labor Law Vision of Archibald Cox" (1981) 4 Ind. Rel. L. J. 483-95

LYND, Staughton, Review of James Atleson, *Values and Assumptions in American Labor Law* (1984) 36 Stan. L. Rev. 1273-98

MENKEL-MEADOW, Carrie, "The Inevitable Interplay of Title VII and the National Labor Relations Act: A New Role for the N.L.R.B." (1974) 123 U. Pa. L. Rev. 158-86

MINDA, Gary, "The Common Law of Employment At-Will in New York: The Paralysis of Nineteenth Century Doctrine" (1985) 36 Syracuse L. Rev. 939-1020

MINDA, Gary, "Decoding Labor Law" [review of James Atleson, *Values and Assumptions in American Labor Law*] (1984) 53 Geo. Wash. L. Rev. 474-87

MINDA, Gary, "The Law and Metaphor of Boycott" (1993) 41 Buffalo L. Rev. 807-931

MUNGER, Frank, "Miners and Lawyers: Law Practice and Class Conflict in Appalachia, 1872-1920" in Maureen Cain and Christine B. Harrington (eds.), *Lawyers in a Postmodern World: Translation and Transgression* (Buckingham: Open University Press, 1994) 185-228

NOTE [David Hoffman], "Protecting Employees at Will Against Wrongful Discharge: The Public Policy Exception" (1983) 96 Harv. L. Rev. 1931-51

NOTE [Stephen B. Presser], "Subjects of Bargaining Under the NLRA and the Limits of Liberal Political Imagination" (1983) 97 Harv. L. Rev. 475-94

OLSEN, Frances, "Employment Discrimination in the New Europe: A Litigation Project for Women" (1993) 20 J. L. & Soc'y 131-44

PETERSON, Hanne, "Perspectives of Women on Work and Law" (1989) 17 Int'l J. Soc. L. 327-46

PITEGOFF, Peter, "Child Care Enterpise, Community Development, and Work" (1993) 81 Geo. L. J. 1897-943

REIFNER, Udo, "Individualistic and Collective Legalization — The Theory and Practice of Legal Advice for Workers in Prefascist Germany" in Richard Abel (ed.), *The Politics of Informal Justice*, vol. 2 (New York: Academic Press, 1982) 81-123

REIFNER, Udo, *The Law of the Illegal State: Labour Law and Constitutional Law in German Fascism* (New York: Campus, 1981)

STONE, Katharine, "The Post-War Paradigm in American Labor Law" (1981) 90 Yale L. J. 1509-80

STONE, Katharine, "Labor and Corporate Structure: Changing Conceptions and Emerging Possibilities" (1988) 55 U. Chi. L. Rev. 73-173

STONE, Katharine, "Re-envisioning Labor Law: A Response to Professor Finkin" (1986) 45 Md. L. Rev. 978-1013

STONE, Katharine, "The Structure of Post-War Labor Relations" (1982-83) 11 N.Y.U. Rev. L. & Soc. Ch. 125-32

TOMLINS, Christopher L., "A Mysterious Power: Industrial Accidents and the Legal Constitution of Employment Relations in Massachusetts, 1800-1850" (1988) 6 L. & Hist. Rev. 375-438

TOMLINS, Christopher L., "The New Deal, Collective Bargaining, and the Triumph of Industrial Pluralism" (1985) 39 Indus. & Lab. Rel. Rev. 19-34

TOMLINS, Christopher L., *The State and the Unions: Law, Labor Relations Policy and the Organized Labor Movement in the United States, 1880-1960* (New York: Cambridge University Press, 1985)

WOODIWISS, Anthony, "The Passing of Modernism and Labor Rights: Lessons from Japan and the United States" (1992) 1 Social & Legal Stud. 477-91

14

Property Law

Critical legal writers have studied the origins of property rules in liberal political theories of the seventeenth century. In particular, they have traced legal treatments of property ownership back to their libertarian roots in Lockean accounts of the labor theory of property and the theory based on first possession. These accounts have also spelled out the importance of evolving and conflicting conceptions of property in the political economy of later figures such as Adam Smith.

Much critical discussion has focused on the assumption that property rules evolved because of, and can be explained and justified by reference to, exogenous conditions or factors, such as the needs of commerce or the economy. Several basic legal principles examined in this light include the freedom of a property owner to alienate resources and the law's bias in favor of protecting the most productive use of those resources. These principles have justified numerous common law rules against restraints on alienation or property use, and they have also been connected to the development of a market economy in property interests. Liberal legal theorists continue to argue that property, conceived as a system of social relations of entitlement over certain valuable interests, reflect a mixture of competing social and economic policies and some degree of historical fortuitousness. In other words, property rules are defended as in some sense "objective" and "neutral," even though those rules in action can lead to significant redistribution of wealth and opportunities.

Some radical critics, such as Gregory Alexander, have found in the common law structure of property rules a pattern of dichotomies and internal contradiction. These include conflicts, for example, between the freedom of a transferor of property to place restrictions (such as a covenant) on the use of the subject of property, and the freedom of the transferee to use and dispose of the land without restriction. As elaborated in common law adjudication, legal doctrines attempt to mediate between these basic values. From a critical legal perspective, judicial decisions can be unpacked for their ideological meaning. Another structural explanation of the rise of modern property rules is contained in Elizabeth Mensch's analysis of competing "social visions" in U.S. pre-revolutionary law.

In their excursions into the historical background of property doctrines, some critical legal writers have rediscovered alternative conceptions to liberal political theory. These have been summed up as a "republican" ideology, with roots in the work, for example, of James Harrington and Thomas Jefferson. By building on the underlying principles of this republican alternative, authors such as William Simon have described a reconstructed, contemporary model of property principles that contrasts with the dominant capitalist regime. At the core of Simon's model are two essential goals: first, the new property regime would ensure a just primary distribution of wealth and income (the equality principle) and, second, under the new regime private individuals could hold property only if they participate in the community that constitutes the property and only if there are restraints on individual accumulation (the participation principle). Organizational forms that would best accomodate these principles are such groups as producer or housing cooperatives.

There is a significant degree of concern in critical legal literature with the consequences of unequal property distribution and the extent to which property law doctrines reinforce past and current social and economic inequalities. The work of Joseph William Singer has re-examined huge disparities in access to and control of property, depending on characteristics of race, gender, disability, and sexuality. None of the liberal legal theories underlying property ownership and distribution account for these inequalities. Radical critics question whether the redistribution accomplished by past property rules has resulted in injustices that invite some form of remedy now. Critical attention has also been paid to the inclusion, in terms of property rights, of entitlements on which poor individuals and families depend to survive. Entitlements such as government-provided social assistance or other public benefits, as well as protections under antidiscrimination laws, have traditionally not been treated as property rights. Critical legal writers have reimagined what property doctrines would look like if issues of distributive justice in relation to these resources were taken seriously.

* * * *

ALEXANDER, Gregory S., "The Dead Hand and the Law of Trusts in the Nineteenth Century" (1985) 37 Stan. L. Rev. 1189-266

ALEXANDER, Gregory S., "History as Ideology in the Basic Property Course" (1986) 36 J. Legal Educ. 381-89

ALEXANDER, Gregory S., "Takings and the Post-modern Dialectic of Property" (1992) 9 Const. Comm. 189-98

ALEXANDER, Gregory S., "Time and Property in the American Republican Legal Culture" (1991) 66 N.Y.U. L. Rev. 273-352

ALEXANDER, Gregory S., "The Transformation of Trusts as a Legal Category, 1800-1914" (1987) 5 L. & Hist. Rev. 303-50

ALEXANDER, Gregory S. and **SKAPSKA**, Grazyna (eds.), *A Fourth Way? Privatization, Property and the Emergence of New Market Economics* (New York: Routledge, 1994)

BEIER, Bryan, "The Perils of Analogical Reasoning: Joseph William Singer, Property, and Sovereignty and Property" (1994) 1 Geo. Mason U. L. Rev. 33-58

BOTTOMLEY, Anne, "Self and Subjectivities: Languages of Claim in Property Law" (1993) 20 J. L. & Soc'y 56-70

BRIGHAM, John, *Property and the Politics of Entitlement* (Philadelphia: Temple University Press, 1990)

CHESTER, Ronald, *Inheritance, Wealth and Society* (Bloomington: Indiana University Press, 1982)

COHEN, David and **HUTCHINSON**, Allan C., "Of Persons and Property: The Politics of Legal Taxonomy" (1990) 13 Dal. L. J. 20-54

COOMBE, Rosemary J., "Author/izing the Celebrity: Publicity Rights, Postmodern Politics, and Unauthorized Genders" (1992) 10 Cardozo Arts & Ent. L. J. 365-95

DAVIES, Margaret, "Feminist Appropriations: Law, Property and Personality" (1994) 3 Social & Legal Stud. 365-91

ELLERMAN, David P., *Property and Contract in Economics: The Case for*

Economic Democracy (Cambridge, Mass.: Blackwell, 1992)

FRUG, Gerald E., Review of Hendrik Hartog, *Public Property and Private Power* [1984] Am. Bar Fdn. Res. J. 673-91

HORWITZ, Morton J., "The Transformation in the Conception of Property in American Law, 1780-1860" (1973) 40 U. Chi. L. Rev. 248-90

KENNEDY, Duncan, "The Effect of the Warranty of Habitability on Low Income Housing: 'Milking' and Class Violence" (1987) 15 Fla. St. U. L. Rev. 485-519

LYND, Staughton, "Investment Decisions and the Quid-Pro-Quo Myth" (1979) 29 Case West. Res. L. Rev. 396-427

LYND, Staughton, "Towards a Not-for-Profit Economy: Public Development Authorities for Acquisition and Use of Industrial Property" (1987) 22 Harv. C.R.-C.L. L. Rev. 13-41

McBRIDE, Michael S., "Critical Legal History and Private Actions Against Public Nuisances, 1800-1865" (1989) 22 Colum. J. L. & Soc. Probs. 307-22

MEIDINGER, Errol, "The 'Public Uses' of Eminent Domain: History and Policy" (1980) 11 Environ. L. 1-66

MENSCH, Elizabeth, "The Colonial Origins of Liberal Property Rights" (1982) 31 Buffalo L. Rev. 635-735

MINDA, Gary, "The Dilemmas of Property and Sovereignty in the Postmodern Era: The Regulatory Takings Problem" (1991) 62 U. Colo. L. Rev. 599-636

PLATER, Zygmunt J. B., "The Takings Issue in a Natural Setting: Floodlines and the Public Power" (1974) 52 Tex. L. Rev. 201-56

PLATER, Zygmunt J. B. and **NORINE**, William L., "Through the Looking Glass of Eminent Domain: Exploring the 'Arbitrary and Capricious' Test and Substantive Rationality Review of Governmental Decisions" (1989) 16 B.C. Envtl. Aff. L. Rev. 661-752

RADIN, Margaret Jane, *Reinterpreting Property* (Chicago: University of Chicago Press, 1993)

ROSE, Carol M., *Property and Persuasion: Essays on the History, Theory, and Rhetoric of Ownership* (Boulder, Co.: Westview Press, 1994)

SCHULTZ, David, "The Locke Republican Debate and the Paradox of Property Rights in Early American Jurisprudence" (1991) 13 West. New Eng. L. Rev. 155-87

SIMON, William H., "Social-Republican Property" (1991) 38 U.C.L.A. L. Rev. 1335-413

SINGER, Joseph William, "Property and Coercion in Federal Indian Law: The Conflict Between Critical and Complacent Pragmatism" (1990) 63 S. Cal. L. Rev. 1821-41

SINGER, Joseph William, "The Reliance Interest in Property" (1988) 40 Stan. L. Rev. 611-751

SINGER, Joseph William, "Re-reading Property" (1992) 26 New Eng. L. Rev. 711-29

SINGER, Joseph William, "Sovereignty amd Property" (1991) 86 Nw. U. L. Rev. 1-56

TIGAR, Michael, "The Right of Property and the Law of Theft" (1984) 62 Tex. L. Rev. 1443-75

VANDEVELDE, Kenneth, "The New Property of the Nineteenth Century: The Development of the Modern Concept of Property" (1980) 29 Buffalo L. Rev. 325-67

VAN DOREN, John W., "Private Property: A Study in Incoherence" (1986) 63 Det. L. Rev. 683-701

WILLIAMS, Robert A., Jr., "Legal Discourse, Social Vision and the Supreme Court's Land Use Planning Law: The Genealogy of the *Lochnerian* Recurrence in *First English Luther Church* and *Nollan*" (1988) 59 U. Colo. L. Rev. 427-94

15

Domestic Relations Law

The preponderance of literature contained under this heading springs from a feminist approach to various traditional and contemporary issues surrounding the institution of the family. There is no single feminist orientation that can be isolated and summarized. Instead, different types of feminism have been developed, including liberal feminism, cultural feminism and radical feminism. No particular typology is offered here. Writers in socialist feminism have often discussed themes that overlap with the leftist critique associated with critical legal studies. This is not to say that one or other type of feminism is simply a subset of the movement. Rather, readers should be aware that radical feminist critiques of the family and of the legal doctrines that relate to it often inform and contribute to other critical political analyses. Though both kinds of critiques concern power and both challenge the conceptual underpinnings of existing legal rules, they are not always congruent, and in fact they often differ sharply.

Traditional rules in the field of family law tended to deal with the legal requirements of marriage and divorce, presumptions governing child custody, adoption rules, and property division and settlement on dissolution of marriage. Critical writing has explored these rules, both as they have been recorded on the law books, and also how they have worked in practice. This writing has fundamentally reexamined central concepts in traditional family law doctrine, including the meaning of "family," "spouse," and "child." These are not assumed to have fixed meanings, nor are they treated as depending solely on biological or affective ties. From a critical perspective, such terms are freighted with changing cultural, historical, and political incidents. In addition, critical writers have enlarged the subject, by discussing the division of labor, care functions, and the impact of education and welfare on how individuals sustain themselves and their dependants.

The institution of the family itself has been criticized by critical writers for its role in the a society marked by systemic inequalities. From one critical perspective, the concept of the family should be broadened to include relationsips which formerly have not been recognized as such under liberal legal regimes. So, for example, gay and lesbian relationships should arguably be treated as familial, so that all individuals would have equal benefits under law. From a different point of view, other critics have attacked the family as the primary site of subordination and exclusion and would discard it from any progressive society.

Critics of traditional family law have challenged attempts to rewrite doctrinal history as if the major flaws in the law have by now been rectified. From a critical perspective, it would be misleading to depict the history of the subject as if the family were formerly a patriarchal institution that has now been significantly reformed. Under the standard liberal legal account, where women and children were once denied basic legal rights, the unjust system has been gradually dismantled and supplanted by new egalitarian system. Various critiques argue that legal rules retain an important element of patriarchal control and coercion. Moreover, the rising tide of employment of women outside the home has had implications for family roles that the law does not always progressively recognize. The value of the vaunted achievement of equality, under modern divorce laws, has been questioned by some writers, who maintain that these laws do not take into account either women's structural disadvantages in the labor market or the extent to which the vast majority of women continue to work both within and outside the home. Liberal legalism continues to be enchanted by this optimistic reformist account because, according to Frances Olsen, certain "structures of consciousness" still grip us. Much of the rhetoric of family law reform continues to rely on conventional dichotomies, for example, between home (sentimentalized as a domestic haven calling for self-sacrifice) and the workplace (the worldly realm that demands self-reliance and competitive behavior in order to succeed in the impersonal market). Olsen has advocated measures to transcend such dualisms.

Critical writers have also inquired into the traditional legal differences between "adult" or "parent" and "child." Again, they have attempted to de-naturalize such distinctions, claiming that the demarcation shifts, depending on changes in social and cultural changes, as well as on legal definitions. These writers have reexamined the series of intricate relationships between adult, child, and the state to determine how the law has occasionally removed legal disabilities or restrictions on children, and also how there have been developments in the other direction. This critical writing has tried to construct, in the words of Martha Minow, a "rich conception of rights as relationships" and affiliation, which differs from the traditional liberal legal view of rights as a matter of autonomy.

* * * *

ASHE, Marie and **CAHN**, Naomi R., "Child Abuse: A Problem for Feminist Theory" (1993) 2 Tex. J. Wom. & L. 75-112

BECKER, Mary, "Strength in Diversity: Feminist Theoretical Approaches to Child Custody and Same-Sex Relationships" (1994) 23 Stetson L. Rev. 701-42

BOYD, Susan B., "Child Custody, Ideologies and Employment" (1989) 3(1) Can. J. Wom. & L. 111-33

BOYD, Susan B., "(Re)Placing the State: Family, Law and Oppression" (1994) 9(1) Can. J. L. & Soc'y 39-73

BOYD, Susan B., "Some Postmodernist Challenges to Feminist Analysis of Law, Family and State: Ideology and Discourse in Child Custody Law" (1991) 10 Can. J. Fam. L. 79-113

BROPHY, Julia and **SMART**, Carol (eds.), *Women-in-Law: Explorations in Law, Family, and Sexuality* (London: Routledge & Kegan Paul, 1985)

COSSMAN, Brenda, "Family Inside/Out" (1994) 44 U. Toronto L. J. 1-39

DAVIS, Peggy C., "Contested Images of Family Values: The Role of the State" (1994) 107 Harv. L. Rev. 1348-73

DELGADO, Richard, "The Politics of Workplace Reforms: Recent Works on Parental Leave and a Father-Daughter Dialogue" (1988) 40 Rutgers L. Rev. 1031-58

DIDUCK, Alison, "Legislating Ideologies of Motherhood" (1993) 2 Social & Legal Stud. 461-85

DONOVAN, Carol, "The Uniform Parentage Act and Nonmarital Motherhood-by-Choice" (1982-83) 11 N.Y.U. Rev. L. & Soc. Change 193-253

DOWD, Nancy E., "A Feminist Analysis of Adoption" (1994) 107 Harv. L. Rev. 913-36

FINEMAN, Martha Albertson, *The Illusion of Equality: The Rhetoric and Reality of Divorce Reform* (Chicago: University of Chicago Press, 1991)

FINEMAN, Martha, "Illusive Equality: On Weitzman's *Divorce Revolution*" [1986] Am. Bar Fdn. Res. J. 781-90

FINEMAN, Martha, "Images of Mothers in Poverty Discourses" [1991] Duke L. J. 274-95

FINEMAN, Martha, "Intimacy Outside of the Natural Family: The Limits of Privacy" (1991) 23 Conn. L. Rev. 955-99

FINEMAN, Martha Albertson, "Legal Stories, Change, and Incentives — Reinforcing the Role of the Father" (1992) 37 N.Y. L. Sch. L. Rev. 227-49

FINEMAN, Martha A., "The Neutered Mother" (1992) 46 U. Mia. L. Rev. 249-68

GAVIGAN, Shelley A. M., "Paradise Lost, Paradox Revisited: The Implications of Familial Ideology for Feminist, Lesbian, and Gay Engagement to Law" (1993) 31 Osgoode Hall L. J. 589-624

IKEMOTO, Lisa C., "The Code of Perfect Pregnancy: At the Intersection of the Ideology of Motherhood, the Practice of Defaulting to Science, and the Internventionist Mindset of Law" (1992) 53 Ohio St. L. J. 1205-306

LACEY, Linda J., "Mimicking the Words, But Missing the Message: The Music of Cultural Feminist Themes in Religion and Family Law Jurisprudence" (1993) 35 B.C. L. Rev. 1-48

LAW, Sylvia A. and **HENNESSEY**, Patricia, "Is the Law Male? The Case of Family Law" (1993) 69 Chi.-Kent L. Rev. 345-58

MINOW, Martha, "Are Rights Right for Children?" [1987] Am. Bar Fdn. Res. J. 203-23

MINOW, Martha, "Beyond State Intervention in the Family: For Baby Jane Doe" (1985) 18 U. Mich. J. L. Ref. 933-1014

MINOW, Martha, "'Forming Underneath Everything That Grows': Toward a History of Family Law" [1985] Wis. L. Rev. 819-98

MINOW, Martha, "The Properties of Family and the Families of Property" [review of Mary Ann Glendon, *The New Family and the New Property*] (1982) 92 Yale L. J. 376-95

MINOW, Martha, "Rights for the Next Generation: A Feminist Approach to Children's Rights" (1986) 9 Harv. Wom. L. J. 1-24

MINOW, Martha, "Why Ask Who Speaks for the Child?" [review of Willard Gaylin and Ruth Macklin, *Who Speaks for the Child?*] (1983) 53 Harv. Educ. Rev. 444-51

MINOW, Martha, "Words and the Door to the Land of Change: Law, Language, and Family Violence" (1990) 43 Vand. L. Rev. 1665-706

O'DONOVAN, Katharine, *Family Law Matters* (London: Pluto Press, 1993)

OLSEN, Frances E., "The Family and the Market: A Study of Ideology and Law Reform" (1983) 96 Harv. L. Rev. 1497-1578

OLSEN, Frances, "The Myth of State Intervention in the Family" (1985) 18 U. Mich. J. L. Ref. 835-64

OLSEN, Frances, "The Politics of Family Law" (1984) 2 L. & Inequality 1-19

RHODE, Deborah L. and MINOW, Martha, "Reforming the Questions, Questioning the Reforms: Feminist Perspectives on Divorce Reform" in Stephen D. Sugarman and Herma Hill Kay (eds.), *Divorce Reform at the Crossroads* (New Haven: Yale University Press, 1990) 191-210

ROSE, Nikolas, "Beyond the Public/Private Division: Law, Power and the Family" in Peter Fitzpatrick and Alan Hunt (eds.), *Critical Legal Studies* (Oxford: Basil Blackwell, 1987) 61-76

SEVENHUIJSEN, Selma, "The Gendered Juridification of Parenthood" (1992) 1 Social & Legal Stud. 71-83

SEVENHUIJSEN, Selma, "Justice, Moral Reasoning and the Politics of Child Custody" in Elizabeth Meehan and Selma Sevenhuijsen (eds.), *Equality Principle and Gender* (London: Sage, 1991) 88-103

SMART, Carol, *The Ties That Bind: Law, Marriage, and the Reproduction of Patriarchal Relations* (London: Routledge & Kegan Paul, 1984)

SMART, Carol (ed.), *Regulating Womanhood: Historical Essays on Marriage, Motherhood, and Sexuality* (London: Routledge, 1992)

SMART, Carol and **SEVENHUIJSEN**, Selma (eds.), *Child Custody and the Politics of Gender* (London: Routledge, 1989)

TAUB, Nadine, "Assessing the Impact of Goldstein, Freud, and Solnit's Proposals: An Introductory Overview" (1984) 12 N.Y.U. Rev. L. & Soc. Ch. 485-94

TAUB, Nadine, "From Parental Leaves to Nurturing Leaves" (1985) 13 N.Y.U. Rev. L. & Soc. Ch. 381-410

16

Environmental Law

Discussions of the normative roots of environmental law and policy have traditionally concentrated on tensions between different moral philosophies that might best underpin environmental protection. The first approach is utilitarian. Moral conceptions in this vein stress the wise use of natural resources based on the goal of maximizing overall social welfare. The social calculus used to measure this incorporates some aggregate measure of costs and benefits associated with possible alternatives. The second approach is deontological. This appeals to the moral ideal that all persons deserve respect, and social decisions should not be justified according to individuals' preferences or desires.

Like some liberal environmentalists themselves, such as Mark Sagoff, critical legal writers view both approaches as consistent with legal liberalism. Because of this liberal background, there are problems with both. The utilitarian approach has the apparent virtue of isolating the crucial factors in weighing social welfare, but it reduces complex and controversial issues to hopelessly simplified forms of economic accounting that tend to omit non-accountable forms of costs, especially such items as lower quality of life or widespread health problems that may not be immediately foreseeable.

The deontological alternative is not much superior, from a critical legal perspective. Under the guidance of this form of ethics, environmentalists have sought to protect the environment by legal recognition of rights. For example, claims have been made to protect wilderness or other natural resources on the basis of the rights of future generations. Another novel type of analysis has attributed rights to animals and other natural objects. Radical critics have challenged the use of rights in this context.

Another orientation to environmental protection that has been rejected by some critical legal writers is the reliance placed on some notion of "public trust." This doctrine assumes that governmental agencies should regard themselves as trustees of depleting natural resources, held in common, and should make decisions by reference to the benefit of all, including both existing and future generations. In the view of Richard Delgado, for example, this influential doctrine is flawed because it is essentially conservative, stifles innovation, and is unable to cope with the exigent conditions that have arisen since the 1960s. It justifies only minor, incremental reforms that are designed to contain problems within manageable levels. As the environment has become degraded, and as we recognize the global implications of such damage (including overpopulaion, global warming, and holes in the ozone layer), more ambitious strategies need to be created and implemented.

Sweeping environmental strategies have been suggested to mold legal doctrine. These all depend on the idea that a "revolution in consciousness" is needed to resist and reverse environmental despoliation. Among the alternatives canvassed is an "earth-centered" ethics, which concentrates on value shifts rather than an enlarged rights consciousness. Appeals have also been made to "ecofeminism" as a source of novel thinking about environmental protection. Ecofeminists have drawn parallels between patriarchy (men's domination of women) and environmental damage (the unfeeling domination of natural things). The challenge to hierarchy represented by ecofeminism has analogues in the critical legal work on environmental issues.

Though critical legal writers, such as Zygmunt Plater, acknowledge that some valuable gains can be made from litigating under environmental protection legislation, they challenge the superficial rhetoric that often informs such disputes. Too often the major principles at stake are obscured behind simplistic clichés or images (for example, in the controversy over the Tellico dam, the fate of the snail darter was pitted against the forces of development).

* * * *

AUSTIN, Regina and **SCHILL**, Michael, "Black, Brown, Poor and Poisoned: Minority Grassroots Environmentalism and the Quest for Eco-Justice" (1991) 1 Kan. J. L. & Pub. Pol'y 69-82

BOYER, Barry and **MEIDINGER**, Errol, "Privatizing Regulatory Enforcement: A Preliminary Assessment of Citizen Suits Under Federal Environmental Laws" (1985) 34 Buffalo L. Rev. 833-964

DELGADO, Richard, "'Our Better Natures': A Revisionist View of Joseph Sax's Public Trust Theory of Environmental Protection, and Some Dark Thoughts on the Possibility of Law Reform" (1991) 44 Vand. L. Rev. 1209-27

FREEMAN, Alan D., "Give and Take: Distributing Local Environmental Control Through Land-Use Regulation" (1976) 60 Minn. L. Rev. 883-970

KING, Joseph H., Jr. and **PLATER**, Zygmunt J. B., "The Right to Counsel Fees in Public Interest Environmental Litigation" (1973) 41 Tenn. L. Rev. 27-92

LUKE, Tim, "The Dreams of Deep Ecology" (1988) 76 Telos 65-92

MEIDINGER, Errol, "The Politics of Emissions Trading in U.S. Air Pollution Policy" in Keith Hawkins and John M. Thomas (eds.), *Making Regulatory Policy* (Pittsburgh: University of Pittsburgh Press, 1989) 153-94

PLATER, Zygmunt J. B., "Coal Law from the Old World: A Perspective on Land Use and Environmental Regulation in the Coal Industries in the United States, Great Britain, and West Germany" (1976) 64 Ky. L. J. 473-506

PLATER, Zygmunt J. B., "In the Wake of the Snail Darter: An Environmental Law Paradigm and Its Consequence" (1986) 19 U. Mich. J. L. Ref. 805-62

PLATER, Zygmunt J. B., "Reflected in a River: Agency Accountability and the TVA Tellico Dam Case" (1982) 49 Tenn. L. Rev. 747-87

PLATER, Zygmunt J. B., "Statutory Violations and Equitable Discretion" (1982) 70 Calif. L. Rev. 524-94

PLATER, Zygmunt J. B., "The Takings Issue in a Natural Setting: Floodlines and the Police Power" (1974) 52 Tex. L. Rev. 201-56

SAGOFF, Mark, "Can Environmentalists Be Liberals? Jurisprudential Foundations of Environmentalism" (1986) 16 Envtl. L. 775-96

SAGOFF, Mark, *The Economy of the Earth: Philosophy, Law, and the Environment* (New York: Cambridge University Press, 1988)

17

Corporations Law

One of the dominant contemporary concepts underlying corporate law doctrine is that the business firm is essentially the product of a series of contracts among various interested parties, including investors, managers and creditors of the firm. It is in the interest of all these parties that the primary goal of the corporation is to maximize profits. On this view, legislation and judicial law-making in relation to corporations can be evaluated by reference to how the law or policy in question reflects what private ordering, through bargaining among informed parties, would otherwise accomplish. The emphasis here is on ensuring that the legal regime promotes "efficiency" by minimally interfering with the relations and expectations among the parties.

This contractual ideology has proved attractive to lawyers and legal academics who broadly favor legislative and judicial deference to market-determined outcomes. It is an ideology consistent with the deregulatory political pressures of the 1980s in the U.S. and elsewhere. Much of the debate over corporate law reform during the same period was concerned with improving the mechanisms for controlling the potential for abuse (damaging the interests of shareholders and creditors) that tempts managers in the exercise of their discretion under current corporate laws. The debate has involved those authors who recommend strengthening internal controls (such as augmenting and enforcing fiduciary duties of managers) and those favoring external controls (for example, the market for corporate control through takeover bids).

Critical legal writing has challenged this perspective from the ground up. The major problem with the contractual model is that it assumes that modern notions of the nature and the functions of the firm are relatively fixed and uncontroversial. Because so much corporate law doctrine frames its analysis according to the profit-making ideal, legal developments in this century have legitimated a particular conception of the business firm and severely reduced the scope for revising corporate law in anything but minor details.

Critical legal writers have studied the evolution of corporate law and retrieved alternative policies and structures for guiding the creation and management of firms. In the nineteenth century, firms were treated as public bodies owing their existence to the state. Chartering a corporation was a matter of public policy. Both the creation of the enterprise and the conferral of specific economic rights, powers and privileges attracted political discussion. In the latter part of that century, public policy makers also became cognizant of the threats to the general polity posed by large, wealthy, impersonal private firms. In part to counter this fear of how the concentration of wealth would distort political processes, laws were enacted to regulate anti-competitive business practices and to tame some of the giant enterprises that had already been assembled.

Critical legal writers have commended concepts of strong economic democracy that might be adopted to revamp corporate law doctrine. The forms of democracy currently used in the corporate organization (for example, voting rights proportionately granted to holders of particular classes of shares) are mere shadows of a radical ideal in which membership in an enterprise would entitle the holder to equal participation, regardless of wealth.

One alternative model that critical legal writers have found appealing is the small-scale cooperative. An association of this type formed by workers or producers or consumers is a relatively non-hierarchical business that permits novel forms of investment, such as labor or patronage, besides capital in the form of money. Decision-making in a cooperative is structured to permit members greater access to information and opportunities to voice their views. A workers cooperative is owned by its employees, so that there is less of a split between management and ownership. With a locally-based cooperative, it is more likely that the business will be attuned to the needs of the community. When a business corporation proposes removing its plant and operations from a particular location, corporate directors are not legally required to consider the interests of either the employees or the community. Although many states in the U.S. have adopted measures permitting business directors to take into account the interests of "special constituencies," these reforms pale into insignificance when compared to a radically reconstructed business law regime.

Some critical legal writing is less visionary in the sense of seeking ways to replace the corporation. Instead, the emphasis by writers such as Robert Gordon has been on assessing the aims and practices of corporate lawyers who choose to work within the existing system. Again, by referring back to nineteenth-century ideals of corporate practice, critics have sought to fashion a contemporary model of the corporate lawyer as a conscientious and professional counsellor (and perhaps policy maker) who, because of the relative openness of the debates surrounding new directions for corporate governance and business policy, should seize the opportunity to educate and influence corporate clients about socially progressive goals.

* * * *

BAUMAN, Richard W., "Liberalism and Canadian Corporate Law" in Richard F. Devlin (ed.), *Canadian Perspectives on Legal Theory* (Toronto: Emond Montgomery, 1991) 75-97

COHEN, Ronnie, "Feminist Thought and Corporate Law: It's Time to Find Our Way Up From the Bottom (Line)" (1994) 2 Am. U. J. Gender & L. 1-36

FRASER, Andrew, "The Corporation as a Body Politic" (1983) 57 Telos 5-40

FRUG, Gerald, "The Ideology of Bureaucracy in American Law" (1984) 97 Harv. L. Rev. 1276-388

GLASBEEK, Harry J., "The Corporate Social Responsibility Movement: The Latest in Maginot Lines to Save Capitalism" (1988) 11 Dal. L. J. 363-402

GLASBEEK, Harry J., "Why Corporate Deviance is Not Treated as a Crime: The Need to Make Profits a Dirty Word" (1984) 22 Osgoode Hall L. J. 393-439

GORDON, Robert W., "Corporate Law Practice as a Public Calling" (1990) 49 Md. L. Rev. 255-92

GORDON, Robert W., "Introduction to the Symposium on the Corporate Law Firm" (1985) 37 Stan. L. Rev. 271-76

HORWITZ, Morton J., "*Santa Clara* Revisited: The Development of Corporate Theory" (1985-86) 88 W. Va. L. Rev. 173-224

IRELAND, Paddy; **GRIGG-SPALL**, Ian; and **KELLY**, Dave, "The Conceptual Foundations of Modern Company Law" in Peter Fitzpatrick and Alan Hunt (eds.), *Critical Legal Studies* (Oxford: Basil Blackwell, 1987) 149-65

LAHEY, Kathleen and **SALTER**, Sarah W., "Corporate Law in Legal Theory and Legal Scholarship: From Classicism to Feminism" (1985) 23 Osgoode Hall L. J. 543-72

PAETZOLD, Ramona L., "Feminism and Business Law: The Essential Interconnection" (1994) 31 Am. Bus. L. J. 699-715

PITEGOFF, Peter, "Organizing Worker Cooperatives" (1985) 7 L. & Policy Rev. 45-49

PITEGOFF, Peter and **ELLERMAN**, David, "The Democratic Corporation: The New Worker Cooperative Statute in Massachusetts" (1982-83) 11 N.Y.U. Rev. L. & Soc. Ch. 441-72

ROELOFS, Joan, "The Warren Court and Corporate Capitalism" (1979) 39 Telos 94-112

SIMON, William H., "Contract Versus Politics in Corporation Doctrine" in David Kairys (ed.), *The Politics of Law: A Progressive Critique*, 2nd rev. ed. (New York: Pantheon Books, 1990) 387-409

SNIDER, Laureen, "Towards a Political Economy of Reform, Regulation and Corporate Crime" (1987) 9 L. & Pol'y 37-68

STANLEY, Christopher, "Corporate Personality and Capitalist Relations: A Critical Study of the Artifice of Company Law" (1988) 19 Cambrian L. Rev. 97-109

STONE, Christopher D., "Corporate Vices and Corporate Virtues: Do Public/Private Distinctions Matter?" (1982) 130 U. Pa. L. Rev. 1441-1501

SUGARMAN, David, "Corporate Groups in Europe: Governance, Industrial Organization, and Efficiency in a Post-Modern World" in David Sugarman and Gunther Teubner (eds.), *Regulating Corporate Groups in Europe* (Baden-Baden: Verlagsgesellschaft, 1990) 13-64

TIGAR, Michael, *Law and the Rise of Capitalism* (New York: Monthly Review Press, 1977)

TUSHNET, Mark, "Corporations and Free Speech" in David Kairys (ed.), *The Politics of Law: A Progressive Critique* (New York: Pantheon Books, 1982) 253-61

18

Commercial Law

Critical legal writers have addressed topics relating to consumer protection laws, transactions covered in the Uniform Commercial Code, standard form contracts, bankruptcy and trade mark legislation. The general heading of commercial law might also include legal issues that arise in the context of banking law, antitrust law, or insurance law.

Peter Winship's article claims that the contribution of critical legal scholars to commercial law has been negligible. Since his article was published, however, critical literature has appeared that examines commercial law doctrine for its ideological assumptions and its efficacy. For example, critical authors have studied strict liability regimes that are designed to protect the public. Under these laws, manufacturers can be held liable for defective products that cause injuries to consumers. Although the strict liability standard was adopted because it would avoid the pitfalls created by a negligence standard, critics such as Stephanie Wildman have argued that this has not been the effect of those laws in certain jurisdictions. Instead, her examination of the evolution of the case law indicates that plaintiffs have been burdened with establishing elements of defect and causation that, in light of judicial interpretation, lead to much the same results as negligence law. Consumer safety has not been enhanced. Strict liability has created a "myth" that the legal system has responded adequately to potential hazards to consumers.

William Whitford's work on consumer protection legislation generally has led him to conclude that in many instances legal rules adopted by statute have had little impact on the way that merchants do business. For example, vague provisions regarding unconscionable transactions (as defined in the U.C.C.) have perhaps merely "symbolic" importance and have functioned largely as a political measure. Whether a statutory rule actually has some bite on business practices depends on the specificity of standards contained in the legislation, as well as on the kinds of remedies available in the event of a breach.

Some legislative measures, though apparently progressive in concept, can be whittled down and made useless by administrative and judicial application. This has been the fate of trade mark use doctrine, according to Michael Davis, who has concluded that the original legal regime has been skewed in a way that favors the rights of those marketing products and against the interests of the public.

Critical legal writing has also responded to arguments that certain types of consumer protection measures are not only ineffective in achieving their purpose, but in fact have consequences that make them unjustifiable. For instance, Whitford has analyzed consumer product warranties, as well as disclosure regulations, and concluded that such measures are useful. They have a positive impact on the behavior of both sellers and consumers. His analysis of disclosure requirements has led him to recommend further empirical studies to determine whether the normative objectives of the legislation are satisfied or not.

The use of empirical data to demonstrate how the law works in action has been an important feature of critical analysis in this area. Whitford's studies have shown, for example, that collection practices by creditors often result in significant bargaining after the debtor's default. Taking this element of bargaining as a socially desirable feature that is preferable to coercive legal practices, Whitford has suggested various strategies (both radical and moderate) to reform the current legal framework for debtor-creditor relationships. These range from creating a free market solution to abolishing coercive execution altogether. The moderate alternatives include encouraging more informal bargaining, changing the priority rules, and reducing the costs of execution. Overall, the goal sought by Whitford's re-envisioning the law in this area is to promote relationships that are "cooperative and humane."

Thoroughly radical critiques, such as that offered by Harry Glasbeek, have doubted whether such noble values as honesty, integrity, good faith, benevolence, and altruism can ever be fitted into the commercial structures and institutions associated with capitalism. From his point of view, capitalism valorizes self-interested behavior, builds economic inequalities into the system, and rejects appeals to substantive equality (in terms, for example, of a fair price principle). Because of these ideological constraints, Glasbeek is skeptical that commercial law can be significantly reoriented.

* * * *

ABROMOWITZ, David, "Post Claimant as Future Victim: Commercial Retaliation and the Erosion of Court Access" (1982) 17 Harv. C.R.-C.L. L. Rev. 209-70

AKAZAKI, Lee, "Source Theory and Guarantee Theory in Anglo-American Trade Mark Policy: A Critical Legal Study" (1990) 72 J. Pat. & Trade Mark Off. Soc'y 255-78

DAVIS, Michael H., "Death of a Salesman's Doctrine: A Critical Look at Trademark Use" (1985) 19 Ga. L. Rev. 223-79

GLASBEEK, Harry J., "Commercial Morality Through Capitalist Law: Limited Possibilities" (1993) 27 Rev. Jur. Thémis 263-308

JOHNSON, Alex M., Jr., "Critiquing the Foreclosure Process: An Economic Approach Based on the Paradigmatic Norms of Bankruptcy" (1993) 79 Va. L. Rev. 959-1024

JOHNSON, Karl, "Commercial Law" (1983) 13 N.M. L. Rev. 293-321

JOHNSON, Karl, "Commercial Law" (1984) 14 N.M. L. Rev. 45-76

KOFFLER, Judith Schenck, "Capital in Hell: Dante's Lesson on Usury" (1979) 32 Rutgers L. Rev. 608-60

KOFFLER, Judith, "Dionysus in Bankruptcy Land" (1976) 7 Rutgers-Camden L. Rev. 655-70

MACAULAY, Stewart, *Law and the Balance of Power: The Automobile Manufacturers and Their Dealers* (New York: Russell Sage Foundation, 1966)

MACAULAY, Stewart, "Lawyers and Consumer Protection Laws" (1979) 14 L. & Soc'y Rev. 115-71

McCOY, Thomas S., "Revoking the Fairness Doctrine: The Year of the Contra" (1989) 11 Comm. & L. 67-83

MENSCH, Elizabeth and **FREEMAN**, Alan, "Efficiency and Image: Advertising as an Antitrust Issue" [1990] Duke L. J. 321-73

PAPKE, David Ray, "Rhetoric and Retrenchment: Agrarian Ideology and American Bankruptcy Law" (1989) 54 Mich. L. Rev. 871-98

WHEELER, Sally, "Capital Fractionalized: The Role of Insolvency Practititoners in Asset Distribution" in Maureen Cain and Christine B. Harrington (eds.), *Lawyers in a Postmodern World: Translation and Transgression* (Buckingham: Open University Press, 1994) 85-104

WHITFORD, William C., "The Appropriate Role of Security Interests in Consumer Transactions" (1986) 7 Cardozo L. Rev. 959-99

WHITFORD, William C., "Comment on A Theory of the Consumer Product Warranty" (1982) 91 Yale L. J. 1371-85

WHITFORD, William C., "A Critique of the Consumer Credit Collection System" [1979] Wis. L. Rev. 1047-1143

WHITFORD, William C., "The Functions of Disclosure Regulation in Consumer Transactions" [1973] Wis. L. Rev. 400-70

WHITFORD, William C., "Law and the Consumer Transaction: A Case Study of the Automobile Warranty" [1968] Wis. L. Rev. 1006-98

WHITFORD, William C., "Strict Products Liability and the Automobile Industry: Much Ado About Nothing" [1968] Wis. L. Rev. 83-171

WHITFORD, William C., "Structuring Consumer Protection Legislation to Maximize Effectiveness" [1981] Wis. L. Rev. 1018-43

WHITFORD, William C. and **KIMBALL**, Spencer L., "Why Process Consumer Complaints? A Case Study of the Office of the Commission of Insurance of Wisconsin" [1974] Wis. L. Rev. 639-720

WILDMAN, Stephanie M. and **FARRELL**, Molly, "Strict Products Liability in California: An Ideological Overview" (1985) 19 U.S.F. L. Rev. 139-58

WINSHIP, Peter, "Contemporary Commercial Law Literature in the United States" (1982) 43 Ohio St. L. J. 643-72

19

Legal Education

Critical legal writers have assessed the purposes, methods, and results of legal education in the modern university. According to this critical assessment, law schools have for the most part created an ideologically tilted environment, where the emphasis is on depoliticized craft training and preparing students for future professional hierarchies. Traditional legal education concentrates on the teaching and learning of rules, as well as a repertoire of techniques for manipulating these rules under the guise of "legal reasoning." The distinctive and specialized reasoning cultivated in law schools is carefully demarcated from ethical or political analysis. Where there is room allowed for disagreement, the choices tend to be confined between conservative and moderate liberal political choices.

As much as possible, the pedagogical ideal is to inculcate a sense that legal materials and techniques can be used to achieve objective, determinable results. Where this is not possible, law teachers tend to use "policy" analysis to fill gaps in legal doctrine or to justify altering rules. Discussion of policies, however, is relatively constrained, for there are only a few policies typically brought into play. These tend to be framed in vague, abstract generalities, such as appeals to the need for certainty, the need for security, or the need to adjust the law to changed social conditions. Those courses which might tolerate broader discussions of issues of justice and values, such as legal philosophy or legal history, are largely treated as peripheral and "soft" subjects in the curriculum.

The classroom teaching methods used in law schools tend to induce passivity on the part of students. They are invited and permitted to participate in limited ways, but this does not include raising fundamental challenges to the content of the legal rules being taught. By carving up law into a range of first-year and upper-year courses, the curriculum fails to provide students with any integrating vision of what law is and how it might be changed in any way other than piecemeal, moderate reforms.

The evaluation devices used in law schools do not generally include timely and detailed feedback. The major method for judging student learning is a single examination at the end of a term, the results of which are used to sort students. This rank ordering creates the impression that there are significant, measurable differences in cognitive capacities and reasoning skills among students. Legal education makes little attempt to give students several chances to acquire the requisite knowledge and bring themselves up to a level of mastery. Instead, the final grade in each course represents a one-shot opportunity for students to demonstrate their competence.

The climate for learning at law schools creates intense pressure (both direct and indirect) for students to conform to the prevailing values within the institution, which tend to reflect those embraced by the profession. Because of the traditional composition of law faculties, the values in question are those that do not threaten the comfortable *modus vivendi* of faculty members, who continue to be largely middle-class white males.

Among the critics' proposals for changing legal education are the following. Pedagogy should be practised without the illusion that law is essentially a system of authoritative rules whose meaning can be discovered and applied without fundamental disagreement. Instead, law should be shown for what it is: replete with contingent and controversial rules and standards which invite contention and critique. Critical legal learning can be used to imagine alternative legal frameworks. Law courses represent an opportunity to inquire into the distribution of wealth and power in various institutions, including the legal system and the legal profession themselves. Legal education could valuably emphasize skills training to a greater extent. The skills in question here would go far beyond case analysis and the manipulation of precedent. They could also include skills at devising and implementing legislative responses to perceived social problems. Other skills could be taught in the context of clinical legal education or neighborhood clinics, where students would benefit from witnessing law's impact on the lives of clients, especially those who are powerless and have learned to fear or distrust the law. A revamped curriculum could create greater opportunities for training in advocacy, negotiating, and counselling. The intellectual and the practical sides of legal education should not be considered antagonistic, but rather mutually reinforcing.

* * * *

ABEL, Richard L., "Evaluating Evaluations: How Should Law Schools Judge Teaching?" (1990) 40 J. Legal Educ. 407-55

ANSLEY, Frances Lee, "Race and the Core Curriculum in Legal Education" (1991) 79 Cal. L. Rev. 1512-97

AUERBACH, Jerold S., "What Has the Teaching of Law to do with Justice?" (1978) 53 N.Y.U. L. Rev. 457-74

BAMBERGER, Clinton, "Debilitating Conformity in 'Local' Law Schools" (1986) 17 Rutgers L. J. 215-20

BAMBERGER, E. Clinton, "Law School's Law Firm" (1985) 18 Md. B. J. 13-15

BARTLETT, Katharine T., "Feminist Perspectives on the Ideological Impact of Legal Education Upon the Profession" (1994) 72 N.C. L. Rev. 1259-70

BOYLE, James, "The PC Harangue" [review of Paul Burman (ed.), *Debating P.C.: The Controversy Over Political Correctness on Campuses*] (1993) 45 Stan. L. Rev. 1457-84

BRAVEMAN, Daan, "A Cubist Vision of Legal Education" (1992) 43 Syracuse L. Rev. 997-1028

BREST, Paul, "The Disorderly University: A Reply to Mark Tushnet" (1992) 4 Yale J. L. & Hum. 381-99

BREST, Paul, "A First-Year Course in the 'Lawyering Process'" (1982) 32 J. Legal Educ. 344-57

BREST, Paul, "On Legal Education: The Advanced Curriculum" (1988) 23 Stan. Law. 2(2)

BURNS, Michael, "The Law School as a Model for Community" (1986) 10 Nova L. J. 329-402

CARRINGTON, Paul, "Of Law and the River" (1984) 34 J. Legal Educ. 222-28

CASSELS, Jamie and **MALONEY**, Maureen, "Critical Legal Education: Paralysis with a Purpose" (1989) 4 Can. J. L. & Soc'y 99-138

CHARLESWORTH, Hilary, "Critical Legal Education" (1988-89) 5 Austl. J. L. & Soc'y 27-34

CHASE, Anthony, "American Legal Education Since 1885: The Case of the Missing Modern" (1985) 30 N.Y.L. Sch. L. Rev. 519-42

CHASE, Anthony, "The Birth of the Modern Law School" (1979) 23 Am. J. Legal Hist. 329-48

CHASE, Anthony, "Lawyer Training in the Age of the Department Store" (1983) 78 Nw. U. L. Rev. 893-909

CHASE, Anthony, "Origins of Modern Professional Education: The Harvard Case Method Conceived as Clinical Instruction in Law" (1981) 5 Nova L. J. 323-63

CHASE, Anthony, Review of William C. Chase, *The American Law School and the Rise of Administrative Government* (1983) 67 Minn. L. Rev. 844-59

CHASE, Anthony, "What Should a Law Teacher Believe?" (1986) 10 Nova L. J. 403-24

CONKLIN, William, "Teaching Critically Within a Modern Legal Genre" (1993) 8 Can. J. L. & Soc'y 33-57

DAVIS, Michael H., "Academic Freedom, Impartiality, and Faculty Governance" (1986) 5 L. & Phil. 263-76

DAVIS, Michael H., "The Courtroom Mystique and Legal Education" (1981) 23 Ariz. L. Rev. 661-88

DELGADO, Richard, "How to Write a Law Review Article" (1986) 20 U.S.F. L. Rev. 445-54

DEVLIN, Richard F., "Legal Education as Political Consciousness-Raising or Paving the Road to Hell" (1989) 39 J. Legal Educ. 213-29

DUNSFORD, John E., "Nihilism and Legal Education — A Response to Sanford Levinson" (1986) 31 St. Louis U. L. J. 27-34

EPSTEIN, Richard and **KENNEDY**, Duncan, "Views on Legal Education: An Exchange" (1985) 8 Harv. J. L. & Pub. Pol'y 269-75

ERICKSON, Nancy S., "Legal Education: The Last Academic Bastion of Sex Bias?" (1986) 10 Nova L. J. 457-64

FARAGO, John M., "The Pedagogy of Community: Trust and Responsibility at CUNY Law School" (1986) 10 Nova L. J. 465-94

FEINMAN, Jay M., "Change in Law Schools" (1986) 16 N. M. L. Rev. 505-12

FEINMAN, Jay M., "The Failure of Legal Education and the Promise of Critical Legal Studies" (1985) 6 Cardozo L. Rev. 739-64

FEINMAN, Jay M., "Reforming and Transforming" (1985) 30 N.Y. L. Sch. L. Rev. 629-35

FEINMAN, Jay M. and **FELDMAN**, Marc, "Achieving Excellence: Mastery Learning in Legal Education" (1985) J. Legal Educ. 528-51

FEINMAN, Jay M. and **FELDMAN**, Marc, "Pedagogy and Politics" (1985) 73 Geo. L. J. 875-930

FELDMAN, Marc, "On the Margins of Legal Education" (1984-85) 13 N.Y.U. Rev. L. & Soc. Ch. 607-46

FELDMAN, Marc and **FEINMAN**, Jay M., "Legal Education: Its Causes and Cure" [review of Robert Stevens, *Law School: Legal Education in America from the 1850s to the 1980s*] (1984) 82 Mich. L. Rev. 914-31

FINMAN, Ted, "Critical Legal Studies, Professionalism, and Academic Freedom: Exploring the Tributaries of Carrington's River" (1985) 35 J. Legal Educ. 180-207

FOSTER, James C., "The 'Cooling Out' of Law Students: Facilitating Market Cooptation of Future Lawyers" in Richard A. L. Gambitta; Marlynn L. May; and James C. Foster (eds.), *Governing Through Courts* (Beverly Hills: Sage Publications, 1981) 177-90

FRASER, Andrew, "Turbulence in the Law School: Republican Civility vs. Patrician Deference" (1988-89) 6 Austl. J. L. & Soc'y 44-52

FRUG, Jerry, "McCarthyism and Critical Legal Studies" [review of Ellen W. Schrecker, *The Ivory Tower: McCarthyism and the Universities*] (1987) 22 Harv. C.R.-C.L. L. Rev. 665-701

GLASBEEK, Harry J. and **HASSON**, Reuben A., "Some Reflections on Canadian Legal Education" (1987) 50 Mod. L. Rev. 777-803

GOLDFARB, Phyllis, "Beyond Cut Flowers: A Clinical Perspective on Critical Legal Theory" (1992) 43 Hast. L. J. 717-47

GOLDFARB, Phyllis, "A Theory-Practice Spiral: The Ethics of Feminism and Legal Education" (1991) 75 Minn. L. Rev. 1599-699

GORDON, Robert W., "Bargaining With the Devil" [review of Richard D. Kahlenberg, *Broken Contract: A Memoir of Harvard Law School*] (1992) 105 Harv. L. Rev. 2041-60

GORDON, Robert W., "Critical Legal Studies as a Teaching Method" (1989) 35 Loy. L. Rev. 383-407

GORDON, Robert W., "Critical Legal Studies as a Teaching Method, Against the Background of the Intellectual Politics of Modern Legal Education in the United States" (1989) 1 Legal Educ. Rev. 59-83

GORDON, Robert W., "Lawyers, Scholars, and the Middle Ground" (1993) 91 Mich. L. Rev. 2075-112

GREENE, Linda S., "Tokens, Role Models, and Pedagogical Politics: Lamentations of an African American Female Law Professor" (1990-910 6 Berk. Wom. L. J. 81-92

HADDON, Phoebe A., "Academic Freedom and Governance: A Call for Increased Dialogue and Diversity" (1988) 66 Tex. L. Rev. 1561-75

HADDON, Phoebe A., "Education for a Public Calling in the 21st Century" (1994) 69 Wash. L. Rev. 573-86

HARRIS, Angela P., "On Doing the Right Thing: Education Work in the Academy" (1990) 15 Vt. L. Rev. 125-37

HARRIS, Angela P., "Women of Color in Legal Education: Representing *La Mestiza*" (1990-91) 6 Berk. Wom. L. J. 107-12

HARRIS, Angela P. and **SCHULTZ**, Marjorie M., "'A(nother) Critique of Pure Reason': Toward Civic Virtue in Legal Education" (1993) 45 Stan. L. Rev. 1773-805

HARRISON, Melissa, "A Time of Passionate Learning: Using Feminism, Law, and Literature to Create a Learning Community" (1993) 60 Tenn. L. Rev. 393-429

HOEFLICH, M. H., "The Americanization of British Legal Education in the Nineteenth Century" (1987) 8 J. Legal Hist. 244-59

HORWITZ, Morton J., "Are Law Schools Fifteen Years Out of Date?" (1986) 54 U.M.K.C. L. Rev. 385-98

HUNT, Alan, "The Case for Critical Legal Education" (1986) 20 L. Teach. 10-20

HUNT, Alan, "Conservatism and Vocationalism in Legal Education: A Case Study" (1987) 21 L. Teach. 72-80

JAFF, Jennifer, "Frame-Shifting: An Empowering Methodology for Teaching and Learning Legal Reasoning" (1986) 36 J. Legal Educ. 249-67

JOHNSON, Karl and **SCALES**, Ann, "An Absolutely, Positively True Story: Seven Reasons Why We Sing" (1986) 16 N.M. L. Rev. 433-78

KENNEDY, David, "International Legal Education" (1985) 26 Harv. Int'l L. J. 361-84

KENNEDY, Duncan, "How the Law School Fails: A Polemic" (1970) 1 Yale Rev. L. & Soc. Action 71-90

KENNEDY, Duncan, *Legal Education and the Reproduction of Hierarchy: A Polemic Against the System* (Cambridge, Mass.: Afar, 1983)

KENNEDY, Duncan, "Legal Education and the Reproduction of Hierarchy" (1982) 32 J. Legal Educ. 591-615

KENNEDY, Duncan, "Legal Education as Training for Hierarchy" in David Kairys (ed.), *The Politics of Law: A Progressive Critique* (New York: Pantheon Books, 1982) 40-61

KENNEDY, Duncan, "Legal Education as Training for Hierarchy" in David Kairys (ed.), *The Politics of Law: A Progressive Critique*, 2nd rev. ed. (New York: Pantheon Books, 1990) 38-58

KENNEDY, Duncan, "Liberal Values in Legal Education" (1986) 10 Nova L. J. 603-17

KENNEDY, Duncan, "The Political Significance of the Structure of the Law School Curriculum" (1983) 14 Seton Hall L. Rev. 1-16

KENNEDY, Duncan, "Positive and Normative Elements in Legal Education: A Response" (1985) 8 Harv. J. L. & Pub. Pol'y 263-67

KENNEDY, Duncan, *Sexy Dressing, Etc.* (Cambridge, Mass.: Harvard University Press, 1993)

KLARE, Karl, "The Law-School Curriculum in the 1980s: What's Left?" (1982) 32 J. Legal Educ. 336-43

KONEFSKY, Alfred and **SCHLEGEL**, John Henry, "Mirror, Mirror on the Wall: Histories of American Law Schools" (1982) 95 Harv. L. Rev. 833-51

LEPOW, C. Garrison, "Deconstructing Los Angeles or a Secret Fax from Magritte Regarding Postliterate Legal Training: A Critique of Legal Training" (1992) 26 U. Mich. J. L. Ref. 69-124

LESNICK, Howard, "The Integration of Responsibility and Values: Legal Education in an Alternative Consciousness of Lawyering and Law" (1986) 10 Nova L. J. 633-44

LESNICK, Howard, "Legal Education's Concern With Justice: A Conversation With a Critic" (1985) 35 J. Legal Educ. 414-20

LESNICK, Howard, Contribution to "Reassessing Law Schooling: The Sterling Forest Group" (1978) 53 N.Y.U. L. Rev. 565-70

LESNICK, Howard; **DVORKIN**, Elizabeth; and **HIMMELSTEIN**, Jack, *Becoming a Lawyer: A Humanistic Perspective on Legal Education and Professionalism* (St. Paul, Minn.: West Pub. Co. 1981)

LETWIN, Leon, "Teaching First-Year Students: The Inevitability of a Political Agenda" (1986) 10 Nova L. J. 645-46

LEVINSON, Sanford, "Professing Law: Commitment of Faith or Detached Analysis?" (1986) 31 St. Louis U. L. J. 3-26

LÓPEZ, Gerald P., "Training Future Lawyers to Work With the Politically and Socially Subordinated: Anti-Generic Legal Education" (1989) 91 W. Va. L. Rev. 305-87

MENKEL-MEADOW, Carrie, "The Legacy of Clinical Education: Theories About Lawyering" (1980) 29 Clev. St. L. Rev. 555-74

MENKEL-MEADOW, Carrie, "Narrowing the Gap by Narrowing the Field: What's Missing From the MacCrate Project — Of Skills, Legal Science and Being Like a Human Being" (1994) 69 Wash. L. Rev. 593-624

MENKEL-MEADOW, Carrie, "Too Little Theory, Too Little Practice? Stevens's *Law School*" [1985] Am. Bar Fdn. Res. J. 675-90

MENKEL-MEADOW, Carrie, "Two Contradictory Criticisms of Clinical Education: Dilemmas and Directions in Lawyering Education" (1986) 4 Antioch L. Rev. 287-99

MENKEL-MEADOW, Carrie, "Women as Law Teachers: Toward the Feminization of Legal Education" in *Humanistic Education in Law: Essays on the Application of a Humanistic Perspective to Law Teaching* (New York: Columbia University School of Law, 1981) 16-32

MINDA, Gary, "Of Law, the River and Legal Education" (1986) 10 Nova L. J. 705-21

MINDA, Gary, "Phenomenology, Tina Turner and the Law" (1986) 16 N.M. L. Rev. 479-93

MINDA, Gary, "The Politics of Professing Law" (1986) 31 St. Louis U. L. J. 61-71

PICKARD, Toni, "Experience as Teacher: Discovering the Politics of Law Teaching" (1983) 33 U. Toronto L. J. 279-314

POST, Debra Waire, "Reflections on Identity, Diversity and Morality" (1990-91) 6 Berk. Wom. L. J. 136-66

PRILLAMAN, Hunter L., "'Critical' Law School Faculty: A Practice Perspective" (1989) 14 J. Legal Prof. 3-20

RESNIK, Judith, "Ambivalence: The Resiliency of Legal Culture in the United States" (1993) 45 Stan. L. Rev. 1525-46

RESNIK, Judith, "Revising the Canon: Feminist Help in Teaching Procedure" (1993) 61 U. Cin. L. Rev. 1181-99

RHODE, Deborah L., "Missing Questions: Feminist Perspectives on Legal Education" (1993) 45 Stan. L. Rev. 1547-69

SCALES, Ann C., "Surviving Legal De-Education: An Outsider's Guide" (1990) 15 Vt. L. Rev. 139-64

SCALES-TRENT, Judy, "Sameness and Difference in a Law School Classroom: Working at the Crossroads" (1992) 4 Yale J. L. & Fem. 415-38

SCHLEGEL, John Henry, "Between the Harvard Founders and the American Legal Realists: The Professionalization of the American Law Professor" (1985) 35 J. Legal Educ. 311-25

SCHLEGEL, John Henry, "Langdell's Legacy or, the Case of the Empty Envelope" (1984) 36 Stan. L. Rev. 1517-33

SCHLEGEL, John Henry, "Revenge, Or Moon(Over) Your Law School" (1990) 40 J. Legal Educ. 467-72

SCHLEGEL, John Henry, "Searching for Archimedes — Legal Education, Legal Scholarship and Liberal Ideology" (1984) 34 J. Legal Educ. 103-10

SCHNEIDER, Elizabeth M., "Political Interference in Law School Clinical Programs: Reflections on Outside Interference and Academic Freedom" (1984) 11 J. C. & U. L. 179-213

SCHNEIDER, Elizabeth M., "Rethinking the Teaching of Civil Procedure" (1987) 37 J. Legal Educ. 41-45

SCHNEIDER, Elizabeth M., "Academic Freedom and Law School Clinical Programs" in Craig Kaplan and Ellen Schrecker (eds.), *Regulating the Intellectuals: Perspectives on Academic Freedom in the 1980's* (New York: Praeger, 1983) 209-39

THOMAS, Richard M., "Deprofessionalization and the Postmodern State of Administrative Law Pedagogy" (1992) 42 J. Legal Educ. 75-96

THOMSON, Alan, "Critical Legal Education in Britain" in Peter Fitzpatrick and Alan Hunt (eds.), *Critical Legal Studies* (Oxford: Basil Blackwell, 1987) 183-97

TORRES, Gerald, "Teaching and Writing: Curriculum Reform as an Exercise in Critical Education" (1986) 10 Nova L. J. 867-78

TORREY, Morrison, "Teaching Law in a Feminist Manner: A Commentary From Experience" (1990) 13 Harv. Wom. L. J. 87-135

TRILLIN, Calvin, "Reporter at Large: Harvard Law" (March 26, 1984) The New Yorker 53-56, 59, 64-67, 69-70, 75-76, 80-83

TRUBEK, David and **PLAGER**, Sheldon Jay, "The Place of Law and Social Science in the Structure of Legal Education" (1985) 35 J. Legal Educ. 483-88

TUSHNET, Mark, "Political Correctness, the Law, and the Academy" (1992) 4 Yale J. L. & Hum. 127-63

TUSHNET, Mark, "Scenes from the Metropolitan Underground: A Critical Perspective on the Status of Clinical Education" (1984) 52 Geo. Wash. L. Rev. 272-79

WORDEN, K. C., "Overshooting the Target: A Feminist Deconstruction of Legal Education" (1985) 34 Am. U. L. Rev. 1141-56

WORDEN, K. C., "A Student Polemic" (1986) 16 N.M. L. Rev. 573-84

20

International Law

One of the major contributions of critical legal writing in public international law has been to revise the historiography of the field. From the point of view of David Kennedy, for example, the analysis that yields the most illuminating results is to treat international law (including its sources, its doctrines, and its institutions) as a type of practice and argument. His work relies heavily on treating the discipline as form of rhetoric, or an area of discourse. By examining this discourse closely, he has tried to reveal the submerged elements of contradiction and tension within public international law materials and debates.

Subjected to Kennedy's method, the traditional narrative associated with the growth of the field takes on new meaning. Prior to this century, the main preoccupation of international legal theorists was to account for the relationship between the law (as a body of normative principles) and state power (conceived in terms of sovereign political will). The debates between proponents of natural law theory and positivism are a rich source of material for a critical analysis of hidden dominant rhetorical structures. The modern emphasis in the field on procedures (as opposed to substance) are, viewed from this perspective, a failed attempt to escape from the difficulties of morally justifying international constraints (conceived as a preexisting normative order) on sovereign autonomy. The historically important efforts to define international law, in an essentialist fashion, are just another aspect of this rhetorical debate.

This kind of work interrogates the traditional self-understanding of international law scholars and, in the process, tries to destabilize or unsettle conventional differences and assumptions. It can be applied not only to the history of public international law, but also to its theory and to the institution-building and administration that have been attempted.

According to critical legal writers, the field of public international law has been dominated during this century by liberal political ideas. For instance, theorists have been fond of analogizing international law with domestic constitutional arrangements. Between the two world wars, international law theorists attempted to reduce their discipline to a body of doctrine that was admirable in its coherence and would promote certainty and compliance among international actors. This striving for a formalist model of international law doctrine was relatively untouched by realist challenges that had affected private law subjects.

After the Second World War, international law felt the bite of realism, with its general attack on formalism. The scholarly response was to approach traditional problems from a pragmatist angle. The attempt at Yale by Myres McDougal and Harold Lasswell to develop a "policy science" was one example of this new scholarship. This approach placed great faith in an international bureaucracy to manage problems arising out of "transnational" disagreements. The pragmatist perspective did not offer a comprehensive answer to the question of what is international law. Instead, it relied on sociological and descriptive explanations. In addition, the liberal ideals of international law scholars emphasized the importance of individual rights as expressive of the core values of a humanitarian philosophy.

The structuralist approach to public international law stresses that long-standing conflicts and contradictions within the field are incapable of resolution. Thus, arguments about the relative authority of such sources as treaties, custom, general principles of law, or resolutions by (arguably) authoritative bodies like the United Nations cannot be finally resolved. Similarly, the development of a fully integrated international legal order, marked by sharing, cooperation, and non-violent modes of solving disputes, remains largely aspirational. These prospects are merely promises without substance. Kennedy claims that current discursive practices in public international law juxtapose contradictory rhetorical claims: for example, firm assertions of an international legal regime (with a "very humble and deferential tone"); a sense of progress and momentum (though this relies on repetition of promises); and loose and contradictory doctrines (that are relatively indeterminate).

Critical legal writers have sought to account for the relative marginality of public international law in the law school curriculum and in legal scholarship. To make it more relevant and central, various critics have proposed a renewal of public international law as a field vitally concerned with discovering the ways in which law is used to create and perpetuate domination and powerlessness. This requires a fundamental re-examination of the extent to which internationalism as an ideology has been animated by a form of political liberalism liable to be unthinkingly imposed on other societies. Although critical legal writers have followed Kennedy's lead in uncovering the structural contradictions embedded in international law doctrines and institutions, there have also been calls (for example, by James Boyle) to engage in "highly contextualized, politicized" studies, which may be made part of a clinical program of education for law students. They would benefit from integrating their theoretical learning with clinical assignments at international agencies and non-governmental organizations.

* * * *

ABEL, Richard L., "Transnational Law Practice" (1994) 44 Case West. Res. L. Rev. 737-870

ALLOTT, Philip; **CARTY**, Tony; **KOSKENNIEMI**, Martti; and **WARBRICK**, Colin, *Theory and International Law: An Introduction* (London: British Institute of International and Comparative Law and International Law Group, Society of Public Teachers of Law, 1991)

ANDERSON, Ken and **ANDERSON**, Richard, "Limitations of the Liberal-Legal Mode of International Human Rights: Six Lessons from El Salvador" (1985) 64 Telos 91-104

BARTHOLEMEW, Mary Elizabeth and **CORNELL**, Drucilla, "Women, Law and Inequality: Rethinking International Human Rights" (1994) 16 Cardozo L. Rev. 153-68

BEDERMAN, David J., "The Cautionary Tale of Alexander McLeod: Superior Orders and the American Writ of Habeas Corpus" (1992) 41 Emory L. J. 515-39

BEDERMAN, David J., Review of Oscar Schachter, *International Law in Theory and Practice* (1992) 33 Va. J. Int'l L. 238-52

BEDERMAN, David J., "Revivalist Canons and Treaty Interpretation" (1994) 41 U.C.L.A. L. Rev. 953-1034

BERMAN, Nathaniel, "But the Alternative is Despair: European Nationalism and the Modernist Renewal of International Law" (1993) 106 Harv. L. Rev. 1792-903

BERMAN, Nathaniel, "Modernism, Nationalism, and the Rhetoric of Reconstruction" (1992) 4 Yale J. L. & Hum. 351-80

BERMAN, Nathaniel, "Nationalism Legal and Linguistic: The Teachings of European Jurisprudence" (1992) 24 N.Y.U. J. Int'l L. & Pol. 1515-78

BERMAN, Nathaniel, "A Perilous Ambivalence: Nationalist Desire, Legal Autonomy, and the Limits of the Interwar Framework" (1992) 33 Harv. Int'l L. J. 353-79

BERMAN, Nathaniel, "Sovereignty in Abeyance: Self-Determination and International Law" (1988) 7 Wis. Int'l L. J. 51-105

BOYLE, James, "Ideals and Things: International Legal Scholarship and the Prison-House of Language" (1985) 26 Harv. Int'l L. J. 327-59

CAMPBELL, David, *Politics Without Principle: Sovereignty, Ethics and the Narratives of the Gulf War* (Boulder, Co.: Lynne Rienner, 1993)

CARTY, Anthony, "Social Theory and the 'Vanishing' of International Law: A Review Article" [review of T. M. Franck, *The Power of Legitimacy Among Nations* and Philip Allott, *Eunomia: New Order for a New World*] (1992) 41 Int'l & Comp. L. Q. 939-45

CHARLESWORTH, Hilary, "The Public/Private Distinction and the Right to Development" (1992) 12 Austl. Y.B. Int'l L. 190-204

CHARLESWORTH, Hilary; **CHINKIN**, Christine; and **WRIGHT**, Shelley, "Feminist Approaches to International Law" (1991) 85 Am. J. Int'l L. 613-45

CHAYES, Abram, "Nicaragua, the United States, and the World Court" (1985) 85 Colum. L. Rev. 1445-82

CHINKIN, Christine, "The Challenge of Soft Law: Development and Change in International Law" (1989) 38 Int'l & Comp. L. Q. 850-66

CHINKIN, Christine, "A Gendered Perspective to the International Use of Force" (1992) 12 Austl. Y.B. Int'l L. 279-93

ENGLE, Karen, "Female Subjects of Public International Law: Human Rights and the Exotic Other Female" (1992) 26 New Eng. L. Rev. 1509-26

ENGLE, Karen, "International Human Rights and Feminism: When Discourses Meet" (1992) 13 Mich. J. Int'l L. 517-610

ENGLE, Karen, "Views From the Margins: A Response to David Kennedy" [1994] Utah L. Rev. 105-18

FRANKENBERG, Günter and **KNIEPER**, Rolf, "Legal Problems of the Overindebtedness of Developing Countries: The Current Relevance of the Doctrine of Odious Debts" (1984) 12 Int'l J. Soc. L. 415-38

GARDHAM, Judith G., "A Feminist Analysis of Certain Aspects of International Humanitarian Law" (1992) 12 Austl. Y.B. Int'l L. 265-78

GROSSFELD, Bernard and **ROGERS**, C. Paul, "A Shared Values Approach to Jurisdictional Conflicts in International Economic Law" (1983) 32 Int'l & Comp. L. Q. 931-47

KENNEDY, David, "A Critical Approach to the Nuclear Weapons Problem" (1983) 9 Brooklyn J. Int'l L. 307-10

KENNEDY, David, "International Legal Education" (1985) 26 Harv. Int'l L. J. 361-84

KENNEDY, David L., *International Legal Structures* (Baden-Baden: Nomos, 1987)

KENNEDY, David, "International Refugee Protection" (1986) 8 Hum. Rts. Q. 1-69

KENNEDY, David, "The International Style in Postwar Law and Policy" [1994] Utah. L. Rev. 7-103

KENNEDY, David, "McDougal's Jurisprudence: Utility, Influence, Controversy" (April, 1985) Am. Soc'y Intl L. Proc. 266-88

KENNEDY, David, "The Move to Institutions" (1987) 8 Cardozo L. Rev. 841-988

KENNEDY, David, "A New Stream of International Law Scholarship" (1988) 7 Wis. Int'l L. J. 1-49

KENNEDY, David, "Primitive Legal Scholarship" (1986) 27 Harv. Int'l L. J. 1-98

KENNEDY, David, "Receiving the International" (1994) 10 Conn. J. Int'l L. 1-26

KENNEDY, David, Review of Louis Henkin, *How Nations Behave*, 2nd ed. (1980) 21 Harv. Int'l L. J. 301-21

KENNEDY, David, Review of I. von Munch (ed.), *Staatsrecht-Völkrecht-Europarecht: Festschrift für Hans-Jürgen Schlochauer zum 75* (1981) 22 Harv. Int'l L. J. 730-34

KENNEDY, David, "Spring Break (Visiting a Political Prisoner in Uruguay)" (1985) 63 Tex. L. Rev. 1377-423

KENNEDY, David, "Theses About International Law Discourse" (1980) 23 German Y.B. Int'l L. 353-91

KENNEDY, David and **TENNANT**, Chris, "New Approaches to International Law: A Bibliography" (1994) 35 Harv. Int'l L. J. 417-60

KOSKENNIEMI, Martti, *From Apology to Utopia: The Structure of International Legal Argument* (Helsinki: Finnish Lawyers' Pub. Co., 1989)

KOSKENNIEMI, Martti, "The Future of Statehood" (1991) 32 Harv. Int'l L. J. 397-410

KOSKENNIEMI, Martti, "National Self-Determination Today: Problems of Legal Theory and Practice" (1994) 43 Int'l & Comp. L. Q. 241-69

KOSKENNIEMI, Martti, "The Politics of International Law" (1990) 1 Eur. J. Int'l L. 4-32

MORGAN, Edward M., "Aliens and Process Rights: The Open and Shut Case of Legal Sovereignty" (1988) 7 Wis. Int'l L. J. 107-47

PAUL, Joel R., "Comity in International Law" (1991) 32 Harv. Int'l L. J. 1-79

PAUL, Joel R., "The Isolation of Private International Law" (1988) 7 Wis. Int'l L. J. 149-78

ROMANY, Celina, "Women as Aliens: A Feminist Critique of the Public/Private Distinction in International Human Rights Law" (1993) 6 Harv. Hum. Rts. J. 87-125

SANDS, Philippe, "Enforcing Environmental Security: The Challenges of Compliance With International Obligations" (1993) 46 J. Int'l Aff. 367-90

SATHIRATHAI, Surakiart, "An Understanding of the Relationship Between International Legal Discourse and Third World Countries" (1984) 25 Harv. Int'l L. J. 395-419

SOIFER, Aviam, "Protecting Posterity" (1982) 7 Nova L. J. 39-51 [reprinted in Arthur Selwyn Miller and Martin Feinrider (eds.), *Nuclear Weapons and Law* (Greenwich, Conn.: Greenwood Press, 1984) 273-85]

TARULLO, Daniel K., "Beyond Normalcy in the Regulation of International Trade" (1987) 100 Harv. L. Rev. 546-628

TARULLO, Daniel K., "Indeterminacy and Legitimation Problems in the Regulation of International Trade" (1983) 77 Am. Soc'y Int'l L. Proc. 140-46

TARULLO, Daniel K., "Law and Politics in Twentieth Century Tariff History" (1986) 34 U.C.L.A. L. Rev. 285-370

TARULLO, Daniel K., "Logic, Myth, and the International Economic Order" (1985) 26 Harv. Int'l L. J. 533-52

TRIMBLE, Phillip R., "International Law, World Order, and Critical Legal Studies" [review of Lung-Chu Chen, *An Introduction to Contemporary International law: A Policy-oriented Perspective*; Richard A. Falk, *Revitalizing International Law*; and David L. Kennedy, *International Legal Structures*] (1990) 42 Stan. L. Rev. 811-45

TRUBEK, David, "Economic, Social and Cultural Rights in the Third World: Human Rights Law and Human Needs Programs" in Theodor Meron (ed.), *Human Rights in International Law: Legal and Policy Issues*, vol. 1 (New York: Oxford University Press, 1984) 205-71

TRUBEK, David M.; **DEZALAY**, Yves; **BUCHANAN**, Ruth; and **DAVIS**, John R., "Global Restructuring and the Law: Studies of the Internationalization of Legal Fields and the Creation of Transnational Arenas" (1994) 44 Case West. Res. L. Rev. 407-98

WRIGHT, Shelley, "Economic Rights and Social Justice: A Feminist Analysis of Some International Human Rights Conventions" (1992) 12 Austl. Y.B. Int'l L. 241-64

21

Comparative Legal Studies

One of the key problems with comparative studies in law is the dilemma created by trying to understand a foreign legal culture, while trying at the same time to transcend the comparatist's domestic legal culture. Critical legal writers have criticized conventional models that guide comparative legal studies, especially those in which the comparatist assumes the role of a neutral spectator interested in the discovery and delineation of legal universals.

Radical critics have argued that comparatists have largely failed to examine rigorously the methodological and theoretical assumptions underlying their field. In particular, traditional modes of investigation do not provide a self-critical and reflective discussion of such questions as, what is the proper subject for comparative studies; what are the benefits that result from such inquiry; and what precisely is meant by "law" and legal forms of behavior and knowledge in the culture to be studied? Instead, critics claim that comparatists have too often relied on implicit theoretical assumptions that turn out to be some variation on the theme of conceptual or evolutionary functionalism. This latter perspective is inadequate to the extent that it incorporates uncritically many of the comparatist's own values, world-view, language, and biases.

An adequate theory for comparative legal studies has to come to grips with language barriers, unique cultural histories, hermeneutic difficulties, and inescapable ideological visions, all of which condition the kind of comparative work being attempted. Radical critics have taken their conventional colleagues to task for tending to impose a cognitive grid on the foreign culture under examination. In this process, law is understood as a formalist enterprise that supplements social institutions. Legal practices and discourses are not viewed as constitutive of society. Moreover, there is a reliance on labeling and on ethnocentric interpretation of data which is chosen selectively to back up the allegedly objective and non-evaluative standpoint of the comparatist. Among the targets of this critique is the division of legal cultural characteristics into "families of law," reflecting criteria such as historical antecedents, legal style or technique, race, and ideology. In such studies, law is usually understood as a set of institutions, techniques and regulations designed to recognize and protect individual rights. Legal doctrine is assumed to be a coherent structure.

Comparatists are fond of using various dichotomies to illustrate the cognitive categories which they impose on this material. Such dichotomous typologies include: common law/civil law; capitalist law/socialist law; primitive system/modern system; common core/radically different cultures; developed nations/developing nations; and parent system/derivative system. These ready-made categories are liable to lead to over-simplication and distortion. Furthermore, law is often treated as primarily existing in a written text, including statutes, judicial decisions, and legal scholarship. When a comparatist confines the study to comparing foreign and domestic texts, the result is a positivist conception of law that abstracts legal institutions from their social and political environment. Also, formal law is typically viewed as the sole means of dispute resolution in society.

Critical legal writers self-consciously depart from this conventional pattern by seeing the point of comparative studies in terms of how law forms a part of the foreign culture and how law is used to distribute, impose, and change power in that culture. These writers are also keenly aware of the dangers of assuming the superiority of one culture over another. Comparatists should not presuppose the necessity, functionality or universality of particular legal forms. As part of their project to be self-critical, radical comparatists have to review the existing scholarly discourse, and reevaluate their own socialization in their domestic legal culture. They must acknowledge limitations in their own perspectives and be wary of claims that a particular interpretation is authentic or has universal implications.

* * * *

ABEL, Richard L., "A Comparative Theory of Dispute Institutions in Society" (1973) 8 L. & Soc'y Rev. 217-347

ABEL, Richard L., "The Transformation of Civil Lawyers" [1987] B.Y.U. L. Rev. 587-94

ABEL, Richard L., "Western Courts in Non-Western Settings: Patterns of Court Use in Colonial and Neo-Colonial Africa" in Sandra B. Burman and Barbara E. Harrell-Bond (eds.), *The Imposition of Law* (New York: Academic Press, 1979) 167-200

ALFORD, William P., "On the Limits of 'Grand Theory' in Comparative Law" (1986) 61 Wash. L. Rev. 945-56

FRANKENBERG, Günter, "Critical Comparisons: Re-thinking Comparative Law" (1985) 26 Harv. Int'l L. J. 411-55

FRANKENBERG, Günter, "In the Beginning of All the World was America: AIDS Policy and Law in West Germany" (1991) 23 N.Y.U. J. Int'l L. & Pol. 1079-109

FRANKENBERG, Günter, "Poland, Of Course, is a Critical Case!" (1982) 51 Telos 131-34

FRASER, David, "The Day the Music Died: The Civil Law Tradition From a Critical Legal Studies Perspective" (1987) 32 Loy. L. Rev. 861-94

GLENDON, Mary Ann, "Individualism and Communitarianism in Contemporary Legal Systems: Tensions and Accomodations" [1993] B.Y.U. L. Rev. 385-419

HILL, Jonathan, "Comparative Law, Law Reform, and Legal Theory" (1989) 9 Oxford J. Legal Stud. 101-15

OTTLEY, Bruce L. and **ZORN**, Jean G., "Criminal Law in Papua New Guinea: Code, Custom and the Courts in Conflict" (1983) 31 Am. J. Comp. L. 251-300

PARKER, Richard B., "Law, Language, and the Individual in Japan and the United States" (1988) 7 Wis. Int'l L. J. 179-203

SANTOS, Boaventura de Sousa, "Law and Revolution in Portugal: The Experience of Popular Justice after the 25th of April 1974" in Richard L. Abel (ed.), *The Politics of Informal Justice*, vol. 2: *Comparative Studies* (New York: Academic Press, 1982) 251-80

SCHMIDHAUSER, John R., "Power, Legal Imperialism, and Dependency" (1989) 23 L. & Soc'y Rev. 857-78

SNYDER, Frederick E., "State of Siege and Rule of Law in Argentina: The Politics and Rhetoric of Vindication" (1984) 15 Law. Americas 503-20

STARR, June, *Dispute and Settlement in Rural Turkey: An Ethnography of Law* (Leiden: Brill, 1978)

STARR, June, "The Legal and Social Transformation of Rural Women in Aegean Turkey" in Renée Hirschon (ed.), *Women and Property / Women as Property* (London: Croom Helm, 1984) 92-116

STARR, June, "Folk Law in Official Courts in Turkey" in Anthony Allott and Gordon R. Woodman (eds.), *People's Law and State Law: The Bellagio Papers* (Dordrecht: Foris Publications, 1985) 123-41

STARR, June, *Law as Metaphor: From Islamic Courts to the Palace of Justice* (Albany: State University of New York Press, 1992)

STARR, June, "The Role of Turkish Secular Law in Changing the Lives of Rural Muslim Women, 1950-1970" (1989) 23 L. & Soc'y Rev. 497-523

STARR, June and **COLLIER**, Jane F. (eds.), *History and Power in the Study of Law: New Directions in Legal Anthropology* (Ithaca: Cornell University Press, 1989)

STARR, June and **POOL**, Jonathan, "The Impact of a Legal Revolution in Rural Turkey" (1974) 8 L. & Soc'y Rev. 533-60

22

Feminism and Law

It would dismayingly inaccurate to portray feminist thinking about law as merely a branch of critical legal studies. Although there may be parallels or intersections among feminism and critical legal work, and although there may be some degree of shared political commitment between the two, not all types of feminist thinking have common themes, methods or aims with critical analysis. Indeed, many feminists have challenged critical legal assumptions and preoccupations. Students of both contemporary perspectives should be aware of the tension that exists, as well as some elements of commonality, in the varieties of feminist and critical legal thinking.

While critical legal writers are committed to exposing and removing the sources and effects of oppression and domination, feminism is particularly interested in men's oppression and domination of women. Feminists who examine the law from a radical perspective have noted the systematic exclusion and devaluation of women's concerns and experiences. Like critical legal writers, some feminists also have lamented the extent to which legal doctrine and traditional legal theory have been predicated on a liberal foundation, in which the basic values are personal autonomy, rational choice, and an assumed devotion to individuals' maximization of their particular preferences. Feminists have criticized these normative ideals as essentially masculine. This is not to say that legal doctrines should be reinscribed on the basis of some alleged biological imperatives that make men and women different. Against the liberal picture of human flourishing, feminists have emphasized the values of affiliation, interpersonal connectedness, and the ways in which human identities are constructed by social and cultural factors. But radical feminists have asked further questions about the legal difference that gender differences should make. They have examined the extent to which legal distinctions can reinforce or remove gender disparities in relation to social status and economic and political power.

Feminists have questioned other liberal legal assumptions. For example, feminists have been skeptical of the view that law is primarily a matter of formal procedure in which ascertainable and determinate rules are deployed to reach a correct answer. A similar skepticism applies to the liberal legal separation of law (as objective and neutral) from politics (as a matter of subjective and partisan will). In the work of Frances Olsen, the dualisms incorporated into law that turn on privileging one side of the pair over the other are striking for how they exemplify the masculine foundations of the legal system. On the male side, she lists: rational, active, thought, reason, culture, power, objective, abstract, and principled. On the female side are projected: irrational, passive, feeling, emotion, nature, sensitivity, subjective, contextualized, and personalized. A great deal of the feminist literature listed in this chapter investigates legal material with the purpose of showing how women's values and interests have traditionally been excluded or depreciated.

Feminist writers have queried the value of theorizing, in the sense that this involves building abstract theories or defending broad principles. Many radical feminists have chosen instead to emphasize experiential, rather than theoretical, analysis. Instead of starting with a comprehensive theory that seeks to explain data, feminists have proposed and used a different methodology which starts with the concrete experiences of individuals or groups who have labored under systemic disadvantages and injustices. The feminist interest in practical perspectives and everyday, pervasive problems has drawn them to narrative styles of presentation.

Feminist legal approaches have evolved during the 1970s and 80s. Where it was once important to address women's issues as if they constituted a particular group of problems common to all women, there is now a heightened awareness of diversity among women, reflecting differences of culture, race, ethnic background, class, age, and sexuality. Theorizing which takes for granted that all women must share some kind of essential nature has been heavily criticized in radical feminist literature. Also, writers who attempt to construct a "relational" feminism, for example Carol Gilligan's work in the unique developmental psychology of females compared with males, have been taken to task for asserting an indefensible "universalism."

Some feminist writers have challenged critical legal critiques of rights discourse. From the different perspectives of Patricia Williams, Kimberlé Crenshaw, and Elizabeth Schneider, social movements that press for recognition and enforcement of rights have been catalyzed by this discourse and have managed to achieve considerable gains. Rights strategies are not inevitably reactionary: they have proved to be empowering and progressive for both disadvantaged individuals and the subordinated groups to which they belong. Two of the major issues in feminist dialogue over the use of rights rhetoric have been: first, the best way to frame rights claims, including the content of those rights, and second, the strengths and limitations that arise when conceiving of a claim in the form of a right.

This section does not incorporate all the feminist literature which has some bearing on, or responds to, critical legal themes. That literature is so vast that what is selected for inclusion here is a mere smattering of all that is available. Also, it should be noted that under many other headings in this guide can be found feminist contributions that illuminate legal issues in distinctive and important ways.

* * * *

ABU-ODEH, Lama, "Post-Colonial Feminism and the Veil: Considering the Difference" (1992) 26 New Eng. L. Rev. 1527-37

ARRIOLA, Elvia R., "Gendered Inequality: Lesbians, Gays, and Feminist Legal Theory" (1994) 9 Berk. Wom. L. J. 103-43

ASHE, Marie, "Inventing Choreographies: Feminism and Deconstruction" (1990) 90 Colum. L. Rev. 1123-45

ASHE, Marie, "Law-Language of Maternity: Discourse Holding Nature in Contempt" (1988) 22 New Eng. L. Rev. 521-59

ASHE, Marie, "Mind's Opportunity: Birthing a Poststructuralist Feminist Jurisprudence" (1987) 38 Syracuse L. Rev. 1129-73

ASHE, Marie, "Zig-Zag Stitching and the Seamless Web: Thoughts on 'Reproduction' and the Law" (1989) 13 Nova L. J. 355-83

AUSTIN, Regina, "Black Women, Sisterhood, and the Difference/Deviance Dvivide" (1992) 26 New Eng. L. Rev. 877-87

BAER, Judith A., "How is Law Male? A Feminist Perspective on Constitutional Interpretation" in Leslie Friedman Goldstein (ed.), *Feminist*

Jurisprudence: The Difference Debate (Lanham, Md.: Rowman and Littlefield, 1992) 147-71

BALBUS, Isaac D., "Disciplining Women: Michel Foucault and the Power of Feminist Discourse" in Seyla Benhabib and Drucilla Cornell (eds.), *Feminism as Critique* (Minneapolis: University of Minnesota Press, 1987) 110-27

BARRON, Anne, "Legal Discourse and the Colonization of the Self in the Modern State" in Anthony Carty (ed.), *Post-Modern Law: Enlightenment, Revolution and the Death of Man* (Edinburgh: Edinburgh University Press, 1990) 107-25

BARTHOLEMEW, Amy, "'Achieving a Place for Women in a Man's World': Or, Feminism With No Class" (1993) 6 Can. J. Wom. & L. 465-90

BARTLETT, Katharine T., "Feminist Legal Methods" (1990) 103 Harv. L. Rev. 829-88

BARTLETT, Katharine T., "MacKinnon's Feminism: Power on Whose Terms?" [review of Catharine MacKinnon, *Feminism Unmodified*] (1987) 75 Cal. L. Rev. 1559-70

BENHABIB, Seyla, "The Generalized and the Concrete Other: The Kohlberg-Gilligan Controversy and Feminist Theory" in Seyla Benhabib and Drucilla Cornell (eds.), *Feminism as Critique* (Minneapolis: University of Minnesota Press, 1987) 77-95

BERKOWITZ, Roger, "Risk of the Self: Drucilla Cornell's Transformative Philosophy" (1994) 9 Berk. Wom. L. J. 175-205

BOTTOMLEY, Anne and **CONAGHAN**, Joanne (eds.), *Feminist Theory and Legal Strategy* (Oxford: Blackwell, 1993)

BOTTOMLEY, Anne; **GIBSON**, Susie; and **METEGARD**, Belinda, "Dworkin; Which Dworkin? Taking Feminism Seriously" in Peter Fitzpatrick and Alan Hunt (eds.), *Critical Legal Studies* (Oxford: Basil Blackwell, 1987) 47-60

BROWN, Beverley, "Debating Pornography: The Symbolic Dimensions" (1990) 1 L. & Critique 131-54

BUMILLER, Kristin, "Fallen Angels: The Representation of Violence Against Women in Legal Culture" (1990) 18 Int'l J. Soc. L. 125-42

CAHN, Naomi R., "Inconsistent Stories" (1993) 81 Geo. L. J. 2475-531

CAIN, Patricia A., "Feminism and the Limits of Equality" (1990) 24 Ga. L. Rev. 803-47

CAIN, Patricia A., "Feminist Jurisprudence: Grounding the Theories" (1989-90) 4 Berk. Wom. L. J. 191-214

CLARKE, Lorenne M. G., "Women and the State: Critical Theory — Oasis or Desert Island?" (1992) 5 Can. J. Wom. & L. 166-78

COLE, David, "Strategies of Difference: Litigating for Women's Rights in a Man's World" (1984) 2 L. & Inequality 33-96

COLKER, Ruth, "Abortion and Dialogue" (1989) 63 Tul. L. Rev. 1363-403

COLKER, Ruth, *Abortion and Dialogue: Pro-Choice, Pro-Life, and American Law* (Bloomington: Indiana University Press, 1992)

COLKER, Ruth, "The Example of Lesbians: A Posthumous Reply to Professor Mary Joe Frug" (1992) 105 Harv. L. Rev. 1084-95

COLKER, Ruth, "Feminism, Sexuality, and the Self: A Preliminary Inquiry Into the Politics of Authenticity" (1988) 68 B.U. L. Rev. 217-64

COLKER, Ruth, "Feminism, Theology, and Abortion: Toward Love, Compassion and Wisdom" (1989) 77 Calif. L. Rev. 1011-75

COLKER, Ruth, "Feminist Consciousness and the State: A Basis for Cautious Optimism" (1990) 90 Colum. L. Rev. 1146-70

COLKER, Ruth, "Feminist Litigation: An Oxymoron?" (1990) 13 Harv. Wom. L. J. 137-88

COLKER, Ruth, "The Practice of Theory" (1993) 87 Nw. U. L. Rev. 1273-85

COLKER, Ruth, "Pregnant Men" (1993) 3 Colum. J. Gender & L. 449-93

COOMBE, Rosemary J., "Publicity Rights and Political Aspiration: Mass Culture, Gender Identity, and Democracy" (1992) 26 New Eng. L. Rev. 1221-80

CORNELL, Drucilla, *Beyond Accomodation: Ethical Feminism, Deconstruction, and the Law* (New York: Routledge, 1991)

CORNELL, Drucilla, "The Doubly-Prized World: Myth, Allegory and the Feminine" (1990) 75 Cornell L. Rev. 644-99

CORNELL, Drucilla, *The Philosophy of the Limit* (New York: Routledge, 1992)

CORNELL, Drucilla, "The Philosophy of the Limit, Systems Theory and Feminist Legal Reform" (1992) 26 New Eng. L. Rev. 783-804

CORNELL, Drucilla, "Sexual Difference, the Feminine, and Equivalency: A Critique of MacKinnon's *Toward a Feminist Theory of the State*" (1991) 100 Yale L. J. 2247-75

CORNELL, Drucilla, *Transformations: Recollective Imagination and Sexual Difference* (New York: Routledge, 1993)

CORNELL, Drucilla and **THURSCHWELL**, Adam, "Femininity, Negativity, Intersubjectivity" in Seyla Benhabib and Drucilla Cornell (eds.), *Feminism as Critique* (Minneapolis: University of Minnesota Press, 1987) 143-62

DALTON, Clare, "Where We Stand: Observations on the Situation of Feminist Legal Thought" (1987-88) 3 Berk. Wom. L. J. 1-13

DAVIS, Adrienne D. and **WILDMAN**, Stephanie M., "The Legacy of Doubt: Treatment of Sex and Race in the Hill-Thomas Hearings" (1992) 65 S. Cal. L. Rev. 1367-91

DAVIS, Peggy C., "Contextual Legal Criticism: A Demonstration Exploring Hierarchy and 'Feminist Style'" (1991) 66 N.Y.U. L. Rev. 1635-81

DEVLIN, Richard F., "Demanding Difference (But Doubting Discourse): A Review Essay" (1994) 7 Can. J. Wom. & L. 156-72

DOBROWOLSKY, Alexandra and **DEVLIN**, Richard F., "The Big Mac Attack: A Critical Affirmation of MacKinnon's Unmodified Theory of Patriarchal Power" (1991) 36 McGill L. J. 575-608

DUCLOS, Nitya, "Lessons of Difference: Feminist Theory on Cultural Diversity" (1990) 38 Buffalo L. Rev. 325-81

EISENSTEIN, Zillah, *The Female Body and the Law* (Berkeley: University of California Press, 1988)

EPSTEIN, Cynthia Fuchs, *Women in Law* (New York: Basic Books, 1981)

ERICKSON, Nancy, "Equality Between the Sexes in the 1980's" (1979) 28 Clev. St. L. Rev. 591-610

ERICKSON, Nancy, "The Feminist Dilemma Over Unwed Parents' Custody Rights: The Mother's Rights Must Take Priority" (1984) 2 L. & Inequality 447-72

ERICKSON, Nancy S., "*Kahn, Ballard* and *Weisenfeld*: A New Equal Protection Test in 'Reverse' Sex Discrimination Cases?" (1975) 42 Brooklyn L. Rev. 1-54

ERICKSON, Nancy S., "Reproduction and the Law" (1985) 32 Med. Trial Tech. Q. 165-74

ERICKSON, Nancy S., "Women and the Supreme Court: Anatomy is Destiny" (1974) 41 Brooklyn L. Rev. 209-82

FINEMAN, Martha L. A., "Feminist Legal Scholarship and Women's Gendered Lives" in Maureen Cain and Christine B. Harrington (eds.), *Lawyers in a Postmodern World: Translation and Transgression* (Buckingham: Open University Press, 1994) 229-46

FINEMAN, Martha A., "A Legal (and Otherwise) Realist Response to 'Sex as Contract': Abortion and Expanded Choice" (1994) 4 Colum. J. Gender & L. 128-42

FINEMAN, Martha A., "The Neutered Mother" (1991) 46 U. Mia. L. Rev. 653-69

FINEMAN, Martha Albertson and **THOMADSEN**, Nancy Sweet (eds.), *At the Boundaries of Law: Feminism and Legal Theory* (New York: Routledge, 1991)

FINLEY, Lucinda, "Breaking Women's Silence in Law: The Dilemma of the Gendered Nature of Legal Reasoning" (1989) 64 Notre Dame L. Rev. 886-910

FINLEY, Lucinda, "The Nature of Domination and the Nature of Women: Reflections on Feminism Unmodified" (1988) 82 Nw. U. L. Rev. 352-85

FINLEY, Lucinda, "Transcending Equality Theory: A Way Out of the Maternity and the Workplace Debate" (1986) 86 Colum. L. Rev. 1118-82

FOX-GENOVESE, Elizabeth, *Feminism Without Illusions: A Critique of Individualism* (Chapel Hill: University of North Carolina Press, 1991)

FOX-GENOVESE, Elizabeth, "Women's Rights, Affirmative Action, and the Myth of Individualism" (1986) 54 Geo. Wash. L. Rev. 338-74

FRASER, David, "What's Love Got to Do With It? Critical Legal Studies, Feminist Discourse, and the Ethic of Solidarity" (1988) 11 Harv. Wom. L. J. 53-82

FREEDMAN, Ann, "Sex Equality, Sex Differences, and the Supreme Court" (1983) 92 Yale L. J. 913-68

FRIEDMAN, Marilyn, "Impracticality of Impartiality" (1989) 86 J. Phil. 645-56

FRUG, Mary Joe, *Postmodern Legal Feminism* (New York: Routledge, 1992)

FRUG, Mary Joe, "A Postmodern Feminist Legal Manifesto (An Unfinished Draft)" 105 Harv. L. Rev. 1045-83

FRUG, Mary Joe, "Progressive Feminst Legal Scholarship: Can We Claim 'A Different Voice'?" (1992) 15 Harv. Wom. L. J. 37-64

FRUG, Mary Joe, "Re-Reading Contracts: A Feminist Analysis of a Contracts Casebook" (1985) 34 Am. U. L. Rev. 1065-1140

FRUG, Mary Joe, "Rescuing Impossibility Doctrine: A Postmodern Feminist Analysis of Contract Law" (1992) 140 U. Pa. L. Rev. 1029-47

FRUG, Mary Joe, "Sexual Equality and Sexual Difference in American Law" (1992) 26 New Eng. L. Rev. 665-82

GERTNER, Nancy, "Bakke on Affirmative Action for Women: Pedestal or Cage?" (1979) 14 Harv. C.R.-C.L. L. Rev. 173-214

GERTNER, Nancy, "Thoughts on Comparable Worth Litigation and Organizational Strategies" (1986) 20 U. Mich. J. L. Ref. 163-82

GILLIGAN, Carol, "Getting Civilized" (1994) 63 Fordham L. Rev. 17-31

GILLIGAN, Carol, *In a Different Voice: Psychological Theory and Women's Development* (Cambridge, Mass.: Harvard University Press, 1982)

GILMORE, Angela D., "It is Better to Speak" (1990-91) 6 Berk. Wom. L. J. 74-80

GOLDFARB, Phyllis, "From the Worlds of 'Others': Minority and Feminist Responses to Critical Legal Studies" (1992) 26 New Eng. L. Rev. 683-710

GOODRICH, Peter, "Gynaetopia: Feminine Genealogies of the Common Law" (1993) 20 J. L. & Soc'y 276-308

GREENBERG, Jude; **MINOW**, Martha; **SCHNEIDER**, Elizabeth M., "Contradiction and Revision: Progressive Feminist Legal Scholars Respond to Mary Joe Frug" (1992) 15 Harv. Wom. L. J. 65-77

GRESCHNER, Donna, "Feminist Concerns with the New Communitarians: We Don't Need Another Hero" in Allan C. Hutchinson and Leslie J. M. Green (eds.), *Law and the Community: The End of Individualism?* (Toronto: Carswell, 1989) 119-50

HARRIS, Angela P., "Categorical Discourse and Dominance Theory" (1990) 5 Berk. Wom. L. J. 181-96

HARRIS, Angela P., "Race and Essentialism in Feminist Legal Theory" (1990) 42 Stan. L. Rev. 581-616

HENDERSON, Lynne N., "Legality and Empathy" (1987) 85 Mich. L. Rev. 1674-653

HERMAN, Didi, "Beyond the Rights Debate" (1993) 2 Social & Legal Stud. 25-43

HIRSHMAN, Linda, "The Rape of the Locke: Race, Gender, and the Loss of Liberal Virtue" (1992) 44 Stan. L. Rev. 1133-62

HUNTER, Nan D. and **LAW**, Sylvia A., "Brief Amici Curiae of Feminist Anti-Censorship Task Force, et al., in *American Booksellers Association* v. *Hudnut*" (1987) 26 Judges' J. 69-136

JACKSON, Emily, "Contradictions and Coherence in Feminist Responses to Law" (1993) 20 J. L. & Soc'y 398-426

JOHNSON, Barbara, "The Postmodern in Feminism" (1992) 105 Harv. L. Rev. 1076-93

KARLAN, Pamela S. and **ORTIZ**, Daniel R., "In a Diffident Voice: Relational Feminism, Abortion Rights, and the Feminist Legal Agenda" (1993) 87 Nw. U. L. Rev. 858-96

KINGDOM, Elizabeth, *What's Wrong With Rights? Problems for a Feminist Politics of Law* (Edinburgh: Edinburgh University Press, 1991)

KLINE, Marlee, "Complicating the Ideology of Motherhood: Child Welfare Law and First Nation Women" (1993) 18 Queen's L. J. 306-42

LACEY, Nicola, "Feminist Legal Theory" (1989) 9 Oxford J. Legal Stud. 383-94

LAHEY, Kathleen, "On Silences, Screams and Scholarship: An Introduction to Feminist Legal Theory" in Richard F. Devlin (ed.), *Canadian Perspectives on Legal Theory* (Toronto: Emond Montgomery, 1991) 319-38

LAW, Sylvia A., "Equality: The Power and Limits of the Law" [review of Zillah Eisenstein, *Feminism and Sexual Equality*] (1986) 95 Yale L. J. 1769-86

LAW, Sylvia A., "Family, Gender and Sexuality: What Our Founding Fathers Had to Say" (1987) 26 Judges' J. 22-27

LAW, Sylvia A., "'Girls Can't Be Plumbers' — Affirmative Action for Women in Construction: Beyond Goals and Quotas" (1989) 24 Harv. C.R.-C.L. L. Rev. 45-77

LAW, Sylvia A., "Homosexuality and the Social Meaning of Gender" [1988] Wis. L. Rev. 187-235

LAW, Sylvia A., "Rethinking Sex and the Constitution" (1984) 132 U. Pa. L. Rev. 955-1040

LAW, Sylvia A., "Women, Work, Welfare, and the Preservation of Patriarchy" (1983) 131 U. Pa. L. Rev. 1249-1339

LAW, Sylvia A. and **RACKNER**, Lisa F., "Gender Equality and the Mexico City Policy" (1987) 20 N.Y.U. J. Int'l L. & Pol'y 193-228

LEVIN, Stephanie A., "Women and Violence: Reflections on Ending the Combat Exclusion" (1992) 26 New Eng. L. Rev. 805-21

LITTLETON, Christine A., "Feminist Jurisprudence: The Difference Method Makes" [review of Catharine MacKinnon, *Feminism Unmodified*] (1989) 41 Stan. L. Rev. 751-84

LITTLETON, Christine A., "Reconstructing Sexual Equality" (1987) 75 Cal. L. Rev. 1279-351

LITTLETON, Christine A., "Women's Experience and the Problem of Transition: Perspectives on Male Battering of Women" [1989] U. Chi. Legal F. 23-57

MacKINNON, Catharine, "Complicity: An Introduction to Andrea Dworkin, 'Abortion,' Chapter 3, Right-Wing Women" (1983) 1 L. & Inequality 89-93

MacKINNON, Catharine, "Excerpts from MacKinnon/Schlafly Debate" (1983) 1 L. & Inequality 341-53

MacKINNON, Catharine, "Feminism, Marxism, Method and the State: An Agenda for Theory" (1982) 7 Signs: J. of Women in Culture & Soc'y 515-44 and (1983) 8 Signs 635-58

MacKINNON, Catharine, *Feminism Unmodified: Discourses on Life and Law* (Cambridge, Mass.: Harvard University Press, 1987)

MacKINNON, Catharine, "Not a Moral Issue" (1984) 2 Yale L. & Pol'y Rev. 321-45

MacKINNON, Catharine, *Only Words* (Cambridge, Mass.: Harvard University Press, 1993)

MacKINNON, Catharine, "Pornography, Civil Rights, and Speech" (1985) 20 Harv. C.R.-C.L. L. Rev. 1-70

MacKINNON, Catharine A., "Rape, Genocide, and Women's Human Rights" (1994) 17 Harv. Wom. L. J. 5-16

MacKINNON, Catharine A., "Reflections on Sex Equality Under Law" (1991) 100 Yale L. J. 1281-328

MacKINNON, Catharine A., "Sex Equality and Nation-Building in Canada: The Meech Lake Accord" (1990) 25 Tulsa L. J. 735-57

MacKINNON, Catharine, *Sexual Harassment of Working Women: A Case of Sexual Discrimination* (New Haven: Yale University Press, 1979)

MacKINNON, Catharine A., *Toward a Feminist Theory of the State* (Cambridge, Mass.: Harvard University Press, 1989)

MacKINNON, Catharine, "Toward Feminist Jurisprudence" [review of Ann Jones, *Women Who Kill*] (1982) 34 Stan. L. Rev. 703-37

MacKINNON, Catharine, "Unthinking ERA Thinking" (1987) 54 U. Chi. L. Rev. 759-71

MATSUDA, Mari J., "Affirmative Action and Legal Knowledge: Planting Seeds in Plowed-Up Ground" (1988) 11 Harv. Women's L. J. 1-17

MATSUDA, Mari J., "Liberal Jurisprudence and Abstracted Visions of Human Nature: A Feminist Critique of Rawls' Theory of Justice" (1986) 16 N.M. L. Rev. 613-30

MATSUDA, Mari J., "When the First Quail Calls: Multiple Consciousness as Jurisprudential Method" (1989) 11 Wom. Rts. L. Rep. 7-10

McINTYRE, Sheila, "Promethea Unbound: A Feminist Perspective on Law in the University" (1989) 38 U.N.B. L. J. 157-73

MENKEL-MEADOW, Carrie, "The Comparative Sociology of Women Lawyers: The Feminization of the Legal Profession" (1986) 24 Osgoode Hall L. J. 897-918

MENKEL-MEADOW, Carrie, "Exploring a Research Agenda of the Feminization of the Legal Profession: Theories of Gender and Social Change" (1989) 14 L. & Soc. Inquiry 289-310

MENKEL-MEADOW, Carrie, "Excluded Voices: New Voices in the Legal Profession Making New Voices in the Law" (1987) 42 U. Mia. L. Rev. 29-53

MENKEL-MEADOW, Carrie, "Feminist Legal Theory, Critical Legal Studies and Education: The 'Fem-Crits' Go to Law School" (1988) 38 J. Legal Educ. 61-85

MENKEL-MEADOW, Carrie, "Portia in a Different Voice: Speculations on a Women's Lawyering Process" (1985) 1 Berk. Wom. L. J. 39-63

MENKEL-MEADOW, Carrie, "Women in Law?" [1983] Am. Bar Fdn. Res. J. 189-202

MINOW, Martha, "Beyond Universality" [1989] U. Chi. Legal F. 115-38

MINOW, Martha, "Feminist Reason: Getting It and Losing It" (1988) 38 J. Legal Educ. 47-60

MINOW, Martha, "Foreword: Justice Engendered" (1987) 101 Harv. L. Rev. 10-95

MINOW, Martha, "Incomplete Correspondence: An Unsent Letter to Mary Joe Frug" (1992) 105 Harv. L. Rev. 1090-105

MINOW, Martha, *Making All the Difference: Inclusion, Exclusion, and American Law* (Ithaca: Cornell University Press, 1990)

MINOW, Martha, "Putting Up and Putting Down: Tolerance Reconsidered" (1990) 28 Osgoode Hall L. J. 409-48

MINOW, Martha, "Rights for the Next Generation: A Feminist Approach to Children's Rights" (1986) 9 Harv. Women's L. J. 1-24

MINOW, Martha and **SPELMAN**, Elizabeth V., "In Context" (1990) 63 S. Cal. L. Rev. 1597-652

MORAN, Leslie, "A Reading in Sexual Politics and Law: *Gillick* v. *West Norfolk and Wisbech Area Health Authority and Another*" (1986) 8 Liverpool L. Rev. 83-94

MOSSMAN,, Mary Jane, "Feminism and Legal Method: The Difference It Makes" (1987) 3 Wis. Wom. L. J. 147-68

NEDELSKY, Jennifer, "Reconceiving Autonomy: Sources, Thoughts and Possibilities" in Allan C. Hutchinson and Leslie J. M. Green (eds.), *Law and the Community: The End of Individualism?* (Toronto: Carswell, 1989) 219-52

NOONAN, Sheila, "Pertaining to Connection: Abortion and Feminist Theory" in Jonathan Hart and Richard W. Bauman (eds.), *Explorations in Difference: Law, Culture and Politics* (Toronto: University of Toronto Press, 1995) 137-68

O'DONOVAN, Katharine, "Engendering Justice: Women's Perspectives and the Rule of Law" (1989) 39 U. Toronto L. J. 127-48

O'DONOVAN, Katharine, *Sexual Divisions in Law* (London: Weindenfeld and Nicolson, 1985)

O'DONOVAN, Katharine and **SZYSZCAK**, Erika, *Equality and Sex Discrimination Law* (Oxford: Basil Blackwell, 1988)

OKIN, Susan Moller, *Justice, Gender, and the Family* (New York: Basic Books, 1989)

OLSEN, Frances, "Constitutional Law: Feminist Critiques of the Public/Private Distinction" (1993) 10 Const. Comm. 319-27

OLSEN, Frances, "Feminism and Critical Legal Theory: An American Perspective" (1990) 18 Int'l J. Soc. L. 199-215

OLSEN, Frances, "Feminist Theory in Grand Style" [review of Catharine MacKinnon, *Feminism Unmodified*] (1989) 89 Colum. L. Rev. 1147-78

OLSEN, Frances, "From False Paternalism to False Equality: Judicial Assaults on Feminist Community, Illinois 1869-1895" (1986) 84 Mich. L. Rev. 1518-41

OLSEN, Frances, "The Sex of Law" in David Kairys (ed.), *The Politics of Law: A Progressive Critique*, 2nd rev. ed. (New York: Pantheon Books, 1990) 453-67

OLSEN, Frances, "Statutory Rape: A Feminist Critique of Rights Analysis" (1981) 63 Tex. L. Rev. 389-432

PATEMAN, Carole, *The Sexual Contract* (Cambridge: Polity Press, 1988)

POLAN, Diane, "Toward a Theory of Law and Patriarchy" in David Kairys (ed.), *The Politics of Law: A Progressive Critique* (New York: Pantheon Books, 1982) 294-303

POWERS, Kathryn, "Sex Segregation and the Ambivalent Directions of Sex Discrimination Law" [1979] Wis. L. Rev. 55-124

RAZACK, Sherene, *Canadian Feminism and the Law: The Women's Legal Education and Action Fund and the Pursuit of Equality* (Toronto: Second Story Press, 1991)

RESNIK, Judith, "Ambivalence: The Resiliency of Legal Culture in the United States" (1993) 45 Stan. L. Rev. 1525-46

RESNIK, Judith, "Complex Feminist Conversations" [1989] U. Chi. Legal F. 1-7

RHODE, Deborah L., "Association and Assimilation" (1987) 81 Nw. U. L. Rev. 106-45

RHODE, Deborah L., "Feminism and the State" (1994) 107 Harv. L. Rev. 1181-208

RHODE, Deborah L., "Feminist Critical Theories" (1990) 42 Stan. L. Rev. 617-38

RHODE, Deborah L., "Gender and Jurisprudence: An Agenda for Research" (1987) 56 U. Cin. L. Rev. 521-34

RHODE, Deborah L., "The 'No-Problem' Problem: Feminist Challenges and Cultural Change" (1991) 100 Yale L. J. 1731-93

RHODE, Deborah L. (ed.), *Theoretical Perspectives on Sexual Difference* (New Haven: Yale University Press, 1990)

RIFKIN, Janet, "Toward a Theory of Law and Patriarchy" (1980) 3 Harv. Wom. L. J. 83-95

ROBINSON, Ruthann, "Embodiment(s): The Possibilities of Lesbian Legal Theory in Bodies Problematicized By Postmodernisms and Feminisms" (1992) 2 L. & Sex. 37-80

SCALES, Ann C., "The Emergence of Feminist Jurisprudence: An Essay" (1986) 95 Yale L. J. 1373-403

SCALES, Ann C., "Feminists in the Field of Time" (1990) 42 U. Fla. L. Rev. 95-123

SCALES, Ann C., "Midnight Train to Us" (1990) 75 Cornell L. Rev. 710-26

SCALES-TRENT, Judy, "Women in the Lawyering Process: The Complications of Categories" (1990) 35 N.Y. L. Sch. L. Rev. 337-42

SCHNEIDER, Elizabeth M., "Describing and Changing: Women's Self-Defense Work and the Problem of Expert Testimony in Battering" (1992) 14 Wom. Rts. L. Rep. 213-41

SCHNEIDER, Elizabeth, "The Dialectic of Rights and Politics: Perspectives From the Women's Movement" (1986) 61 N.Y.U. L. Rev. 589-652

SCHNEIDER, Elizabeth, "Equal Rights to Trial for Women: Sex Bias in the Law of Self-Defense" (1980) 15 Harv. C.R.-C.L. L. Rev. 623-47

SCHNEIDER, Elizabeth M., "Violence Against Women and Legal Education: An Essay for Mary Joe Frug" (1992) 26 New Eng. L. Rev. 843-75

SCHNEIDER, Elizabeth M. and **JORDAN**, Susan B., "Representation of Women Who Defend Themselves in Response to Physical or Sexual Assault" (1978) 4 Nat. J. Crim. Def. 141-69

SCHULTZ, Vicki, "Room to Maneuver (f)or a Room of One's Own? Practice Theory and Feminist Practice" (1989) 14 L. & Soc. Inquiry 123-47

SMART, Carol, "Feminism and Law: Some Problems of Analysis and Strategy" (1986) 14 Int'l J. Soc. L. 109-23

SMART, Carol, *Feminism and the Power of Law* (London and New York: Routledge, 1989)

SMART, Carol, "Feminist Jurisprudence" in Peter Fitzpatrick (ed.), *Dangerous Supplements: Resistance and Renewal in Jurisprudence* (Durham: Duke University Press, 1991) 133-58

SMART, Carol, "Law, Feminism and Sexuality: From Essence to Ethics" (1994) 9(1) Can. J. L. & Soc'y 15-38

SMART, Carol, *The Ties That Bind: Law, Marriage, and the Reproduction of Patriarchal Relations* (London: Routledge & Kegan Paul, 1984)

SMART, Carol, "The Women of Legal Discourse" (1992) 1 Social & Legal Stud. 29-44

SPELMAN, Elizabeth V., *Inessential Woman: Problems of Exclusion in Feminist Thought* (Boston: Beacon Press, 1988)

SPELMAN, Elizabeth V. and **MINOW**, Martha, "Outlaw Women: An Essay on Thelma and Louise" (1992) 26 New Eng. L. Rev. 1281-96

STROSSEN, Nadine, "A Feminist Critique of 'The' Feminist Critique of Pornography" (1993) 79 Va. L. Rev. 1099-190

TAUB, Nadine, "Thoughts on Living and Moving with the Recurring Divide" (1990) 24 Ga. L. Rev. 965-84

TAUB, Nadine and **SCHNEIDER**, Elizabeth, "Perspectives on Women's Subordination and the Role of Law" in David Kairys (ed.), *The Politics of Law: A Progressive Critique* (New York: Pantheon Books, 1982) 117-39

TAUB, Nadine and **SCHNEIDER**, Elizabeth M., "Women's Subordination and the Role of Law" in David Kairys (ed.), *The Politics of Law: A Progressive Critique*, 2nd rev. ed. (New York: Pantheon Books, 1990) 151-76

TAUB, Nadine and **WILLIAMS**, Wendy W., "Will Equality Require More Than Assimilation, Accomodation or Separation from the Existing Social Structure?" (1985) 37 Rutgers L. Rev. 825-44

WARD, Cynthia V., "A Kinder, Gentler Liberalism? Visions of Empathy in Feminist and Communitarian Literature" (1994) 61 U. Chi. L. Rev. 929-55

WEST, Robin, "Deconstructing the CLS-Fem Split" (1986) 2 Wis. Wom. L. J. 85-92

WEST, Robin, "The Difference in Women's Hedonic Lives: A Phenomenological Critique of Feminist Legal Theory" (1987) 3 Wis. Wom. L. J. 81-145 [reprinted in Robin L. West, *Narrative, Authority, and Law* (Ann Arbor: University of Michigan Press, 1993) 179-249]

WEST, Robin, "Economic Man and Literary Woman: One Contrast" (1988) 39 Mercer L. Rev. 867-78 [reprinted in Robin L. West, *Narrative, Authority, and Law* (Ann Arbor: University of Michigan Press, 1993) 251-63]

WEST, Robin, "Feminism, Critical Social Theory, and Law" [1989] U. Chi. Legal F. 59-97

WEST, Robin L., "The Feminist-Conservative Anti-Pornography Alliance and the 1986 Attorney General's Commission on Pornography Report" [1987] Am. Bar Fdn. Res. J. 681-711

WEST, Robin, "Jurisprudence and Gender" (1988) 55 U. Chi. L. Rev. 1-70

WHISNER, Mary, "Gender-Specific Clothing Regulation: A Study in Patriarchy" (1982) 5 Harv. Women's L. J. 73-119

WILDMAN, Stephanie M., "The Legitimation of Sex Discrimination: A Critical Response to Supreme Court Jurisprudence" (1984) 63 Oregon L. Rev. 265-307

WILLIAMS, Joan C., "Deconstructing Gender" in Leslie Friedman Goldstein (ed.), *Feminist Jurisprudence: The Difference Debate* (Lanham, Md.: Rowman and Littlefield, 1992) 41-98

WILLIAMS, Patricia J., "A Case Study of Muleheadedness and Men" in Toni Morrison (ed.), *Race-ing Justice, En-gendering Power: Essays on Anita Hill, Clarence Thomas, and the Construction of Social Reality* (New York: Pantheon, 1992) 159-71

WILLIAMS, Patricia J., "On Being the Object of Property" (1988) 14 Signs 5-24

WILLIAMS, Susan H., "Feminist Legal Epistemology" (1993) 8 Berk. Wom. L. J. 63-105

WILLIAMS, Wendy W., "The Equality Crisis: Some Reflections on Culture, Courts, and Feminism" (1982) 7 Wom. Rts. L. Rep. 175-200 [reprinted in (1992) 14 Wom. Rts. L. Rep. 151-74]

WILLIAMS, Wendy W., "Equality's Riddle: Pregnancy and the Equal Treatment/Special Treatment Debate" (1983) 13 N.Y.U. Rev. L. & Soc. Change 325-80

WILLIAMS, Wendy W., "Notes From a First Generation" [1989] U. Chi. Legal F. 99-113

WISHIK, Heather Ruth, "To Question Everything: The Inquiries of Feminist Jurisprudence" (1986) 1 Berk. Wom. L. J. 64-77

YOUNG, Iris M., "Difference and Context: Some Reflections in the Context of New Social Movements" (1987) 56 U. Cin. L. Rev. 535-50

YOUNG, Iris Marion, "Gender as Seriality: Thinking About Women as a Social Collective" (1994) 19 Signs 713-38

YOUNG, Iris Marion, "Impartiality and the Civic Public: Some Implications of Feminist Critiques of Moral and Political Theory" in Seyla Benhabib and Drucilla Cornell (eds.), *Feminism as Critique* (Minneapolis: University of Minnesota Press, 1987) 56-76

YOUNG, Iris Marion, *Justice and the Politics of Difference* (Princeton: Princeton University Press, 1990)

YOUNG, Iris Marion, "Polity and Group Difference: A Critique of the Ideal of Universal Citizenship" (1989) 99 Ethics 250-74

23

Critical Race Theory

As the 1980s unfolded, critics of contemporary antidiscrimination law in the U.S. developed an acute sense that, while the critical legal attack on liberalism was useful to understand the political background of legal doctrine, the radical work by critics failed to account for the continuing presence of racism in common practices and institutions. The critical legal challenge to rights discourse, for example, seemed to underestimate the importance (both real and symbolic) of rights rhetoric for minorities seeking equality through legal intervention. As a result, a new series of approaches, roughly grouped under the heading of critical race theory, has emerged. That literature has given rise to the following general themes and methods.

Critical commentators on antidiscrimination doctrine in the U.S. have argued that the law assumes a typically abstract liberal shape. Historically, the point of antidiscrimination law has been the pursuit of formal equality, so that all citizens, regardless of color for example, should be treated the same in the eyes of the law. This concept of equality is an abstract norm that requires particular applications, but as an ideal, it is at the core of liberal ideology. Another liberal assumption about racial discrimination was that it should be viewed as essentially a matter of benighted individuals (or, sometimes, institutions) exhibiting a prejudiced attitude that could be remedied in the short term by an appropriate judicial remedy, and in the long term, by education and the process of reason. Overall, the campaign to promote the enforcement of civil rights in respect of political participation, education, employment, and housing would lead eventually to everyone, regardless of race, having the same equality of opportunity.

Despite several cycles of gains and setbacks that have marked the civil rights movement in the U.S. since the 1950s, critics of antidiscrimination law doubt whether the law has been an effective instrument for removing deep-seated racial inequalities. Racism has not turned out to be a mere aberration, in an otherwise just society, that has been overcome with legislative or judicial action. From the perspective of some critics, racism remains an intractable, ineradicable problem. We should not expect that it will gradually be erased through education or general enlightenment. Instead, racism is viewed as a pervasive, unconscious, culturally transmitted feature of legal and social structures in the U.S. Moderate, reformist measures to deal superficially with some of the more obvious consequences of racism simply ignore the extent to which fundamental and substantive issues of racial justice are postponed or ignored.

One of the problems with the ideal of the equality of opportunity is that it ultimately requires objective and neutral criteria: the aim is to create and sustain a meritocracy that is strictly color-blind. Critics have attacked this liberal model as a mechanism for preserving existing hierarchical advantages. The formal ideal can be invoked by claimants who wish to avoid redistribution of wealth and privileges, on the ground that their vested rights or expectations are violated by any policy which is race-conscious. Thus, an affirmative action or set-aside program set up to remedy disadvantages suffered by a minority group because of past discrimination can be struck down on the ground that it violates the formal concept of equality.

The persistence of a system of racial subordination and injustice, with an economic and political underclass, is a vexing problem. From the point of view of critical writers, the problem is not even being contained. The inequalities go beyond a "tolerable" level. To illustrate the depth of discrimination still present, these writers have often tried to convey a sense of how people of color labor under the weight of racism as they attempt to deal with everyday tasks: from acquiring accomodation, going to school, being hired and maintaining employment, bidding on and obtaining governing contracts, encountering the police and the court system, to dining out, shopping, joining clubs, and receiving the benefit of social services. Legal discourse tends to omit or devalue reports of these kinds of experiences. This silence has inspired many critical writers to frame their work using chronicles, parables, or autobiographies. These are meant to dispute the standard accounts, under a liberal legal regime, of gradual progress towards a non-racist polity.

Stories are vitally important to some critical authors who argue that our relative position within the social and political structure structures how we see the world. The "plea for narrative" has also been justified on the ground that stories can encourage awareness and empathy among readers. This methodology is one aspect of overlap between critical commentaries on race issues and feminist analyses of women's oppression. From various women who are also members of groups suffering racial discrimination have emerged analyses on the "intersectionality" of their position (to use Kimberlé Crenshaw's expression). They encounter racism differentially in a way that mainstream legal thinking fails to comprehend.

The intractability of legally reinforced modes of racism has prompted some critical writers to break with the civil rights tradition that marked the 1950s and 60s. One of the guiding aims of this movement was the achievement of full integration by minorities into the social and economic privileges enjoyed by the white majority. The norms, practices, and institutions were to be determined by reference to universalist and apparently neutral standards. In fact, according to these critics, the standards imagined were the products of "white" history and ideology. This "assimilationist" model has been rejected by writers such as Derrick Bell, who characterize integration as "romantic," unattainable, and arguably undesirable. In its place, these critics invoke a model of heightened race consciousness, with an emphasis on maintaining various traditions of the minority culture and community. The gains commonly identified with the civil rights movement, in regard to desegregating schools, workplaces, and neighborhoods, were achieved at the expense of the cultural vitality of distinctively black communities and neighborhoods. This new critique appeals to a vision of solidarity and renewed resistance to externally imposed standards of justice.

* * * *

ALEINIKOFF, T. Alexander, "A Case for Race-Consciousness" (1991) 91 Colum. L. Rev. 1060-125

ALEINIKOFF, T. Alexander, "The Constitution in Context: The Continuing Significance of Racism" (1992) 63 U. Colo. L. Rev. 325-73

ANSLEY, Frances Lee, "A Civil Rights Agenda for the Year 2000: Confessions of an Identity Politician" (1992) 59 Tenn. L. Rev. 593-609

ANSLEY, Frances Lee, "Stirring the Ashes: Race, Class, and the Future of Civil Rights Scholarship" (1989) 74 Cornell L. Rev. 993-1077

AUDAIN, Linz, "Critical Cultural Law and Economics, the Culture of Individualization, the Paradox of Blackness" (1995) 70 Ind. L. J. 709-82

AUSTIN, Regina, "'The Black Community,' Its Lawbreakers, and a Politics of Identification" (1992) 65 S. Cal. L. Rev. 1769-817

AUSTIN, Regina, "'A Nation of Thieves': Securing Black People's Right to Shop and Sell in White America" [1994] Utah L. Rev. 147-77

AUSTIN, Regina, "Sapphire Bound!" [1989] Wis. L. Rev. 539-78

BALL, Milner S., "The Legal Academy and Minority Scholars" (1990) 103 Harv. L. Rev. 1855-63

BANKS, Taunya Lovell, "Two Life Stories: Reflections of One Black Woman Law Professor" (1990-91) 6 Berk. Wom. L. J. 46-56

BANKS, Taunya Lovell, "Women and AIDS — Racism, Sexism, and Classism" (1989-90) 17 N.Y.U. Rev. L. & Soc. Ch. 351-85

BARKAN, Steven E., "Legal Control of the Southern Civil Rights Movement" (1984) 49 Am. Soc. Rev. 552-65

BARNES, Robin D., "Black Women Law Professors and Critical Self-Consciousness: A Tribute to Denise S. Carty-Bennia" (1990-91) 6 Berk. Wom. L. J. 57-73

BARNES, Robin D., "Politics and Passion: Theoretically a Dangerous Liaison" [review of Stephen L. Carter, *Reflections of an Affirmative Action Baby* and Patricia J. Williams, *The Alchemy of Race and Rights*] (1992) 101 Yale L. J. 1631-59

BARNES, Robin D., "Race Consciousness: The Thematic Content of Racial Distinctiveness in Critical Race Scholarship" (1990) 103 Harv. L. Rev. 1864-71

BARON, Jane B., "Resistance to Stories" (1994) 67 S. Cal. L. Rev. 255-85

BELL, Derrick A., Jr., "After We're Gone: Prudent Speculations on America in a Post-Racial Epoch" (1990) 34 St. Louis U. L. J. 393-405

BELL, Derrick A., Jr., "An American Fairy Tale: The Income-Related Neutralization of Race Law Precedent" (1984) 18 Suffolk U. L. Rev. 331-45

BELL, Derrick A., Jr., *And We Are Not Saved: The Elusive Quest for Racial Justice* (New York: Basic Books, 1987)

BELL, Derrick A., Jr., "Application of the 'Tipping Point' Principle to Law Faculty Hiring Policies" (1986) 10 Nova L. J. 319-27

BELL, Derrick A., "*Bakke,* Minority Admissions, and the Usual Price of Racial Remedies" (1979) 67 Calif. L. Rev. 3-19

BELL, Derrick A., "*Brown* v. *Board of Education* and the Interest-Convergence Dilemma" (1980) 93 Harv. L. Rev. 518-33

BELL, Derrick A., Jr., "The Dilemmas of the Responsible Law Reform Lawyer in the Post-Free Enterprise Era" (1986) 4 L. & Inequality 231-43

BELL, Derrick A., *Faces at the Bottom of the Well: The Permanence of Racism* (New York: Basic Books, 1992)

BELL, Derrick A., "The Final Report: Harvard's Affirmative Action Allegory" (1989) 87 Mich. L. Rev. 2382-410

BELL, Derrick A., Jr., "Foreword: The Civil Rights Chronicles [The Supreme Court, 1984 Term]" (1985) 99 Harv. L. Rev. 4-83

BELL, Derrick A., "A Hurdle Too High: Class-Based Roadblocks to Racial Remediation" (1984) 33 Buffalo L. Rev. 1-34

BELL, Derrick A., "The Law of Racial Standing" (1991) 2 Yale J. L. & Lib. 117-21

BELL, Derrick A., Jr., *Race, Racism, and American Law*, 3rd ed. (Boston: Little, Brown, 1992)

BELL, Derrick A., Jr., "Racial Realism" (1992) 24 Conn. L. Rev. 363-79

BELL, Derrick A., Jr., "Racial Remediation: An Historical Perspective on Current Conditions" (1976) 52 Notre Dame Law. 5-29

BELL, Derrick A., "Racism: A Prophecy for the Year 2000" (1989) 42 Rutgers L. Rev. 93-108

BELL, Derrick A., Jr., "Reconstruction's Racial Realities" (1992) 23 Rutgers L. J. 261-70

BELL, Derrick A., Jr., "Serving Two Masters: Integration Ideals and Client Interests in School Desegregation Litigation" (1976) 85 Yale L. J. 470-516

BELL, Derrick, "White Superiority in America: Its Legal Legacy, Its Economic Costs" (1988) 33 Villa. L. Rev. 769-79

BELL, Derrick, "Xerces and the Affirmative Action Mystique" (1989) 57 Geo. Wash. L. Rev. 1595-613

BELL, Derrick and **BANSAL**, Preeta, "The Republican Revival and Racial Politics" (1988) 97 Yale L. J. 1609-21

BELL, Derrick; **HIGGINS**, Tracy; and **SUH**, Sung-Hee, "Racial Reflections: Dialogues in the Direction of Liberation" (1990) 37 U.C.L.A. L. Rev. 1037-100

BROOKS, Roy L., "Critical Race Theory: A Proposed Structure and Application to Federal Pleading" 91994) 11 Harv. BlackLetter L. J. 85-113

BROOKS, Roy L. and **NEWBORN**, Mary Jo, "Critical Race Theory and Classical-Liberal Civil Rights Scholarship: A Distinction Without a Difference?" (1994) 82 Cal. L. Rev. 787-845

BURNS, W. Haywood, "Law and Race in America" in David Kairys (ed.), *The Politics of Law: A Progressive Critique* (New York: Pantheon Books, 1982) 89-95

BURNS, W. Haywood, "Law and Race in Early America" in David Kairys (ed.), *The Politics of Law: A Progressive Critique*, 2nd rev. ed. (New York: Pantheon Books, 1990) 115-20

CALDWELL, Paulette M., "A Hair Piece: Perspectives on the Intersection of Race and Gender" [1991] Duke L. J. 365-96

CALMORE, John O., "Critical Race Theory, Archie Shepp, and Fire Music: Securing an Authentic Intellectual Life in a Multicultural World" (1992) 65 S. Cal. L. Rev. 2129-230

CALMORE, John O., "Exploring the Significance of Race and Class in Representing the Black Poor" (1982) 61 Oregon L. Rev. 201-44

CALMORE, John O., "Fair Housing and the Black Poor: An Advocacy Guide" (1984) 18 Clearinghouse Rev. 609-76

CHANG, Robert S., "Toward an Asian American Legal Scholarship: Critical Race Theory, Post-Structuralism, and Narrative Space" (1993) 81 Cal. L. Rev. 1241-323

CHIU, Daina C., "The Cultural Defense: Beyond Exclusion, Assimilation, and Guilty Liberalism" (1994) 82 Cal. L. Rev. 1053-125

COOK, Anthony E., "Beyond Critical Legal Studies: The Reconstructive Theology of Dr. Martin Luther King" (1990) 103 Harv. L. Rev. 985-1044

COOK, Anthony E., "The Spiritual Movement Towards Justice" [1992] U. Ill. L. Rev. 1007-20

CRENSHAW, Kimberlé W., "A Black Feminist Critique of Antidiscrimination Law and Politics" in David Kairys (ed.), *The Politics of Law: A Progressive Critique*, 2nd rev. ed. (New York: Pantheon Books, 1990) 195-218

CRENSHAW, Kimberlé W., "Demarginalizing the Intersection of Race and Sex: A Black Feminist Critique of Antidiscrimination Doctrine, Feminist Theory and Antiracist Politics" [1989] U. Chi. Legal F. 139-67

CRENSHAW, Kimberlé W., "Race, Reform and Retrenchment: Transformation and Legitimation in Antidiscrimination Law" (1988) 101 Harv. L. Rev. 1331-87

CRENSHAW, Kimberlé W., "Toward a Race Conscious Pedagogy in Legal Education" (1989) 11 Nat'l Black L. J. 1-14

CRENSHAW, Kimberlé, "Whose Story Is It Anyway? Feminist and Antiracist Appropriations of Anita Hill" in Toni Morrison (ed.), *Race-ing Justice, En-gendering Power: Essays on Anita Hill, Clarence Thomas, and the Construction of Social Reality* (New York: Pantheon Books, 1992)

CULP, Jerome M., Jr., "Colorblind Remedies and the Intersectionality of Oppression: Policy Arguments Masquerading as Moral Claims" (1994) 69 N.Y.U. L. Rev. 162-96

CULP, Jerome M., Jr., "Diversity, Multiculturalism, and Affirmative Action: Duke, the NAS, and Apartheid" (1992) 41 DePaul L. Rev. 1141-72

CULP, Jerome M., Jr., "Posner on Duncan Kennedy and Racial Difference: White Authority in the Legal Academy" (1992) 41 Duke L. J. 1095-114

CULP, Jerome M., Jr., "Toward a Black Legal Scholarship: Race and Original Understandings" [1991] Duke L. J. 39-105

CULP, Jerome M., Jr., "Voice, Perspective, Truth, and Justice: Race and the Mountain in the Legal Academy" (1992) 38 Loy. L. Rev. 61-81

DALTON, Harlon L., "The Clouded Prism" (1987) 22 Harv. C.R.-C.L. L. Rev. 435-47

DAVIS, Peggy Cooper, "Law as Microaggression" (1989) 98 Yale L. J. 1559-77

DAVIS, Peggy Cooper, "Neglected Stories and the Lawfulness of *Roe* v. *Wade*" (1993) 28 Harv. C.R.-C.L. L. Rev. 299-394

DELGADO, Richard, "Affirmative Action as a Majoritarian Device: Or, Do You Really Want to be a Role Model?" (1991) 89 Mich. L. Rev. 1222-31

DELGADO, Richard, "Approach Avoidance in Law School Hiring: Is the Law a WASP?" (1990) 34 St. L. U. L. J. 631-42

DELGADO, Richard, "Brewer's Plea: Critical Thoughts on Common Cause" (1991) 44 Vand. L. Rev. 1-14

DELGADO, Richard, "Campus Antiracism Rules: Constitutional Narratives in Collision" (1991) 85 Nw. U. L. Rev. 343-87

DELGADO, Richard, "Critical Legal Studies and the Realities of Race: Does the Fundamental Contradiction Have a Corollary?" (1988) 23 Harv. C.R.-C.L. L. Rev. 407-13

DELGADO, Richard, "Derrick Bell and the Ideology of Racial Reform: Will We Ever be Saved?" [review of Derrick Bell, *And We Are Not Saved*] (1988) 97 Yale L. J. 923-47

DELGADO, Richard, "The Ethereal Scholar: Does Critical Legal Studies Have What Minorities Want?" (1987) 22 Harv. C.R.-C.L. L. Rev. 301-22

DELGADO, Richard, "Enormous Anomaly: Left-Right Parallels in Recent Writing About Race" (1991) 91 Colum. L. Rev. 1547-60

DELGADO, Richard, "Fact, Norm and Standard of Review — The Case of Homosexuality" (1985) 10 U. Dayton L. Rev. 575-98

DELGADO, Richard, "The Imperial Scholar: Reflections on a Review of Civil Rights Literature" (1984) 132 U. Pa. L. Rev. 561-77

DELGADO, Richard, "The Imperial Scholar Revisited: How to Marginalize Outsider Writing, Ten Years Later" (1992) 140 U. Pa. L. Rev. 1349-72

DELGADO, Richard, "Mindset and Metaphor" (1990) 103 Harv. L. Rev. 1872-77

DELGADO, Richard, "Minority Law Professors' Lives: The Bell-Delgado Survey" (1989) 24 Harv. C.R.-C.L. L. Rev. 349-92

DELGADO, Richard, *The Rodrigo Chronicles: Conversations About America and Race* (New York: New York University Press, 1995)

DELGADO, Richard, "Rodrigo's Chronicle [review of Dinesh D'Souza, *Illiberal Education: The Politics of Race and Sex on Campus*] (1992) 101 Yale L. J. 1357-80

DELGADO, Richard, "Rodrigo's Fourth Chronicle: Neutrality and Stasis in Antidiscrimination Law" (1993) 45 Stan. L. Rev. 1133-60

DELGADO, Richard, "Rodrigo's Sixth Chronicle: Intersections, Essences, and the Dilemmas of Social Reform" (1993) 68 N.Y.U. L. Rev. 639-74

DELGADO, Richard, "Rodrigo's Seventh Chronicle: Race, Democracy, and the State" (1994) 41 U.C.L.A. L. Rev. 721-57

DELGADO, Richard, "Rodrigo's Ninth Chronicle: Race, Legal Instrumentalism, and the Rule of Law" (1994) 143 U. Pa. L. Rev. 379-416

DELGADO, Richard, "Storytelling for Oppositionists and Others: A Plea for Narrative" (1989) 87 Mich. L. Rev. 2411-41

DELGADO, Richard, "When a Story is Just a Story: Does Voice Really Matter?" (1990) 76 Va. L. Rev. 95-111

DELGADO, Richard, "Words That Wound: A Tort Action for Racial Insults, Epithets and Name-Calling" (1982) 17 Harv. C.R.-C.L. L. Rev. 133-81

DELGADO, Richard, "Zero-Based Racial Politics: An Evaluation of Three Best-Case Arguments on Behalf of the Nonwhite Underclass" (1990) 78 Geo. L. J. 1929-48

DELGADO, Richard, "Zero-Based Racial Politics and an Infinity-Based Response: Will Endless Talking Cure America's Racial Ills?" (1992) 80 Geo. L. J. 1879-90

DELGADO, Richard and **STEFANCIC**, Jean, "Critical Race Theory: An Annotated Bibliography" (1993) 79 Va. L. Rev. 461-516

DELGADO, Richard and **STEFANCIC**, Jean, "Critical Race Theory: An Annotated Bibliography — 1993, A Year of Transition" (1995) 66 U. Colo. L. Rev. 159-93

DELGADO, Richard and **STEFANCIC**, Jean, *Failed Revolutions: Social Reform and the Limits of Legal Imagination* (Boulder, Co.: Westview Press, 1994)

DELGADO, Richard and **STEFANCIC**, Jean, "Hateful Speech, Loving Commitments: Why Our Notion of a 'Just Balance' Changes So Slowly" (1994) 82 Cal. L. Rev. 851-69

DELGADO, Richard and **STEFANCIC**, Jean, "Images of the Outsider in American Law and Culture: Can Free Expression Remedy Systemic Social Ills?" (1992) 77 Cornell L. Rev. 1258-97

DELGADO, Richard and **STEFANCIC**, Jean, "Norms and Narratives: Can Judges Avoid Serious Moral Error?" (1991) 69 Tex. L. Rev. 1929-83

DELGADO, Richard and **YUN**, David H., "Pressure Valves and Bloodied Chickens: An Analysis of Paternalistc Objections to Hate Speech Regulation" (1994) 82 Cal. L. Rev. 871-91

DEVLIN, Richard F., "Towards An/Other Legal Education: Some Critical and Tentative Proposals to Confront the Racism of Modern Legal Education" (1989) 38 U.N.B. L. J. 89-120

DREYFUSS, Joel and **LAWRENCE**, Charles R., III, *The Bakke Case: The Politics of Inequality* (New York: Harcourt Brace Jovanovich, 1979)

DUDZIAK, Mary L., "Desegregation as a Cold War Imperative" (1988) 41 Stan. L. Rev. 61-120

FARBER, Daniel A., "The Outmoded Debate Over Affirmative Action" (1994) 82 Cal. L. Rev. 893-934

FELDMAN, Stephen M., "Whose Common Good? Racism in the Political Community" (1992) 80 Geo. L. J. 1835-77

FITZPATRICK, Peter, "Racism and the Innocence of Law" in Peter Fitzpatrick and Alan Hunt (eds.), *Critical Legal Studies* (Oxford: Basil Blackwell, 1987) 119-32

FLAGG, Barbara J., "Enduring Principle: On Race, Process, and Constitutional Law" (1994) 82 Cal. L. Rev. 935-80

FREEMAN, Alan D., "Antidiscrimination Law: A Critical Review" in David Kairys (ed.), *The Politics of Law: A Progressive Critique* (New York: Pantheon Books, 1982) 96-116

FREEMAN, Alan D., "Antidiscrimination Law: The View From 1989" (1990) 64 Tul. L. Rev. 1407-41 and in David Kairys (ed.), *The Politics of Law: A Progressive Critique*, 2nd rev. ed. (New York: Pantheon Books, 1990) 121-50

FREEMAN, Alan D., "Legitimizing Racial Discrimination Through Antidiscrimination Law: A Critical Review of Supreme Court Doctrine" (1978) 62 Minn. L. Rev. 1049-119

FREEMAN, Alan D., "Race and Class: The Dilemma of Liberal Reform" [review of Derrick Bell, *Race, Racism and American Law*, 2nd ed.] (1981) 90 Yale L. J. 1880-95

FREEMAN, Alan D., "Racism, Rights and the Quest for Equality of Opportunity: A Critical Legal Essay" (1988) 23 Harv. C.R.-C.L. L. Rev. 295-392

FREEMAN, Alan David, "School Desegregation Law: Promise, Contradiction, Rationalization" in Derrick Bell (ed.), *Shades of Brown: New Perspectives on School Desegregation* (New York: Teachers College Press, 1980) 70-89

GATES, Henry Louis, Jr., "Let Them Talk" [review of Mari J. Matsuda, Charles R. Lawrence, III, Richard Delgado, and Kimberlé Williams Crenshaw, *Words That Wound: Critical Race Theory, Assaultive Speech, and the First Amendment*] (Sept. 20 and 27, 1993) New Republic 37-49

GENTILLI, Veronica, "A Double Challenge for Critical Race Scholars: The Moral Context" (1992) 65 S. Cal. L. Rev. 2361-83

GOTANDA, Neil, "A Critique of 'Our Constitution is Color-Blind'" (1991) 44 Stan. L. Rev. 1-68

GREENE, Linda S., "Civil Rights at the Millennium: A Response to Bell's Call for Racial Realism" (1992) 24 Conn. L. Rev. 499-515

GREENE, Linda S., "Multiculturalism as Metaphor" (1992) 41 DePaul L. Rev. 1173-89

GREENE, Linda S., "Race in the 21st Century: Equality Through Law?" (1990) 64 Tul. L. Rev. 1515-41

GREENE, Linda S., "Serving the Community: Aspiration and Abyss for the Law Professor of Color" (1991) 10 St. Louis U. L. Rev. 297-303

GRILLO, Trina and **WILDMAN**, Stephanie M., "Observing the Importance of Race: The Implications of Making Comparisons Between Racism and Sexism (Or Other -Isms)" [1991] Duke L. J. 396-411

HAINES, Andrew W., "The Critical Legal Studies Movement and Racism: Useful Analytics amd Guides for Social Action or An Irrelevant Modern Legal Skepticism and Solipsism?" (1987) 13 Wm. Mitchell L. Rev. 685-736

HARRING, Sidney L., *Crow Dog's Case: American Indian Sovereignty, Tribal Law, and United States Law in the Nineteenth Century* (Cambridge: Cambridge University Press, 1994)

HARRIS, Angela P., "The Jurisprudence of Reconstruction" (1994) 82 Cal. L. Rev. 741-85

HARRIS, Cheryl I., "Whiteness as Property" (1993) 106 Harv. L. Rev. 1709-91

IKEMOTO, Lisa C., "Furthering the Inquiry: Race, Class, and Culture in the Forced Medical Treatment of Pregnant Women" (1992) 59 Tenn. L. Rev. 487-517

INNESS, Julie, "Going to the Bottom" (1994) 9 Berk. Wom. L. J. 162-74

JOHNSON, Alex M., Jr., "Defending the Use of Quotas in Affirmative Action: Attacking Racism in the Nineties" [1992] U. Ill. L. Rev. 1043-73

JOHNSON, Alex M., Jr., "The New Voice of Color" (1991) 100 Yale L. J. 2007-63

JOHNSON, Alex M., Jr., "Racial Critiques of Legal Academia: A Reply in Favor of Context" (1990) 43 Stan. L. Rev. 137-65

KAIRYS, David, "Race Trilogy" (1994) 67 Temp. L. Rev. 1-12

KENNEDY, Duncan, "A Cultural Pluralist Case for Affirmative Action in Legal Academia" [1990] Duke L. J. 705-57

KENNEDY, Duncan, "Race, Racism, and Feminist Legal Theory" (1989) 12 Harv. Wom. L. J. 115-50

KENNEDY, Randall, "Racial Critiques of Legal Academia" (1989) 102 Harv. L. Rev. 1745-819

KLARE, Karl, "The Quest for Industrial Democracy and the Struggle Against Racism: Perspectives From Labor Law and Civil Rights Law" (1982) 61 Oregon L. Rev. 157-200

KLINE, Marlee, "The Colour of Law: Ideological Representations of First Nations in Legal Discourse" (1994) 3 Social & Legal Stud. 451-76

KLINE, Marlee, "Race, Racism and Feminist Legal Theory" (1989) 12 Harv. Wom. L. J. 115-50

LAWRENCE, Charles R., III, "Education for Black Power in the Eighties: Present Day Implications of the *Bakke* Decision" (1987) 10 Nat'l Black L. J. 58-63

LAWRENCE, Charles R., III, "The Id, the Ego, and Equal Protection: Reckoning with Unconscious Racism" (1987) 39 Stan. L. Rev. 317-88

LAWRENCE, Charles R., III, "If He Hollers Let Him Go: Regulating Racist Speech on Campus" [1990] Duke L. J. 431-83

LAWRENCE, Charles R., III, "Minority Hiring in the AALS Schools: The Need For Voluntary Quotas" (1986) 20 U.S.F. L. Rev. 429-44

LAWRENCE, Charles R., III, "The World and the River: Pedagogy as Scholarship as Struggle" (1992) 65 S. Cal. L. Rev. 2231-98

LÓPEZ, Gerald P., *Rebellious Lawyering: One Chicano's Vision of Progressive Law Practice* (Boulder, Co.: Westview Press, 1992)

LÓPEZ, Gerald P., "The Work We Know So Little About" (1989) 42 Stan. L. Rev. 1-13

MACAULAY, Jacqueline and **MACAULAY**, Stewart, "Adoption for Black Children: A Case Study of Expert Discretion" in Rita J. Simon (ed.), *Research in Law and Sociology*, vol. 1 (Greenwich, Conn.: JAI Press, 1978) 265-318

MARTINEZ, George A., "Legal Indeterminacy, Judicial Discretion and the Mexican-American Litigation Experience: 1930-1980" (1994) 27 U.C. Davis L. Rev. 555-618

MATSUDA, Mari J., "Beside My Sister, Facing My Enemy: Legal Theory Out of Coalition" (1991) 43 Stan. L. Rev. 1183-92

MATSUDA, Mari J., "Law and Culture in the District Court of Hawaii, 1844-45: A Case Study of the Rise of Legal Sconsciousness" (1988) 32 Am. J. Legal Hist. 16-41

MATSUDA, Mari J., "Looking to the Bottom: Critical Legal Studies and Reparations" (1987) 22 Harv. C.R.-C.L. L. Rev. 323-99

MATSUDA, Mari J., "Pragmatism Modified and the False Consciousness Problem" (1990) 63 S. Cal. L. Rev. 1763-82

MATSUDA, Mari J., "Public Response to Racist Speech: Considering the Victim's Story" (1989) 87 Mich. L. Rev. 2320-81

MATSUDA, Mari J., "Voices of America: Accent, Antidiscrimination Law, and a Jurisprudence for the Last Reconstruction" (1991) 100 Yale L. J. 1329-407

MATSUDA, Mari J.; **LAWRENCE**, Charles R., III; **DELGADO**, Richard; and **CRENSHAW**, Kimberlé Williams, *Words That Wound: Critical Race Theory, Assaultive Speech, and the First Amendment* (Boulder, Co.: Westview Press, 1993)

McDOUGALL, Harold A., "From Litigation to Legislation in Exclusionary Zoning Law" (1987) 22 Harv. C.R.-C.L. L. Rev. 623-63

McDOUGALL, Harold, "The Role of the Black Lawyer: A Marxist View" (1980) 7 Black L. J. 31-45

MINOW, Martha, "Learning to Live With the Dilemma of Difference: Bilingual and Special Education" (1985) 48 L. & Contemp. Probs. 157-211

MINOW, Martha, "Partial Justice: Law and Minorities" in Austin Sarat and Thomas R. Kearns (eds.), *The Fate of Law* (Ann Arbor: University of Michigan Press, 1991) 15-77

MINOW, Martha, "Putting Up and Putting Down: Tolerance Reconsidered" in Mark Tushnet (ed.), *Comparative Constitutional Federalism: Europe and America* (New York: Greenwood Press, 1990) 77-113

MINOW, Martha, "When Difference Has Its Home: Group Homes for the Mentally Retarded, Equal Protection, and Legal Treatment of Difference" (1987) 22 Harv. C.R.-C.L. L. Rev. 111-89

NAN, Carlos J., "Adding Salt to the Wounded: Affirmative Action and Critical Race Theory" (1994) 12 L. & Inequality 553-72

OLIVAS, Michael A., "The Chronicles, My Grandfather's Stories, and Immigration Law: The Slave Traders Chronicle as Racial History" (1990) 10 St. Louis U. L. J. 425-41

OVERTON, Spencer A., "The Threat Diversity Poses to African Amercians: A Black Nationalist Critique of Outsider Ideology" (1994) 37 How. L. J. 465-93

PELLER, Gary, "Notes Toward a Postmodern Nationalism" [1992] U. Ill. L. Rev. 1095-102

PELLER, Gary, "Race Consciousness" [1990] Duke L. J. 758-847

PELLER, Gary, "Reel Time/Real Justice" (1993) 70 Den. U. L. Rev. 283-96

POST, Deborah W., "Critical Thoughts About Race, Exclusion, Oppression, and Tenure" (1994) 15 Pace L. Rev. 69-110

ROELOFS, Joan, "The Supreme Court as Superlegislature: Taking Into Account Brown and Bakke" in Steven Spitzer (ed.), *Research in Law and Sociology*, vol. 3 (Greenwich, Conn: JAI Press, 1980) 257-78

ROSS, Thomas, "Innocence and Affirmative Action" (1990) 43 Vand. L. Rev. 297-316

ROSS, Thomas, "The Rhetorical Tapestry of Race: Innocence and Black Abstraction" (1990) 32 Wm. & Mary L. Rev. 1-40

ROSS, Thomas, "The Richmond Narratives" (1989) 68 Tex. L. Rev. 381-413

ROTHSTEIN, Lawrence E., "The Politics of Legal Reasoning: Conceptual Contexts and Racial Segregation" (1980) 15 Val. U. L. Rev. 81-136

RUSSELL, Margaret M., "Entering Great America: Reflections on Race and the Convergence of Progressive Legal Theory and Practice" (1992) 43 Hast. L. J. 749-67

RUSSELL, Margaret M., "'A New Scholarly Song': Race, Storytelling, and the Law" (1993) 33 Santa Clara L. Rev. 1057-63

RUSSELL, Margaret M., "Race and the Dominant Gaze: Narratives of Law and Inequality in Popular Film" (1991) 15 Legal Stud. F. 243-54

SCALES-TRENT, Judy, "Commonalties: On Being Black and White, Different and the Same" (1990) 2 Yale J. L. & Fem. 305-27

SCALES-TRENT, Judy, "Black Women and the Constitution: Finding Our Place, Asserting Our Rights (Voices of Experience: New Responses to Gender Discourse)" (1989) 24 Harv. C.R.-C.L. L. Rev. 9-44

SCALES-TRENT, Judy, "A Judge Shapes and Manages Institutional Reform: School Desegregation in Buffalo" (1989-90) 17 N.Y.U. Rev. L. & Soc. Change 119-69

SHIFFRIN, Steven H., "Racist Speech, Outsider Jurisprudence, and the Meaning of America" (1994) 80 Cornell L. Rev. 43-103

SINGER, Joseph William, "Property and Coercion in Federal Indian Law: The Conflict Between Critical and Complacent Pragmatism" (1990) 63 S. Cal. L. Rev. 1821-41

SOIFER, Aviam, "Confronting Deep Structures: Robinson, Rickey, and Racism" (1985) 6 Cardozo L. Rev. 865-69

SOIFER, Aviam, "On Being Overly Discrete and Insular: Involuntary Groups and the Anglo-American Judicial Tradition" (1991) 48 Wash. & Lee L. Rev. 381-418

SPANN, Girardeau A., "Pure Politics" (1990) 88 Mich. L. Rev. 1971-2033

SPANN, Girardeau A., *Race Against the Court: The Supreme Court and Minorities in Contemporary America* (New York: New York University Press, 1993)

STRICKLAND, Rennard, "Indian Law and the Miner's Canary: The Signs of Poison Gas" (1991) 39 Clev. St. L. Rev. 483-504

TAIBI, Anthony D., "Racial Justice in the Age of the Global Economy: Community Empowerment and Global Strategy" (1995) 44 Duke L. J. 928-84

THOMAS, Kendall, "A House Divided Against Itself: A Comment on 'Mastery, Slavery, and Emancipation'" (1989) 10 Cardozo L. Rev. 1481-515

THOMAS, Kendall, "Strange Fruit" in Toni Morrison (ed.), *Race-ing Justice, En-gendering Power: Essays on Anita Hill, Clarence Thomas, and the Construction of Social reality* (New York: Pantheon Books, 1992) 364-87

TORRES, Gerald, "Critical Race Theory: The Decline of the Universalist Ideal and the Hope of Plural Justice: Some Observations and Questions of an Emerging Phenomenon" (1991) 75 Minn. L. Rev. 993-1007

TORRES, Gerald, "Local Knowledge, Local Color: Critical Legal Studies and the Law of Race Relations" (1988) 25 San Diego L. Rev. 1043-70

TORRES, Gerald and **MILUN**, Kathryn, "Translating *Yonnondio* by Precedent and Evidence: The Mashpee Indian Case" [1990] Duke L. J. 625-59

TURPEL, Mary Ellen, "Patriarchy and Paternalism: The Legacy of the Canadian State for First Nations Women" (1993) 6 Can. J. Wom. & L. 174-92

TUSHNET, Mark, *The NAACP's Legal Strategy Against Segregated Education, 1925-1950* (Chapel Hill: University of North Carolina Press, 1987)

TUSHNET, Mark, "What Really Happened in *Brown* v. *Board of Education*" (1991) 91 Colum. L. Rev. 1867-930

WEST, Cornel, *Keeping Faith: Philosophy and Race in America* (New York: Routledge, 1993) 251-91

WEST, Cornel, "Marxist Theory and the Specificity of Afro-American Oppression" in Cary Nelson and Lawrence Grossberg (eds.), *Marxism and the Interpretation of Culture* (Urbana and Chicago: University of Illinois Press, 1988) 17-33

WEST, Robin L., "Murdering the Spirit: Racism, Rights, and Commerce" [review of Patricia J. Williams, *The Alchemy of Race and Rights*] (1992) 90 Mich. L. Rev. 1771-96

WILDMAN, Stephanie, "Integration in the 1980s: The Dream of Diversity and the Cycle of Exclusion" (1990) 64 Tul. L. Rev. 1625-76

WILLIAMS, Patricia J., "Alchemical Notes: Reconstructing Ideals from Deconstructed Rights" (1987) 22 Harv. C.R.-C.L. L. Rev. 401-33

WILLIAMS, Patricia J., *The Alchemy of Race and Rights: Diary of a Law Professor* (Cambridge, Mass.: Harvard University Presss, 1991)

WILLIAMS, Patricia J., "Fetal Fictions: An Exploration of Property Archetypes in Racial and Gendered Context" (1990) 42 U. Fla. L. Rev. 81-94

WILLIAMS, Patricia J., "*Metro Broadcasting, Inc.* v. *FCC*: Regrouping in Singular Times" (1990) 104 Harv. L. Rev. 525-46

WILLIAMS, Patricia J., "The Obliging Shell: An Informal Essay on Formal Equal Opportunity" (1989) 87 Mich. L. Rev. 2128-51

WILLIAMS, Patricia J., "Spirit-Murdering the Messenger: The Discourse of Fingerpointing as the Law's Response to Racism" (1987) 42 U. Mia. L. Rev. 127-57

WILLIAMS, Robert A., Jr., "The Algebra of Federal Indian Law: The Hard Trail of Decolonizing and Americanizing the White Man's Jurisprudence" [1986] Wis. L. Rev. 219-99

WILLIAMS, Robert A., Jr., *The American Indian in Western Legal Thought: The Discourses of Conquest* (New York: Oxford University Press, 1989)

WILLIAMS, Robert A., Jr., "Columbus Legacy: The Rehnquist's Perpetuation of European Cultural Racism Against American Indian Tribes" (1992) 39 Fed. Bar News & J. 358-69

WILLIAMS, Robert A., Jr., "Columbus's Legacy: Law as an Instrument of Racial Discrimination Against Indigenous Peoples' Rights of Self-Determination" (1991) 8 Ariz. J. Int'l & Comp. L. 51-75

WILLIAMS, Robert A., Jr., "Documents of Barbarism: The Contemporary Legacy of European Racism and Colonialism in the Narrative Traditions of Federal Indian Law" (1989) 31 Ariz. L. Rev. 237-78

WILLIAMS, Robert A., Jr., "Encounters on the Frontiers of International Human Rights Law: Redefining the Terms of Indigenous Peoples' Survival in the World" [1990] Duke L. J. 660-704

WILLIAMS, Robert A., Jr., "Gendered Checks and Balances: Understanding the Legacy of White Patriarchy in an American Indian Cultural Context" (1989) 24 Ga. L. Rev. 1019-44

WILLIAMS, Robert A., Jr., "Jefferson, the Norman Yoke, and American Indian Lands" (1987) 29 Ariz. L. Rev. 165-94

WILLIAMS, Robert A., Jr., "Linking Arms Together: Multicultural Constitutionalism in a North American Indigenous Vision of Law and Peace" (1994) 82 Cal. L. Rev. 981-1049

WILLIAMS, Robert A., Jr., "Sovereignty, Racism, Human Rights: Indian Self-Determination and the Postmodern World Legal System" (1995) 2 Rev. Const. Stud. 146-202

WILLIAMS, Robert A., Jr., "Taking Rights Aggressively: The Perils and Promise of Critical Legal Theory for Peoples of Color" (1987) 5 L. & Inequality 103-34

WRIGGINS, Jennifer, "Rape, Racism and the Law" (1983) 6 Harv. Women's L. J. 103-41

24

Marxism and Law

Particularly in their work in the late 1970s, critical legal authors drew on some of the concepts and arguments associated with Marxist analyses of law. Inspired by vigorous debates within the political left over the previous two decades, radical legal critics often identified issues and problems in a way that would be instantly recognizable to participants in New Left politics. The primary problem for critical legal writers has been to explain how law creates, sustains, and reproduces the marked inequalities present in modern societies. On this issue, critical legal writing has tapped into Marx's own work, as well as into subsequent Marxist interpretations, and, without arriving at any particular theory that commands consensus, has frequently enlightened the debates by acutely analyzing legal form and legal doctrine.

Like Marxist theorists of state and society, a few critical writers, especially early in the literature, shared a preoccupation with explaining the form and content of laws by reference to a material basis. Various theories have been offered to show how law stands in relation to the economic system, cultural forms of production, and the political system.

Some critical work has treated the law as primarily a tool which serves the interests of the dominant or ruling class. This so-called "instrumentalist" perspective has been invoked to show how common law rules of contract, tort, or criminal law can be understood as either directly or subtly assisting a particular class, such as the bourgeoisie in maintaining its dominance over the working class. Many radical critics condemn this kind of analysis as implausible (as a claim of strict causality) or as too crude. The main criticism is that many aspects of the law are inconsistent with the situation that the instrumentalist view would predict. Some laws (for example, those imposing labor standards) appear to represent political victories by a subordinate class.

Some critical writers have tried to vindicate the claim that law, while inextricably linked with politics, is "relatively autonomous" from the state, the economic order, and any particular social classes. This view has also been criticized from within the movement, on the ground that the concept of relative autonomy is used without any adequate clarification of the precise relationship between law and other phenomena. The description of law as relatively autonomous would permit a limited amount of scope for the courts and for lawyers to operate somewhat independently of state control. They would not simply respond reflexively to the political will of the ruling class. Instead, law would arguably have a internal logic and procedure in which disputes to be argued out without a pre-determined result. This does not mean that law is neutral, but that it often operates indirectly to favor class-specific values. This leftist perspective imagines some room for at least short-term political gains through class struggle. Without such concessions, the working class would not accept the existing system as "legitimate."

One important strand of critical legal thinking (exemplified particularly in the early work of Peter Gabel and Duncan Kennedy) focused on the ways in which economic relations in a society generate distinctive forms of consciousness, or clusters of beliefs about politics, economics, hierarchies, work, and prevailing values. That is, legal forms of consciousness arise and dominate the ways of interpreting the world so as to sustain existing practices of domination. On this view, as the modes and relations of production have changed while capitalism has evolved, the types of consciousness or structures of legal thought change in response. This type of critique claimed to expose the contradictions that are contained in such structures. It was on this ideological terrain that struggles over the directions of the law were worked out.

Because radical critics are devoted to social transformation and the replacement of liberal legal ideals, some of this writing has made use of Gramsci's work on the role of intellectuals in a revolutionary context. Critical legal authors have used Gramsci's description of the "organic" intellectual as a model for the progressive lawyer and law teacher. Organic intellectuals are capable of thinking creatively and propagating their ideas among the particular class they serve. That class, if it is powerful in its own right or because of alliances with other classes, can lead the struggle for change and help break up the settled bourgeois state. Intellectuals can play a key role in achieving working-class hegemony.

As with Marxist theory generally, there is little in critical legal writing about what a society would look like that had dispensed with the need for law altogether. Critics appear to be more fond of describing the proliferation of law, for example, in many different institutions of civil society (schools, churches, clubs, informal community associations), rather than foreseeing the withering away of legal constraints. In other words, from this critical standpoint, law is not necessarily irredeemably associated with capitalism.

Finally, critical legal writers have generally rejected the suggestion that Marxism can constitute a science, while all other forms of knowledge are viewed as merely ideological. Within the critical literature, there is a broad acceptance that legal practices and institutions are part of social relations generally. Legal phenomena can be understood as in an important sense "constitutive" of those social relations. That is, law can be used to create, govern or change the relationships among various parties. Some critical literature has gone so far as to put a "socialist" spin on traditional liberal concepts (such as rights), in order to demonstrate that legal doctrines are more than superstructural phenomena: they can transform the matrix in which social life takes place.

* * * *

ABEL, Richard L., "Capitalism and the Rule of Law: Precondition or Cntradiction?" (1990) 15 L. & Soc. Inquiry 685-97

ANDERSON, Nancy E. and **GREENBERG**, David F., "From Substance to Form: The Legal Theories of Pashukanis and Edelman" (1983) 7 Social Text 69-84

BALBUS, Isaac, "Commodity Form and Legal Form: An Essay on the 'Relative Autonomy' of the Law" (1977) 11 L. & Soc'y Rev. 571-88

BALBUS, Isaac D., *Marxism and Domination: A Neo-Hegelian, Feminist, Psychoanalytic Theory of Sexual, Political, and Technological Liberation* (Princeton: Princeton University Press, 1982)

BARTHOLEMEW, Amy and **BOYD**, Susan, "The Political Economy of Law" in Wallace Clement and Glyn Williams (eds.), *The New Canadian Political Economy* (Kingston: McGill-Queen's University Press, 1989) 212-39

BEIRNE, Piers, "Marxism and the Sociology of Law: Theory or Practice?" (1975) 2 Brit. J. L. & Soc'y 78-81

BEIRNE, Piers and **HUNT**, Alan, "Law and the Constitution of Soviet Society: The Case of Comrade Lenin" (1988) 22 L. & Soc'y Rev. 575-614

CAIN, Maureen, "Gramsci, the State, and the Place of Law" in David Sugarman (ed.), *Legality, Ideology and the State* (New York: Academic Press, 1983) 95-117

COLLINS, Hugh, *Marxism and Law* (Oxford: Oxford University Press, 1982)

DOUZINAS, Costas and **WARRINGTON**, Ronnie, "Domination, Exploitation, and Suffering: Marxism and the Opening of Closed Systems" [review of Hugh Collins, *Marxism and Law* and Allen E. Buchanan, *Marx and Justice*] [1986] Am. Bar Fdn. Res. J. 801-43

DOUZINAS, Costas; **WARRINGTON**, Ronnie; and **McVEIGH**, Shaun, *Postmodern Jurisprudence: The Law of Text in the Texts of Law* (London: Routledge, 1991)

FITZPATRICK, Peter, "Is it Simple to be a Marxist in Legal Anthropology?" [review of Katharine S. Newman, *Law and Economic Organization: A Comparative Study of Preindustrial Societies*] (1985) 48 Mod. L. Rev. 472-85

FITZPATRICK, Peter, "Marxism and Legal Pluralism" (1983) 1 Aust'l J. L. & Soc'y 45-59

FITZPATRICK, Peter, *The Mythology of Modern Law* (London: Routledge, 1992)

FOLEY, Michael A., "Critical Legal Studies: New Wave Utopian Socialism" (1986) 91 Dick. L. Rev. 467-96

FRASER, Andrew, "The Legal Theory We Need Now" (1978) 40/41 Socialist Rev. 147-87

FREEMAN, Alan, "The Politics of Truth: On Sugarman's *Legality, Ideology and the State*" [1986] Am. Bar Fdn. Res. J. 829-43

FUDGE, Judy, "Marx's Theory of History and a Marxist Analysis of Law" in Richard F. Devlin (ed.), *Canadian Perspectives on Legal Theory* (Toronto: Emond Montgomery, 1991) 151-75

GREENBERG, David F. (ed.), *Crime and Capitalism: Readings in Marxist Criminology* (Palo Alto: Mayfield Pub. Co., 1981)

GREENBERG, Edward S., "Liberal Culture and Capitalist Hegemony" in Michael J. G. McGrath (ed.), *Liberalism and the Modern Polity* (New York: Dekker, 1978) 251-71

GREER, Edward, "Antonio Gramsci and 'Legal Hegemony'" in David Kairys (ed.), *The Politics of Law: A Progressive Critique* (New York: Pantheon Books, 1982) 304-9

HEYDEBRAND, Wolf and **SERON**, Carroll, "The Double Bind of the Capitalist Judicial System" (1981) 9 Int'l J. Soc. L. 407-37

HIRST, Paul Q., *Associative Democracy: New Forms of Economics and Social Governance* (Amherst: University of Massachusetts Press, 1994)

HIRST, Paul Q., *Law, Socialism and Democracy* (London: Allen and Unwin, 1986)

HIRST, Paul Q., *On Law and Ideology* (London: Macmillan, 1979)

HUMPHRIES, Drew and **GREENBERG**, David F., "Social Control and Social Formation: A Marxian Analysis" in Donald Black (ed.), *Toward a General Theory of Social Control*, vol. 2 (New York: Academic Press, 1984) 171-208

HUNT, Alan, "Marxism, Law, Legal Theory and Jurisprudence" in Peter Fitzpatrick (ed.), *Dangerous Supplements: Resistance and Renewal in Jurisprudence* (Durham: Duke University Press, 1991) 102-32

HUNT, Alan, "Marxist Legal Theory and Legal Positivism" (1983) 46 Mod. L. Rev. 236-43

HUNT, Alan, "On Legal Relations and Economic Relations" in Robert N. Moles (ed.), *Law and Economics* (Stuttgart: Franz Steiner, 1988) 57-82

JOURNES, Claude, "The Crisis of Marxism and Critical Legal Studies: a View from France" (1982) 10 Int'l J. Soc. L. 2-8

KENNEDY, Duncan, "Antonio Gramsci and the Legal System" (Winter, 1982) 6(1) A.L.S.A. Forum 32-37

KERRUISH, Valerie, *Jurisprudence as Ideology* (London: Routledge, 1991)

KLARE, Karl, "The Citizens of Everyday Life, the New Left, and the Unrecognizable Marxism" in Dick Howard and Karl E. Klare (eds.), *The Unknown Dimension: European Marxism Since Lenin* (New York: Basic Books, 1972) 3-33

KLARE, Karl, "Law-Making as Praxis" (1979) 40 Telos 123-35

KRYGIER, Martin, "Marxism and the Rule of Law: Reflections After the Collapse of Communism" (1990) 15 L. & Soc. Inquiry 633-63

MANDEL, Michael, "Marxism and the Rule of Law" (1986) 35 U.N.B. L. J. 7-33

ROBERTSON, Michael, "Critical Legal Studies and Socialism" (1991) 14 N.Z. U. L. Rev. 355-74

ROTHSTEIN, Lawrence E., "A Marxist View of Equal Opportunity as a Doctrine for Social Change" (1984) 8 A.L.S.A. Forum 203-24

SANTOS, Boaventura de Sousa, "Law and Community: The Changing Nature of State Power in Late Capitalism" (1980) 8 Int'l J. Soc. L. 379-97

STONE, Alan, "The Place of Law in the Marxian Structure-Superstructure Archetype" (1985) 19 L. & Soc'y Rev. 39-67

SUMNER, Colin, *Reading Ideologies: An Investigation Into the Marxist Theory of Ideology and Law* (London: Academic Press, 1979)

SYPNOWICH, Christine, *The Concept of Socialist Law* (Oxford: Clarendon Press, 1990)

SYPNOWICH, Christine, "Law as a Vehicle of Altruism" (1985) 5 Oxford J. Legal Stud. 276-84

TURKEL, Gerald, "The Public/Private Distinction: Approaches to the Critique of Legal Ideology" (1988) 22 L. & Soc'y Rev. 801-23

TUSHNET, Mark, "Marxism as Metaphor" (1983) 68 Cornell L. Rev. 281-90

TUSHNET, Mark, "A Marxist Analysis of American Law" (1978) 1 Marxist Perspectives 96-117

VINCENT, Andrew, "Marx and Law" (1993) 20 J. L. & Soc'y 371-97

YOUNG, Gary, "Justice and Capitalist Production: Marx and Bourgeois Theory" (1978) 8 Can. J. Phil. 421-55

YOUNG, Gary, "Marx on Bourgeois Law" in Steven Spitzer (ed.), *Research in Law and Sociology*, vol. 2 (Greenwich, Conn: JAI Press, 1979) 133-67

25

Alternative Forms of
Dispute Resolution

Owing to perceived problems or crises surrounding the work of courts and "formal" justice, there has been a proliferation in recent years of alternative processes of dispute resolution. These include the use of mediation panels, arbitration boards, ombudspersons, neighborhood justice centers, and consumer complaint agencies. The work of courts and judges has been characterized as slow, expensive, and inflexible. These formal mechanisms are encrusted with rules of procedure and evidence which laypeople often cannot understand. The alternative, "informal" dispute resolution devices have been promoted as decentralized and responsive institutions that can quickly and cheaply address community disputes. They can be more accessible than courts and less hidebound by formalities. The atmosphere can be less intimidating and the process of resolution can depend more on compromise and consensus than on winning. The process can lead to a greater and more imaginative range of solutions than the standard court-ordered remedies. The process does not have to result in a coercive judgment. One intriguing prospect of the ADR movement is that its success would help alleviate court dockets of some of the more minor and troublesome cases.

Critics have challenged both the goals and the impact of ADR activity. First, from an empirical perspective, various studies of the actual performance of ADR panels and their clients' expectations and satisfaction do not indicate a substantial reduction in court congestion. Nor do these studies show that ADR is always speedier or less expensive. Finally, the vaunted hope that the widespread use of ADR would strengthen the values of the community has not been conclusively demonstrated. The lofty aspirations of ADR proponents have not measured up well against the actual practices of "deformalized" justice.

Critical legal writers have problems also with the normative assumptions underlying ADR. The role of the state in establishing, encouraging, funding, and sending clients to ADR processes means that, instead of representing a withdrawal of the state from local or private life, ADR increases the role of the state in managing conflict. From the perspective of Richard Delgado, for instance, the point of ADR has been to maintain social order, rather than to achieve substantive justice. With its emphasis on decision by consensus, ADR is a device to defuse and avoid confrontation rather than to resolve it in the most just fashion.

Although ADR is supposed to be a non-coercive and popular alternative to formal justice, critics also point to studies showing that the bulk of ADR clients use the process only after a referral from, for example, a court or a government agency. The spectre of coercion and enforced participation remains present in the background.

The dispute subject to ADR is typically framed as an interpersonal conflict between individual parties. In other words, disputants are "disaggregated" and the solutions reached may not address the collective problems of the community, which may form the real background of the conflict in question.

Other critiques of ADR have questioned whether informal processes of dispute resolution have not been hurtful to women in the context of divorce or domestic proceedings.

Finally, some critics have lamented the dangers contained in informal processes that dispense with procedural and evidentiary safeguards. This lack of boundaries to contain discretion creates more opportunities for prejudice (based on race or class) to influence the proceedings. Without the formalities of the courtroom, informal justice can, in this sense, present greater risks that bias will infiltrate the process.

* * * *

ABEL, Richard, "Conservative Conflict and the Reproduction of Capitalism: The Role of Informal Justice" (1981) 9 Int'l J. Soc. L. 245-67

ABEL, Richard L., "Informalism: A Tactical Equivalent to Law?" (1985) 19 Clearinghouse Rev. 375-83

ABEL, Richard, "Mediation in Pre-Capitalist Societies" (1983) 3 Windsor Y.B. Acc. Just. 175-85

ABEL, Richard L. (ed.), *The Politics of Informal Justice*, two vols.: Vol. 1 — *The American Experience*; Vol. 2 — *Comparative Studies* (New York: Academic Press, 1982)

AUERBACH, Jerold S., *Justice Without Law?* (New York: Oxford University Press, 1983)

AUERBACH, Jerold S., "The Quest for Justice Under the Rule of Law" (1985) 19 Suffolk U. L. Rev. 560-76

CAIN, Maureen and **KULCSÁR**, Kálmán, *Disputes and the Law* (Budapest: Akadémiai Kiadó, 1983)

CAIN, Maureen and **KULCSÁR**, Kálmán, "Thinking Disputes: An Essay on the Origins of the Dispute Industry" (1982) 16 L. & Soc'y Rev. 375-402

DELGADO, Richard, "ADR and the Dispossessed: Recent Books About the Deformalization Movement" [review of Richard Hofrichter, *Neighborhood Justice in Capitalist Society*; Christine B. Harrington, *Shadow Justice*; and Steven B. Goldberg, Eric D. Green, and Frank A. E. Sander, *Dispute Resolution*] (1988) 13 L. & Soc. Inquiry 145-54

DELGADO, Richard and **DUNN**, Christopher, "Fairness and Formality: Minimizing the Risk of Prejudice in Alternative Dispute Resolution" [1985] Wis. L. Rev. 1359-1404

FELSTINER, William; **ABEL**, Richard; and **SARAT**, Austin, "The Emergence and Transformation of Disputes: Naming, Blaming, Claiming . . ." (1981) 15 L. & Soc'y Rev. 631-54

FITZGERALD, J. M., Review of Richard Abel (ed.), *The Politics of Informal Justice* [1984] Am. Bar Fdn. Res. J. 637-57

FITZPATRICK, Peter, "The Impossiblity of Popular Justice" (1992) 1 Social & Legal Stud. 199-215

FRUG, Gerald, "The Ideology of Bureaucracy in American Law" (1984) 97 Harv. L. Rev. 1276-1388

GRILLO, Trina, "The Mediation Alternative: Process Dangers for Women" (1991) 100 Yale L. J. 1545-610

HARRINGTON, Christine B., "The Politics of Participation and Nonparticipation in Dispute Processes" (1984) 6 L. & Pol'y 203-30

HARRINGTON, Christine B., "Popular Justice, Populist Politics: Law in Community Organizing" (1992) 1 Social & Legal Stud. 177-98

HARRINGTON, Christine B., *Shadow Justice: The Ideology and Institutionalization of Alternatives to Court* (Westport: Greenwood Press, 1985)

HARRINGTON, Christine B. and **MERRY**, Sally Engle, "Ideological Production: The Making of Community Mediation" (1989) 22 L. & Soc'y Rev. 709-35

HARRINGTON, Christine B. and **RIFKIN**, Janet, *The Gender Organization of Mediation: Implications for the Feminization of Legal Practice* (Madison: Institute for Legal Studies, University of Wisconsin, 1989)

HOFRICHTER, Richard, *Neighborhood Justice in Capitalist Society: The Expansion of the Informal State* (Westport, Conn.: Greenwood Press, 1987)

LEFCOURT, Carol, "Women, Mediation and Family Law" (1984) 18 Clearinghouse Rev. 266-69

LERMAN, Lisa G., "Mediation of Wife Abuse Cases: The Adverse Impact of Informal Dispute Resolution" (1984) 7 Harv. Wom. L. J. 57-113

MATHER, Lynn and **YNGVESSON**, Barbara, "Language, Audience, and the Transformations of Disputes" (1981) 15 L. & Soc'y Rev. 775-822

MENKEL-MEADOW, Carrie, "For and Against Settlement: Uses and Abuses of the Mandatory Settlement Conference" (1985) 33 U.C.L.A. L. Rev. 485-514

MENKEL-MEADOW, Carrie, "Judges and Settlement: What Part Should Judges Play?" (1985) 21 Trial 24-29

MENKEL-MEADOW, Carrie, "Toward Another View of Legal Negotiation: The Structure of Problem Solving" (1984) 31 U.C.L.A. L. Rev. 754-842

MERRY, Sally Engle, "The Discourse of Mediation and the Power of Naming" (1990) 2 Yale J. L. & Hum. 1-36

MERRY, Sally Engle, *Getting Justice and Getting Even: Legal Consciousness Among Working-Class Americans* (Chicago: University of Chicago Press, 1990)

MERRY, Sally Engle, "Popular Justice and the Ideology of Social Transformation" (1992) 1 Social & Legal Stud. 161-76

MERRY, Sally Engle, "The Social Organization of Mediation in Nonindustrial Societies: Implications for Informal Community Justice in America" in Richard L. Abel (ed.), *The Politics of Informal Justice*, vol. 2: *Comparative Studies* (New York: Academic Press, 1982) 17-45

MERRY, Sally Engle and **MILNER**, Neal (eds.), *The Possibility of Popular Justice: A Case Study of Community Mediation in the United States* (Ann Arbor: University of Michigan Press, 1993)

MINOW, Martha, "Some Thoughts on Dispute Resolution and Civil Procedure" (1984) 34 J. Legal Educ. 284-97

NADER, Laura, "Disputing Without the Force of Law" (1979) 88 Yale L. J. 998-1021

QUADE, Vicki, "Are Lawyers Really Necessary?" [an interview with Duncan Kennedy] (Fall, 1987) 14 (No. 4) Barrister 10-13, 16-17, 36-37

REIFNER, Udo, "Types of Legal Needs and Modes of Legalization: The Example of the Berlin Tenants Initiative" in Erhard Blankenburg (ed.), *Innovations in the Legal Services* (Cambridge, Mass.: Oelgeschlager, Gunn & Hain, 1980) 37-52

RIFKIN, Janet, "Mediation From a Feminist Perspective: Promise and Problems" (1984) 2 L. & Inequality 21-31

SANTOS, Boaventura de Sousa, "Law and Community: The Changing Nature of State Power in Late Capitalism" (1980) 8 Int'l J. Soc. L. 379-97

SARAT, Austin and **FELSTINER**, William L. F., "Law and Social Relations: Vocabularies of Motive in Lawyer/Client Interaction" (1988) 22 L. & Soc'y Rev. 739-69

SCHNEIDER, Elizabeth M., "Gendering and Engendering Process" (1993) 61 U. Cin. L. Rev. 1223-35

SIBLEY, Susan and **SARAT**, Austin, "Dispute Processing in Law and Legal Scholarship: From Institutional Critique to the Reconstruction of the Juridical Subject" (1989) 66 Den. U. L. Rev. 437-98

SPITZER, Steve, "The Dialectics of Formal and Informal Control" in Richard Abel (ed.), *The Politics of Informal Justice*, vol. 1: *The American Experience* (New York: Academic Press, 1982) 167-205

TRUBEK, David, "The Construction and Deconstruction of a Disputes-Focused Approach: An Afterword" (1980-81) 15 L. & Soc'y Rev. 727-47

TRUBEK, David, "Turning Away from Law?" [review of Richard Abel (ed.), *The Politics of Informal Justice* and Jerold Auerbach, *Justice Without Law*] (1984) 82 Mich. L. Rev. 824-35

26

Legal Aid

Critical legal writers have reexamined the standard accounts of the rise of legal aid as a state-sponsored form of public service in Western societies. Richard Abel, for example, has argued that traditional descriptions of the origins of the legal aid movement have obscured or underestimated the political struggles that preceded the adoption of legal aid programs. Instead, the accounts are often written from an apolitical perspective, in which liberal legal assumptions about a consensual recognition of the need for procedural justice and the desire for "equal access" to the courts are treated as underpinning the provision of legal aid services. Abel has criticized the very concept of a spontaneous "need" underlying the legitimation of legal aid schemes. From his perspective, this functionalist explanation is itself an ideological disguise of the real history of the struggle for broader provision of legal services.

Against this liberal conception of the premises of legal aid work, critical authors have assessed the interests and influences of various constituencies in the rise (and, to some extent, the decline) of legal assistance services through storefront agencies, pro bono work by legal firms, and clinical legal education programs in the law schools. These studies have identified the different interests of the legal profession, legal aid practitioners, clients, and the government. Critiques have also focused on the quantity and quality of legal services, using empirical studies to illustrate who uses such services and for what purposes.

Critical legal authors have questioned the traditional modes for measuring the success of legal aid programs. If these programs have not significantly contributed to the reduction of levels of poverty, are they then a failure? These issues have led to discussions about whether there are institutional limitations on legal aid schemes. These may be due to the political context in which legal aid programs are situated (that is, they may be heavily dependent on the state for funding and for staffing policies). There may also be serious structural flaws, such as economic constraints, location of programs, psychological impediments to using such services, ignorance of legal rights, and inadequate training for lawyers.

At a normative level, critics have challenged whether legal assistance programs do not rest on a set of inconsistent principles or values. In light of this, the existence of such programs continues to be ideologically controversial. For example, it is unclear whether legal aid programs are supposed to reduce or channel conflict, or promote litigation through access to the courts. Also, the establishment of legal aid schemes tends to be on the basis of procedural justice, rather than substantive norms. Within legal aid programs, there is often tension between those who favor strategies based on existing legal rights, and those who envision their role as pushing for the creation of new rights (for example, the expansion of welfare rights). Another area of conflict is over the line to be drawn in determining eligibility for legal aid representation. Sometimes this takes the form of demarcating where poverty begins. In other contexts, small business operators or creditors are specifically disqualified from participating in legal aid programs.

One of the major drawbacks of modern legal aid programs, from a critical perspective, has been the legalization of issues that might better be treated as political matters inviting widespread organization and mobilization. Legal aid litigation has tended to atomize parties and their conflicts and claims. According to some critical legal authors, this has undermined the potential for collective action. Furthermore, legal aid practitioners are sometimes caught in a dilemma, for their professional training inclines them toward reasonable litigation strategies, while their inclination to social activism propels them toward more transformative goals. They have to choose between routine legal work and more heroic, activist visions. Another critique has been aimed at the danger of creating hierarchical legal aid bureaucracies and local offices.

Critics have proposed radical changes to the methods and goals of providing legal assistance to various groups. The recipients include, besides the poor, members of minorities, children and juveniles, prisoners, refugees, the aged, the mentally and physically disabled, and those afflicted by AIDS. To accomodate the interests of all these groups, the criteria for legal assistance need to be reviewed and expanded. In addition, critics have called for a type of radical practice that breaks down the tendency toward passive dependency on the part of legal aid clients. Legal aid practitioners have been advised to allow clients' own voices to be heard in the process, rather than to represent them in a reconceived form. Also, legal aid schemes might be transformed so that they are not merely specialized forms of crisis intervention (that is, legal emergency rooms). Rather, these programs should focus more on long-term remedies regarding housing, health, child care, support for the elderly, education, employment, and immigration. Finally, legal strategies should be reoriented to ensure that political mobilization of socio-economic classes is fostered, rather than undermined. This calls for fresh alliances and strategies other than litigation. To promote the "empowerment" of client groups, critics have recommended client representation on governing boards, employment of members of the client community (for example, as paralegals), and more creative adaptation of legal technology, so that clients might be enabled to represent themselves.

* * * *

ABEL, Richard L., "Law Without Politics: Legal Aid Under Advanced Capitalism" (1985) 32 U.C.L.A. L. Rev. 474-642

ABEL, Richard L., "What is the Assistance of Effective Counsel For?" (1986) 14 N.Y.U. Rev. L. & Soc. Change 165-71

ABELL, Jennie, "Ideology and the Emergence of Legal Aid in Saskatchewan" (1993) 16 Dal. L. J. 125-68

ALFIERI, Anthony V., "The Antinomies of Poverty Law and a Theory of Dialogic Empowerment" (1988) 16 N.Y.U. Rev. L. & Soc. Ch. 659-712

ALFIERI, Anthony V., "Disabled Clients, Disabling Lawyers" (1992) 43 Hast. L. J. 769-851

ALFIERI, Anthony V., "Reconstructive Poverty Law Practice: Learning Lessons of Client Narrative" (1991) 100 Yale L. J. 2107-47

BELLOW, Gary, "Legal Aid in the United States" (1980) 14 Clearinghouse Rev. 337-45

BELLOW, Gary and **KETTLESON**, Jeanne, "From Ethics to Politics: Confronting Scarcity in Public Interest Practice" (1978) 58 B.U. L. Rev. 337-90

BESHAROV, Douglas J., "The Feminization of Poverty: Has Legal Services Failed to Respond?" (1990) 24 Clearinghouse Rev. 210-18

BEZDEK, Barbara L., "'Legal Theory and Practice' Development at the University of Maryland: One Teacher's Experience in Programmatic Context" (1992) 42 Wash. U. J. Urb. & Contemp. Law 127-45

BLANKENBURG, Erhard, "Comparing Legal Aid Schemes in Europe" (1992) 11 Civ. Just. Q. 106-14

BLANKENBURG, Erhard and **REIFNER**, Udo, "Conditions of Legal and Political Culture Limiting the Transferability of Access-to-Law Innovations" in Mauro Cappelletti (ed.), *Access to Justice and the Welfare State* (Florence: European University Institute, 1981) 217-48

CAHN, Edgar S., "Reinventing Poverty Law" (1994) 103 Yale L. J. 2133-55

GILKERSON, Christopher P., "Poverty Law Narratives: The Critical Practice and Theory of Receiving and Translating Client Stories" (1992) 43 Hast. L. J. 861-945

KESSLER, Mark, "The Politics of Legal Representation: The Influence of Local Politics on the Behavior of Poverty Lawyers" (1986) 8 L. & Pol'y 149-67

KLAWITER, Richard F., "La Tierra es Nuestra! The Compesino Struggle in El Salvador and a Vision of Community-Based Lawyering" (1990) 42 Stan. L. Rev. 1625-89

LEE, Paul E. and **LEE**, Mary M., "Reflections From the Bottom of the Well: Racial Bias in the Provision of Legal Services to the Poor" (1993) 27 Clearinghouse Rev. 310-21

MEADOW, Robert and **MENKEL-MEADOW**, Carrie, "Personalized or Bureaucratized Justice in Legal Services: Resolving Sociological Ambivalence in the Delivery of Legal Aid to the Poor" (1982) 9 L. & Hum. Behavior 397-413

MENKEL-MEADOW, Carrie, *The Fifty-Ninth Street Legal Clinic: Evaluation of an Experiment* (Chicago: American Bar Association, 1979)

MENKEL-MEADOW, Carrie, "Legal Aid in the United States: The Professionalization and Politicization of Legal Services in the 1980's" (1984) 22 Osgoode Hall L. J. 29-67

MENKEL-MEADOW, Carrie, "Nonprofessional Advocacy: The Paralegalization of Legal Services for the Poor" (1985) 19 Clearinghouse Rev. 403-11

MENKEL-MEADOW, Carrie and **MEADOW**, Robert, "Resource Allocation in Legal Services" (1983) 5 L. & Pol'y Q. 237-56

MILOVANOVIC, Dragan, "Jailhouse Lawyers and Jailhouse Lawyering" (1988) 16 Int'l J. Soc. L. 455-75

MILNER, Neal, "The Dilemmas of Legal Mobilization: Ideologies and Strategies of Mental Patient Liberation Groups" (1986) 8 L. & Pol'y 105-29

MOSSMAN, Mary Jane, "Gender Equality and Legal Aid Services: A Research Agenda for Institutional Change" (1993) 15 Sydney L. Rev. 30-58

NADER, Laura, "Process of Constructing (No) Access to Justice (For Ordinary People)" (1990) 10 Windsor Y.B. Acc. Just. 496-513

powell, john a., "Race and Poverty: A New Focus for Legal Services" (1993) 27 Clearinghouse Rev. 298-309

ROJAS, Fernando, "A Comparison of Change-oriented Legal Services in Latin America with Legal Services in North America and Europe" (1988) 16 Int'l J. Soc. L. 203-56

ROTHSTEIN, Lawrence E., "The Myth of Sisyphus: Legal Services Efforts on Behalf of the Poor" (1974) 7 U. Mich. J. L. Ref. 493-515

TREMBLAY, Paul R., "Impromptu Lawyering and De Facto Guardians" (1994) 62 Ford. L. Rev. 1429-45

TREMBLAY, Paul R., "Rebellious Lawyering, Regnant Lawyering, and Street-Level Bureaucracy" (1992) 43 Hast. L. J. 947-70

TREMBLAY, Paul R., "Toward a Community-Based Ethic for Legal Services Practice" (1990) 37 U.C.L.A. L. Rev. 1101-56

TRUBEK, David, Review of Council for Public Interest Law, *Balancing the Scales of Justice: Financing Public Interest Law in America* [1977] Wis. L. Rev. 303-15

WHITE, Lucie E., "*Goldberg* v. *Kelly* and the Paradox of Lawyering for the Poor" (1990) 56 Brook. L. Rev. 861-87

WHITE, Lucie E., "Mobilization on the Margins of the Lawsuit: Making Space for Clients to Speak" (1987-88) 16 N.Y.U. Rev. L. & Soc. Ch. 535-64

27

The Welfare State

The enactment of welfare programs earlier in this century in the U.S., their subsequent application and interpretation, and the political vulnerability of such programs, have all been commented on by critical legal writers. According to these analyses, government-funded and administered social welfare schemes such as unemployment insurance, medicare, public assistance, old-age and other social security measures, all constitute a progressive liberal response to serious exigencies associated with the Depression. Critical authors have examined the ideological assumptions at the root of welfare reformism. In particular they have tried to clarify the concepts of "right," "entitlement," or "privilege" that characterize different stages in the legal implementation of welfare benefits. One of the major features of welfare ideology, according to these authors, is that the different views about who is eligible for assistance, what levels should be provided, on what conditions, and who should make those decisions, are all fraught with contestable normative values.

Owing to the liberal background of welfare schemes, there has been a tendency to frame these issues in terms of whether the poor, the disabled, or parents with dependent children have a right to government aid. Most of the conceptual debate about welfare has turned on whether statutory or constitutional provisions give rise to some kind of legitimate expectation or entitlement which the courts will recognize as legally enforceable. While this debate resulted in progressive judicial decisions during a brief period in the late 1960s, for the most part the debate has shifted attention away from larger issues of social justice. From a critical legal point of view, there have been a few court victories followed by a much longer period of insecurity over the future of social welfare programs.

The high-water mark of social welfare rights (understood as something analogous either to property or contract rights or to civil rights) occurred when courts were willing to limit the discretion of administrators in determining the eligibility of welfare applicants. Also, this was a time when courts stepped in to protect the recipients' fundamental rights of privacy and family autonomy. Throughout this period, the thinking underlying social welfarism was to try to place individuals in a position where they could participate (or return to their role) in the economy. Some programs (such as unemployment insurance) were organized as involving contributions (through payroll deductions) and earnings (that is, benefits are paid out), as if the welfare scheme itself were market-based.

From a critical perspective, this welfare entitlement model did not last long. It was succeeded by the present approach in which courts narrowly construe statutory provisions and detect privileges which are always susceptible to legislative alteration. According to this account, governmental attitudes in the U.S. have increasingly become hardened toward the poor, treating their lack of economic success as primarily due to their own lack of effort, rather than to lack or withdrawal of opportunity. In interpreting welfare legislation, judges emphasize the value of market-based and privatized solutions to social problems, rather than state intervention. That the state is assumed to have no affirmative duty to intervene to relieve the misfortunes of the needy is grounded in a concept of liberal neutrality.

Some critical legal authors have tried to retrieve other welfare ideologies from the past. William Simon has investigated the progressive "social work" critique of welfare policies that arose in the 1940s, but which was subsequently submerged by the movement to treat social benefits as one type of the "new property" (the ideology popularized in the 1960s). Under the social work jurisprudence, welfare should be predicated on notions of "interdependence" (rather than narrow, individualist values) and solidarity. The fundamental premise of eligibility would be "need" rather than "effort." The earlier progressive approach would, according to Simon, have legitimized the guarantee of a minimally adequate income.

Another type of welfare alternative has been suggested by Rand Rosenblatt. He emphasizes that when the government claims to act for the general welfare, this should be interpreted broadly and not just as a reference to the need to protect and defer to market-based processes. His model would require governments, first, to take responsiblity for the problems of the poor, and, second, to respect their own commitments, so that in delivering legislative programs the government would not undermine the policy goals by inadequate levels of staffing and funding.

Rights and entitlements would be allocated on more than an individual basis: governments would be forced to understand the structural determinants of poverty and to organize relief in a form that identifies particularly vulnerable groups. The overall objective would be to seek greater egalitarian and cooperative results.

Critical authors clearly envision welfare schemes as worthwhile only to the extent that such schemes accomplish a substantial degree of economic redistribution. If the welfare system is organized with an aversion to direct or explicit redistribution, then from a critical perspective, it is merely another type of liberal reform that stands in the way of achieving social justice.

* * * *

AUSTIN, Regina, "The Problem of the Legitimacy of the Welfare State" (1982) 130 U. Pa. L. Rev. 1510-18

CALMORE, John O., "Fair Housing vs. Fair Housing: The Problems with Providing Increased Housing Opportunities Through Spatial Deconcentration" (1980) 14 Clearinghouse Rev. 7-18

CALMORE, John O., "North Carolina's Retreat From Fair Housing: A Critical Examination of North Carolina Human Relations v. Weaver Realty Co." (1987) 16 N.C. L. Rev. 154-70

CHESTER, C. Ronald, "The Effects of a Redistribution of Wealth on Property Crime" (1977) 23 Crime & Delinq. 272-89

CHESTER, Ronald, *Inheritance, Wealth and Society* (Bloomington, Ind.: Indiana University Press, 1982)

CHESTER, C. Ronald, "Perceived Relative Deprivation as a Cause of Property Crime" (1976) 22 Crime & Delinq. 17-30

CLUNE, William, III, "The Supreme Court's Treatment of Wealth Discriminations Under the Fourteenth Amendment" [1975] Sup. Ct. Rev. 289-354

CLUNE, William, III, "Unreasonableness and Alienation in the Continuing Relationships of Welfare State Bureaucracy: From Regulatory Complexity to Economic Democracy" [1985] Wis. L. Rev. 707-40

HANDLER, Joel F., "Community Care for the Frail Elderly: A Theory of Empowerment" (1989) 50 Ohio St. L. J. 541-60

HANDLER, Joel F., *The Conditions of Discretion: Autonomy, Community, Bureaucracy* (New York: Russell Sage Foundation, 1986)

HANDLER, Joel F., "'Constructing the Social Spectacle': The Interpretation of Entitlements, Legalization, and Obligations in Social Welfare History" (1990) 56 Brook. L. Rev. 899-974

HANDLER, Joel F., "Dependent People, the State, and the Modern/Postmodern Search for the Dialogic Community" (1988) 35 U.C.L.A. L. Rev. 999-1113

HANDLER, Joel F., *Law and the Search for Community* (Philadelphia: University of Pennsaylvania Press, 1990)

HANDLER, Joel F., "The Transformation of Aid to Families with Dependent Children: The Family Support Act in Historical Context" (1987-88) 16 N.Y.U. Rev. L. & Soc. Change 457-533

HANDLER, Joel F. and **HASENFELD**, Yeheskel, *The Moral Construction of Poverty: Welfare Reform in America* (Newbury Park, Ca.: Sage Pub., 1991)

HANDLER, Joel F. and **SOSIN**, Michael, *Last Resorts: Emergency Assistance and Special Needs Programs in Public Welfare* (New York: Academic Press, 1983)

LAW, Sylvia A., "Health Care and Social Change" (1985) 19 Clearinghouse Rev. 419-24

MINOW, Martha, Review of Joel F. Handler, *The Conditions of Discretion* (1987) 34 U.C.L.A. L. Rev. 981-1001

MINOW, Martha, "When Difference Has Its Home: Group Homes for the Mentally Retarded, Equal Protection and Legal Treatment of Difference" (1987) 22 Harv. C.R.-C.L. L. Rev. 111-89

ROSENBLATT, Rand, "Dual Track Health Care — The Decline of the Medicaid Cure" [review of Robert Stevens and Rosemary Stevens, *Welfare Medicine in America: A Case Study of Medicaid*] (1975) 44 U. Cin. L. Rev. 643-61

ROSENBLATT, Rand, "Health Care, Markets, and Democratic Values" (1981) 34 Vand. L. Rev. 1067-1115

ROSENBLATT, Rand, "Health Care Reform and Administrative Law: A Structured Approach" (1978) 88 Yale L. J. 243-336

ROSENBLATT, Rand, "Legal Entitlement and Welfare Benefits" in David Kairys (ed.), *The Politics of Law: A Progressive Critique* (New York: Pantheon Books, 1982) 262-78

ROSENBLATT, Rand, "Medicaid Primary Care Case Management, the Doctor-Patient Relationship, and the Politics of Privatization" (1985-86) 36 Case West. Res. L. Rev. 915-68

ROSENBLATT, Rand, "Rationing 'Normal' Health Care: The Hidden Legal Issues" (1981) 59 Tex. L. Rev. 1401-20

ROSENBLATT, Rand, "Rationing 'Normal' Health Care Through Market Mechanisms: A Response to Professor Blumstein" (1982) 60 Tex. L. Rev. 919-32

ROSENBLATT, Rand E., "Social Duties and the Problem of Rights in the American Welfare State" in David Kairys (ed.), *The Politics of Law: A Progressive Critique*, 2nd rev. ed. (New York: Pantheon Books, 1990) 90-114

ROSS, Thomas, "The Rhetoric of Poverty: Their Immorality, Our Helplessness" (1991) 79 Geo. L. J. 1499-547

SARAT, Austin, "'. . . The Law is All Over': Power, Resistance and the Legal Consciousness of the Welfare Poor" (1990) 2 Yale J. L. & Hum. 343-79

SIMON, William H., "The Invention and Reinvention of Welfare Rights" (1985) 44 Md. L. Rev. 1-37

SIMON, William H., "Legal Informality and Redistributive Politics" (1985) 19 Clearinghouse Rev. 384-91

SIMON, William H., "Legality, Bureaucracy, and Class in the Welfare System" (1983) 92 Yale L. J. 1198-269

SIMON, William H., "Rights and Redistribution in the Welfare System" (1986) 38 Stan. L. Rev. 1431-516

SPARER, Edward, "Gordian Knots: The Situation of Health Care Advocacy for the Poor Today" (1981) 15 Clearinghouse Rev. 1-23

SPARER, Edward, "The Role of the Welfare Client's Lawyer" (1965) 12 U.C.L.A. L. Rev. 361-80

SPARER, Edward, "Welfare Reform: Which Way is Forward?" (1978) 35 NLADA Briefcase 110-16

TAIBI, Anthony, "Politics and Due Process: The Rhetoric of Social Security Disability Law" [1990] Duke L. J. 913-66

TRUBEK, David M., "Unequal Protection: Thoughts on Legal Services, Social Welfare, and Income Distribution in Latin America" (1978) 13 Tex. Int'l L. J. 243-62

TWEEDY, John and **HUNT**, Alan, "The Future of the Welfare State and Social Rights: Reflections on Habermas" (1994) 21 J. L. 7 Soc'y 288-316

WHITE, Lucie E., "No Exit: Rethinking 'Welfare Dependency' from a Different Ground" (1993) 81 Geo. L. J. 1961-2002

WILLIAMS, Lucy A., "The Ideology of Division: Behavioral Modification Welfare Reform Proposals" (1992) 102 Yale L. J. 719-46

28

Social Theory

Social scientific studies of law in the 1950s and 60s largely took their cue from realist insights into the problems of classical, formalist models of law. To replace the pure study of legal doctrine, members of the law and society movement, which sprang up in the 1960s and continues in various forms to be vigorous today, proposed looking at law as a "social phenomenon." Under the umbrella of this movement, scholars examined the role of law within the entire social system, its impact on individual and group behavior, and the modes through which it served an integrative function. The background of the researchers varies: they may be lawyers collaborating with social scientists, or they may themselves have been trained in several disciplines.

Critical legal writers about social theory frequently see their work as a successor to law and society scholarship. Critical writing deviates from the original law and society model of interdisciplinary research in significant ways. First, the earlier social scientists were extremely optimistic about the power of law to change social life. Law was either credited with an immanent rationality (that is, it was the embodiment of reason), or viewed as a powerful device for making the society better. Radical critics have problems with both these perspectives, for they are severely skeptical about assuming law's normative worth, its neutrality or its effectiveness.

Another problem arises from the tendency within law and society scholarship to treat legal systems as embracing distinctive modes of knowledge independent of bias based on race, class or other factors. This "objectivist" account of legal knowledge contrasts with critical legal assessments of legal rules and doctrines as permeated with ideological traces.

Third, law and society scholars, at least originally, were imbued with a "progressive" mission. Their goal was to conduct academically respectable studies that would provide a sound base for moderate reforms to help solve such nagging social ills as race discrimination and poverty. Those scholars engaged in "development" studies also envisioned using their expertise to transplant "modern" legal systems (that is, modelled after that in the U.S.) in "underdeveloped" countries. In David Trubek's account, such ebullient beliefs formed part of the hegemonizing, imperial legal culture of the 1960s. Radical critics doubt whether these notions of a distinctive modern legal system are either exportable or normatively desirable.

The law and society ideal depended on a view of law as a set of standards that can serve unproblematically as guidelines for social construction, criticism, and transformation. From a critical perspective, law looks quite different. It is composed of complex and contradictory components, in which there is considerable room for argumentative play. Also, law has just as much potential for reproduction and legitimation (even of repressive regimes) as it does for transformation. One of the failings of law and society studies, according to this perspective, is its emphasis on law as a centralizing and controlling force. To this extent, earlier socio-legal scholarship sought to disengage itself from politics. critical legal writers, of course, see the creation of legal doctrine, its interpretation, and its impact on other parts of social life as a matter of political and rhetorical struggle.

Finally, law and society work tended to overrate empirical work, not realizing how this served to reinforce existing structures. The functional sociology of the 1950s and 60s depended on a positivist epistemology, in which the knowledge attained was projected as mirroring an alleged objective reality. Critical scholars have reconceived social relationships as something that law does not merely reflect: rather, law and knowledge about the law are treated as constituting relationships. Thus, the researcher cannot separate knowledge of social life from social life itself. Some kind of phenomenological investigation is called for.

Out of the emerging strands of critical writing are questions about the marginality of law (how legal culture is fragmented and diffuse), so that social studies of law require minute, localized descriptions and interpretations. Transformation through law is not guaranteed. One has to look to individual sites or moments to understand the possibilities for transformative action. Empirical work in socio-legal studies must recognize the "discursive" nature of legal knowledge and be self-critical about any claims (or inclinations) to objectivity and normative disengagement.

* * * *

ABEL, Richard, "Law as Lag: Inertia as a Social Theory of Law" (1982) 80 Mich. L. Rev. 785-809

ABEL, Richard, "Lawyers and the Power to Change" (1985) 7 L. & Pol'y 5-18

ABEL, Richard, "Law Books and Books About Law" [review of Max Rheinstein, *Marriage Stability, Divorce, and the Law*] (1973) 26 Stan. L. Rev. 175-228

ABEL, Richard L., "Redirecting Social Studies of Law" (1980) 14 L. & Soc'y Rev. 805-29

ABEL, Richard, Review of Thomas Mathiesen, *Law, Society and Political Action: Towards a Strategy Under Late Capitalism* (1982) 10 Int'l J. Soc. L. 105-11

ALFIERI, Anthony V., Review of Austin Sarat and Thomas R. Kearns (eds.), *Law's Violence*] (1994) 94 Colum. L. Rev. 1721-50

BACHMANN, Steve, "Lawyers, Law, and Social Change" (1984-85) 13 N.Y.U. Rev. L. & Soc. Change 1-50

BEIRNE, Piers, "Ideology and Rationality in Max Weber's Sociology of Law" in Steven Spitzer (ed.), *Research in Law and Sociology*, vol. 2 (Greenwich, Conn.: JAI Press, 1979) 103-31

BRIGHAM, John and **HARRINGTON**, Christine B., "Realism and Its Consequences: An Inquiry Into Contemporary Sociological Research" (1989) 17 Int'l J. Soc. L. 41-62

CAIN, Maureen, "The Limits of Idealism: Max Weber and the Sociology of Law" in Steven Spitzer (ed.), *Research in Law and Sociology*, vol. 3 (Greenwich, Conn.: JAI Press, 1980) 53-83

CARTY, Anthony, "Post-Modernism in the Theory and the Sociology of Law, or Rousseau and Durkheim as read by Baudrillard" in Anthony Carty (ed.), *Post-Modern Law: Enlightenment, Revolution and the Death of Man* (Edinburgh: Edinburgh University Press, 1990) 71-89

CARTY, Anthony, "Some Post-Modern Perspectives on Law and Society" (1990) 17 J. L. & Soc'y 395-410

CAUDILL, David S., "Freud and Critical Legal Studies: Contours of a Radical Socio-Legal Psychoanalysis" (1991) 66 Ind. L. J. 651-97

CHAMBLISS, William J., "On Lawmaking" in William J. Chambliss and Marjorie S. Zatz (eds.), *Making Law: The State, the Law, and Structural Contradictions* (Bloomington: Indiana University Press, 1993) 3-35

CLUNE, William, "Courts and Legislatures as Arbitrators of Social Change" (1984) 93 Yale L. J. 763-79

CLUNE, William H., III, *Legal Disintegration and a Theory of the State* (Madison: Institute for Legal Studies, University of Wisconsin, 1987)

CLUNE, William, III, "A Political Method of Evaluating the Education for All Handicapped Children Act of 1975 and the Several Gaps of Gap Analysis" (1985) 48 L. & Contemp. Probs. 7-62

CLUNE, William, III, "A Political Model of Implementation and Implications of the Model for Public Policy, Research, and the Changing Roles of Law and Lawyers" (1983) 69 Iowa L. Rev. 47-125

COOMBE, Rosemary J., "Room for Manoeuver: Toward a Theory of Practice in Critical Legal Studies" (1989) 14 L. & Soc. Inquiry 69-121

d'ERRICO, Peter, "A Critique of Critical Social Thought About Law amd Some Comments on Decoding Capitalist Culture" (1979) 4 A.L.S.A. Forum 39-56

DEVLIN, Richard F., "Law's Centaurs: An Inqury Into the Nature and Relations of Law, State and Violence" (1989) 27 Osgoode Hall L. J. 219-93

EWICK, Patrick and **SIBLEY**, Susan S., "Conformity, Contestation, and Resistance: An Account of Legal Consciousness" (1992) 26 New Eng. L. Rev. 731-49

FITZPATRICK, Peter, "'The Desperate Vacuum': Imperialism and Law in the Experience of Enlightenment" in Anthony Carty (ed.), *Post-Modern Law: Enlightenment, Revolution and the Death of Man* (Edinburgh: Edinburgh University Press, 1990) 90-106

FITZPATRICK, Peter, "Law and Societies" (1984) 22 Osgoode Hall L. J. 115-38

FITZPATRICK, Peter, "Law, Modernization and Mystification" in Steven Spitzer (ed.), *Research in Law and Sociology*, vol. 3 (Greenwich, Conn.: JAI Press, 1980) 161-78

GALANTER, Marc, "Why the 'Haves' Come Out Ahead: Speculations on the Limits of Legal Change" (1974) 9 L. & Soc'y Rev. 95-160

GOODRICH, Peter, *Languages of Law: From Logics of Memory to Nomadic Masks* (London: Weidenfeld and Nicolson, 1990)

GORDON, Robert W., "Law and Disorder" (1989) 64 Ind. L. J. 803-30

GREENBERG, David N., "Law and Economic Development in Light of Dependency Theory" in Steven Spitzer (ed.), *Research in Law and Sociology*, vol. 3 (Greenwich, Conn.: JAI Press, 1980) 129-59

GREENHOUSE, Carol J.; YNGVESSON, Barbara; and ENGEL, David M., *Law and Community in Three American Towns* (Ithaca: Cornell University Press, 1994)

HARRINGTON, Christine B., "Moving From Integrative to Constitutive Theories of Law: Comment on Itzkowitz" (1988) 22 L. & Soc'y Rev. 963-67

HARRINGTON, Christine B. and YNGVESSON, Barbara, "Interpretive Sociolegal Research" (1990) 15 L. & Soc. Inquiry 135-48

HARRINGTON, Christine B. and MERRY, Sally Engle, "Ideological Production: The Making of Community Mediation" (1988) 22 L. & Soc'y Rev. 709-35

HEYDEBRAND, Wolf, "Organization and Praxis" in Gareth Morgan (ed.), *Beyond Method: Strategies for Social Research* (Beverly Hills: Sage Publications, 1983) 306-20

HEYDEBRAND, Wolf, "The Technocatic Administration of Justice" in Steven Spitzer (ed.), *Research in Law and Sociology*, vol. 2 (Greenwich, Conn.: JAI Press, 1979) 29-64

HUNT, Alan, "Foucault's Expulsion of Law: Toward a Retrieval" (1992) 17 L. & Soc. Inquiry 1-39

HUNT, Alan, "The Ideology of Law" (1985) 19 L. & Soc'y Rev. 11-37

HUNT, Alan, "Radical Pluralism and Beyond: Reflections on Law, Order, and Power" [review of William J. Chambliss and Robert Seidman, *Law, Order, and Power*, 2nd ed.] (1984) 2 Austrl. J. L. & Soc'y 132-43

HUNT, Alan, "The Sociology of Law of Gurvitch and Timasheff: A Critique of Theories of Normative Integration" in Steven Spitzer (ed.), *Research in Law and Sociology*, vol. 2 (Greenwood, Conn: JAI Press, 1979) 169-204

HYDE, Alan, "The Concept of Legitimation in the Sociology of Law" [1983] Wis. L. Rev. 379-426

LUBAN, David, *Legal Modernism* (Ann Arbor: University of Michigan Press, 1994)

MACAULAY, Stewart, "Images of law in Everyday Life" (1987) 21 L. & Soc'y Rev. 185-218

MACAULAY, Stewart, "Law and the Behavioral Sciences: Is There Any There There?" (1984) 6 L. & Policy 149-87

McDOUGALL, Harold A., "Social Movements, Law, and Implementation: A Clinical Dimension for the New Legal Process" (1989) 75 Cornell L. Rev. 83-122

MENKEL-MEADOW, Carrie, "Durkheimian Epiphanies: The Importance of Engaged Social Science in Legal Studies" (1990) 18 Fla. St. U. L. Rev. 91-119

MERRY, Sally Engle, "Culture, Power, and the Discourse of Law" (1992) 37 N.Y. L. Sch. L. Rev. 209-25

MERRY, Sally Engle, "Everyday Understandings of the Law in Working-Class America" (1986) 13 Am. Ethnologist 253-70

MERRY, Sally Engle, "Rethinking Gossip and Scandal" in Donald Black (ed.), *Toward a General Theory of Social Control*, vol. 1 (New York: Academic Press, 1984) 271-302

NOTE, "The Faith of the 'Crits': Critical Legal Studies and Human Nature" (1988) 11 Harv. J. L. & Pub. Pol'y 433-59

RAZACK, Sherene, "Using Law for Social Change: Historical Perspectives" (1992) 17 Queen's L. J. 31-53

ROELOFS, Joan, "The Supreme Court as a Superlegislature: Taking Into Account *Brown* and *Bakke*" in Steven Spitzer (ed.), *Research in Law and Sociology*, vol. 3 (Greenwich, Conn.: JAI Press, 1980) 257-78

SANTOS, Boaventura de Sousa, "Law: A Map of Misreading — Toward a Postmodern Conception of Law" (1987) 14 J. L. & Soc'y 279-302

SANTOS, Boaventura de Sousa, "The Law of the Oppressed: The Construction and Reproduction of Legality in Pasargada" (1977) 12 L. & Soc'y Rev. 5-126

SANTOS, Boaventura de Sousa, "Law, State and Urban Struggles in Recife, Brazil" (1992) 1 Social & Legal Stud. 235-55

SANTOS, Boaventura de Sousa, "On Modes of Production of Law and Social Power" (1985) 13 Int'l J. Soc. L. 299-336

SANTOS, Boaventura de Sousa, "The Postmodern Transition: Law and Politics" in Austin Sarat and Thomas R. Kearns (eds.), *The Fate of Law* (Ann Arbor: University of Michigan Press, 1991) 79-118

SANTOS, Boaventura de Sousa, "State, Law and Community in the World System: An Introduction" (1992) 1 Social & Legal Stud. 131-42

SANTOS, Boaventura de Sousa, *Toward a New Common Sense: Law, Science and Politics in the Paradigmatic Tradition* (London: Routledge, 1995)

SANTOS, Boaventura de Sousa, "Towards a Postmodern Understanding of Law" in André Jean Arnaud (ed.), *Legal Culture and Everyday Life* (Onati: Onati International Institute for the Sociology of Law, 1989) 113-23

SARAT, Austin, "Legal Effectiveness and Social Studies of Law: On the Unfortunate Persistence of a Research Tradition" (1985) 9 Legal Stud. Forum 23-31

SARAT, Austin, "Off to Meet the Wizard: Beyond Validity and Reliability in the Search for a Post-Empiricist Sociology of law" (1990) 15 L. & Soc. Inquiry 155-70

SARAT, Austin and **FELSTINER**, William L. F., "Lawyers and Legal Consciousness: Law Talk in the Divorce Lawyer's Office" (1987) 98 Yale L. J. 1663-88

SARAT, Austin and **KEARNS**, Thomas R., "A Journey Through Forgetting: Toward a Jurisprudence of Violence" in Austin Sarat and Thomas R. Kearns (eds.), *The Fate of Law* (Ann Arbor: University of Michigan Press, 1991) 209-73

SARAT, Austin and **SIBLEY**, Susan, "The Pull of the Policy Audience" (1988) 10 L. & Pol'y 97-166

SCHLEGEL, John Henry, "American Legal Realism and Empirical Social Science: From the Yale Experience" (1979) 28 Buffalo L. Rev. 459-586

SCHLEGEL, John Henry, "American Legal Realism and Empirical Social Science: The Singular Case of Underhill Moore" (1980) 29 Buffalo L. Rev. 195-323

SIBLEY, Susan S. and **SARAT**, Austin, "Critical Traditions in Law and Society Research" (1987) 21 L. & Soc'y Rev. 165-74

SPITZER, Steven, "Punishment and Social Organization: A Study of Durkheim's Theory of Penal Evolution" (1975) 9 L. & Soc'y Rev. 613-37

SUGARMAN, David, *In the Spirit of Weber: Law, Modernity and "The Peculiarities of the English"* (Madison: Institute for Legal Studies, University of Wisconsin, 1987)

TRUBEK, David M., *Back to the Future: The Short, Happy Life of the Law and Society Movement* (Madison: Institute for Legal Studies, University of Wisconsin, 1990)

TRUBEK, David, "Complexity and Contradiction in the Legal Order: Balbus and the Challenge of Critical Social Thought About Law" (1977) 11 L. & Soc'y Rev. 529-69

TRUBEK, David, "Max Weber and the Rise of Capitalism" [1972] Wis. L. Rev. 720-53

TRUBEK, David, *Max Weber's Tragic Modernism and the Study of Law in Society* (Madison: Institute for Legal Studies, University of Wisconsin, 1985)

TRUBEK, David, "Toward a Social Theory of Law: An Essay on the Study of Law and Development" (1972) 82 Yale L. J. 1-50

TRUBEK, David, "Where the Action Is: Critical Legal Studies and Empiricism" (1984) 36 Stan. L. Rev. 575-622

TRUBEK, David M. and **ESSER**, John, *Critical Empiricism in American Legal Studies: Paradox, Program, or Pandora's Box* (Madison: Institute for Legal Studies, University of Wisconsin, 1988)

TRUBEK, David and **ESSER**, John, "'Critical Empiricism' in American Legal Studies: Paradox, Program, or Pandora's Box" (1989) 14 L. & Soc. Inquiry 3-52

TRUBEK, David and **GALANTER**, Marc, "Scholars in Self-Estrangement" [1974] Wis. L. Rev. 1062-102

TURKEL, Gerald, "The Public/Private Distinction: Approaches to the Critique of Legal Ideology" (1988) 22 L. & Soc'y Rev. 801-23

WHITFORD, William C., "Critical Empiricism" (1989) 14 L. & Soc. Inquiry 61-67

WHITFORD, William C., "Lowered Horizons: Implementation Research in a Post-CLS World" [1986] Wis. L. Rev. 755-79

YNGVESSON, Barbara, "Legal Ideology and Community Justice in the Clerk's Office" (1985) 9 Legal Stud. F. 71-87

YNGVESSON, Barbara, "Re-examining Continuing Relations and the Law" [1985] Wis. L. Rev. 623-46

YNGVESSON, Barbara, *Virtuous Citizens, Disruptive Subjects: Order and Complaint in a New England Court* (New York: Routledge, 1993)

YNGVESSON, Barbara, "Making Law at the Doorway: The Clerk, the Court, and the Construction of Community in a New England Town" (1988) 22 L. & Soc'y Rev. 409-48

29

Economic Analysis of Law

According to practitioners of law and economics, all aspects of social, political and legal life can be understood as economic phenomena. Under this systematic approach, the basic motivation for individual persons in a world of choice and scarce resources is to engage in a series of tradeoffs that maximizes their utility (or their piece of the economic pie). This account assumes that each of us rationally pursues our own self-interest. Our preferences are treated essentially as given (there is little in the literature on law and economics about how preferences are formed).

This economic perspective is unified in the sense that it detects logical patterns that cut across different doctrinal subjects. It conceives of legal rules as involving costs and benefits. So, for example, one can construe many of the rights and liability rules in tort law as a regime for exacting damages from defendants who should have taken precautions (borne the costs) in respect of conduct that injured the plaintiff while it produced some benefit for those defendants. In a perfect world, social ordering could take place by letting unregulated markets determine what kind of economic conduct is rational. These markets would be guided by clear, general legal rules. In situations where transaction costs (such as information or administration costs) are too high, simple bargaining between the parties affected by an activity is not always possible. This justifies some degree of legal intervention, but in doing so lawmakers should create standards that reward efficient arrangenents and that punish inefficiency.

Efficiency is not the only normative touchstone of economic analysis. "Wealth maximization" (that is, achieving the greatest total satisfaction of preferences) has also been invoked as the primary criterion for assessing whether a particular legal principle or result is "just."

Critical legal writers have offered critiques of several different approaches to law and economics, including the Chicago-school variety associated with Richard Posner and the Yale group. All these contemporary practitioners of economic analysis suffer from the weakness of their liberal assumptions. Not all of them accept this liberal tag, though some, such as Robin Paul Malloy, explicitly claim classical liberal credentials.

From a critical legal perspective, the school's core concepts of individual rationality, utility maximization, and ethical instrumentalism are far from apolitical or objective. Rather, they are acutely ideological constructs. They pose as allegedly neutral descriptions of human behavior, in furtherance of an alluring image of economics as providing a scientific footing to legal decisionmaking. Under the disguise of "rationality" and the free exercise of bargaining power, law-and-economics scholarship preserves and reinforces existing inequalities of wealth and power. Critiques have also been aimed at the distinction between state regulation and market constraints and the economic analyst's presumption in favor of market "solutions" as the proper guide to decide legal outcomes. The ultimate ideological goal of economic analysis, as it has been popularly practised in the last four decades, has been to defend the liberal state against "collectivist" attacks.

Critical legal writers have also taken law-and-economics scholars to task for failing to pay attention to issues of just distribution of wealth. In the field of property law, for example, that scholarship has focused on allocational issues: efficiency is adjudicated by determining who would make most productive use of the resources in question. There is no room to consider competing public values, such as substantive equality or fairness. In addition, critics such as Mark Kelman have lamented the remarkably scant attention paid in law and economics literature to macroeconomic issues or assumptions. For the most part, economic analysis is built on neo-classical, microeconomic premises. A further problematic feature of law and economics, according to Kelman's diagnosis, is that school's failure to distinguish private-regarding preferences from public-regarding preferences.

Because of its scientific pretensions, its reductionist methods, it lack of empirical support, and its dubious normative assumptions, the law-and-economics approach has been disparaged and rejected by its radical critics. Some members of the critical legal studies movement have tried to use different forms of economic analysis to understand how "efficiency" can be deployed as a useful standard of measure. For example, Duncan Kennedy has attempted to show that, for an economic analysis to be illuminating, the rules in question must be related to the specific wants and factual circumstances of individual parties affected by the choice among different possible rules. In other words, settling what is the most efficient legal regime cannot simply be deduced from presuppositions about each individual's rational utility-maximizing conduct.

* * * *

AARON, Nan; **MOULTON**, Barbara; and **OWENS**, Chris, "Economics, Academia, and Corporate Money in America: The 'Law and Economics' Movement" (1992-93) 24(4) Antitrust L. & Econ. Rev. 27-42 and (1994) 25(1) Antitrust L. & Econ. Rev. 37-54

AUDAIN, Linz, "Critical Cultural Law and Economics, the Culture of Individualization, the Paradox of Blackness" (1995) 70 Ind. L. J. 709-82

AUDAIN, Linz, "Critical Legal Studies, Feminism, Law and Economics, and the Veil of Intellectual Tolerance: A Tentative Case for Cross-Jurisprudential Dialogue" (1992) 20 Hofstra L. Rev. 1017-104

BAKER, C. Edwin, "The Ideology of the Economic Analysis of Law" (1975) 5 Phil. & Pub. Aff. 3-48

BAKER, C. Edwin, "Posner's Privacy Mystery and the Failure of the Economic Analysis of Law" (1978) 12 Ga. L. Rev. 475-95

BAKER, C. Edwin, "Starting Points in the Economic Analysis of Law" (1980) 8 Hofstra L. Rev. 939-72

BALKIN, J. M., "Learning Nothing and Forgetting Nothing: Richard Epstein and the Takings Clause" (1986) 18 Urb. Law. 707-32

BARTLETT, Katharine T., "Rumpelstiltskin" [on Richard A. Posner, *Sex and Reason*] (1993) 25 Conn. L. Rev. 473-90

BLACK, Robert A.; **KREIDER**, Rosalie S.; and **SULLIVAN**, Mark, "Critical Legal Studies, Economic Realism, and the Theory of the Firm" (1988) 43 U. Mia. L. Rev. 343-60

BRAUN, Christopher K., "Alternative Rhythms in Law and Economics: The Posner-Malloy Dialectic" (1991) 15 Legal Stud. Forum 153-65

BRIETZKE, Paul H., "Law, Legitimacy and Coercion: One View From Law and Economics" (1991) 25 Val. U. L. Rev. 343-81

BRUNELL, Richard, "Efficiency and a Rule of 'Free Contract': A Critique of Two Models of Law and Economics" (1984) 97 Harv. L. Rev. 978-96

CULP, Jerome M., Jr., "Judex Economicus" (1987) 50(4) L. & Contemp. Probs. 95-140

CURRAN, William J., III, "Antitrust and the Rule of Reason: A Critical Assessment" (1984) 28 St. Louis U. L. J. 745-70

CURRAN, William J., III, "Beyond Economic Concepts and Categories: A Democratic Refiguration of Antitrust Law" (1987) 31 St. Louis U. L. J. 349-78

CURRAN, William J., III, "Corporate Realities, Liberal Myths: Interpreting Section 7 of the Clayton Act" (1985) 30 St. Louis U. L. J. 171-92

DUXBURY, Neil, "Is There a Dissenting Tradition in Law and Economics?" [review of Nicholas Mercuro (ed.), *Law and Economics*] (1991) 54 Mod. L. Rev. 300-11

FINEMAN, Martha A., "The Hermeneutics of Reason: A Commentary on *Sex and Reason*" (1993) 25 Conn. L. Rev. 503-13

GORDON, Robert W., "Hayek and Cooter on Custom and Reason" (1994) 23 Sw. U. L. Rev. 453-60

HAGER, Mark M., "The Emperor's Clothes Are Not Efficient: Posner's Jurisprudence of Class" (1991) 41 Am. U. L. Rev. 7-62

HELLER, Thomas, "The Importance of Normative Decisionmaking: The Limitations of Legal Economics as a Basis for Liberal Jurisprudence — As Illustrated by the Regulation of Vacation Home Development" [1976] Wis. L. Rev. 385-507

HELLER, Thomas, "Is the Charitable Exemption from Property Taxation an Easy Case? General Concerns About Legal Economics and Jurisprudence" in Daniel L. Rubinfeld (ed.), *Essays on the Law and Economics of Local Governments* (Washington, D.C.: The Urban Institute, 1979) 183-251

HONOROFF, Bradley, "Reflections on Richard Posner" [review of Richard Posner, *The Economics of Justice*] (1983) 18 Harv. C.R.-C.L. L. Rev. 287-303

HORWITZ, Morton J., "Law and Economics: Science or Politics?" (1981) 8 Hofstra L. Rev. 905-12

HORWITZ, Morton J., "The Legacy of 1776 in Legal and Economic Thought" (1976) 19 J. L. & Econ. 621-32

KELMAN, Mark, "Choice and Utility" [1979] Wis. L. Rev. 769-96

KELMAN, Mark, "Comment on Hoffman and Spitzer's 'Experimental Law and Economics'" (1985) 85 Colum. L. Rev. 1037-47

KELMAN, Mark, "Consumption Theory, Production Theory, and Ideology in the Coase Theorem" (1979) 52 S. Cal. L. Rev. 669-98

KELMAN, Mark, "Could Lawyers Stop Recessions? Speculations on Law and Macroeconomics" (1993) 45 Stan. L. Rev. 1215-310

KELMAN, Mark, "Misunderstanding Social Life: A Critique of the Core Premises of Law and Economics" (1983) 33 J. Legal Educ. 274-84

KELMAN, Mark, "Personal Deductions Revisited: Why They Fit Poorly in an 'Ideal' Income Tax and Why They Fit Worse in a Far From Ideal World" (1979) 31 Stan. L. Rev. 831-83

KELMAN, Mark, "Spitzer and Hoffman on Coase: A Brief Rejoinder" (1980) 53 S. Calif. L. Rev. 1215-23

KELMAN, Mark, "Taking *Takings* Seriously: An Essay for Centrists" (1986) 74 Calif. L. Rev. 1829-63

KENNEDY, David W., "Turning to Market Democracy: A Tale of Two Architectures" (1991) 32 Harv. Int'l L. J. 373-96

KENNEDY, Duncan, "Cost-Benefit Analysis of Entitlement Problems: A Critique" (1981) 33 Stan. L. Rev. 387-445

KENNEDY, Duncan, "Cost-Reduction Theory as Legitimation" (1981) 90 Yale L. J. 1275-83

KENNEDY, Duncan, "The Role of Law in Economic Thought: Essays on the Fetishism of Commodities" (1985) 34 Am. U. L. Rev. 939-1001

KENNEDY, Duncan and **MICHELMAN**, Frank, "Are Property and Contract Efficient?" (1980) 8 Hofstra L. Rev. 711-70

KITCH, Edmund D., "The Intellectual Foundations of Law and Economics" (1983) 37 J. Legal Educ. 184-96

KORNHAUSER, Lewis A., "The Great Image of Authority" (1984) 36 Stan. L. Rev. 349-89

MALLOY, Robin Paul, "Equating Human Rights and Property Rights: The Need for Moral Judgment in an Economic Analysis of Law and Social Policy" (1986) 47 Ohio St. L. J. 163-77

MALLOY, Robin Paul, "Toward a New Discourse of Law and Economics" (1991) 42 Syracuse L. Rev. 27-73

MINDA, Gary, "The Law and Economics and Critical Legal Studies Movements in American Law" in Nicholas Mercuro (ed.), *Law and Economics* (Boston: Kluwer, 1989) 87-122

MINDA, Gary, "The Lawyer-Economist at Chicago: Richard A. Posner and the Economic Analysis of Law" (1978) 39 Ohio St. L. J. 439-75

SAMUELS, Warren J., "A Consumer View on Financing Nuclear Plant Abandonments" (1985) 115 Pub. Util. Fort. 24-27

SAMUELS, Warren J., "The Economy as a System of Power and Its Legal Bases: The Legal Economics of Robert Lee Hale" (1973) 27 U. Mia. L. Rev. 261-371

SAMUELS, Warren J., "Maximization of Wealth as Justice: An Essay on Posnerian Law and Economics as Policy Analysis" [review of Richard Posner, *The Economics of Justice*] (1981) 60 Tex. L. Rev. 147-72

SAMUELS, Warren J., "The State, Law and Economic Organization" in Steven Spitzer (ed.), *Research in Law and Sociology*, vol. 2 (Greenwich: Conn.: JAI Press, 1979) 65-99

SAMUELS, Warren J., "Welfare Economics, Power and Property" in Warren J. Samuels and A. Allan Schmid (eds.), *Law and Economics: An Institutional Perspective* (Boston: Martinus Nijhoff, 1981) 9-75

SAMUELS, Warren and **MERCURO**, Nicholas, "Posnerian Law and Economics on the Bench" (1984) 4 Int'l Rev. L. & Econ. 107-30

SAMUELS, Warren and **MERCURO**, Nicholas, "Wealth Maximization and Judicial Decision-Making: The Issues Further Clarified" (1986) 6 Int'l Rev. L. & Econ. 133-37

SCHLAG, Pierre, "An Appreciative Comment on Coase's 'The Problem of Social Cost': A View from the Left" [1986] Wis. L. Rev. 919-62

SCHLAG, Pierre, "The Problem of Transaction Costs" (1989) 62 S. Cal. L. Rev. 1661-700

SCHWARTZSTEIN, Linda A., "Austrian Economics and the Current Debate Between Critical Legal Studies and Law and Economics" (1992) 20 Hofstra L. Rev. 1105-37

WEST, Robin L., "Authority, Autonomy, and Choice: The Role of Consent in the Moral and Political Visions of Franz Kafka and Richard Posner" (1985) 99 Harv. L. Rev. 384-428 [reprinted in Robin L. West, *Narrative, Authority, and Law* (Ann Arbor: University of Michigan Press, 1993) 27-78]

WEST, Robin L., "Submission, Choice, and Ethics: A Rejoinder to Judge Posner" (1986) 99 Harv. L. Rev. 1449-56

WEST, Robin L., "Taking Preferences Seriously" (1989) 64 Tul. L. Rev. 659-703 [reprinted in Robin L. West, *Narrative, Authority, and Law* (Ann Arbor: University of Michigan Press, 1993) 299-342]

WIEGERS, Wanda, "Economic Analysis of Law and 'Private Ordering': A Feminist Critique" (1992) 42 U. Toronto L. J. 170-206

30

Law, Narrative and Literature

In several different ways, critical legal writers have drawn attention to the discursive context in which law and its effects are created, presented, interpreted, and assessed. Among critical authors there has been a marked fascination with storytelling: whether it is constructing fresh narratives or rediscovering and analyzing stories already told (which might be descriptive, experiential or fictional). No single approach dominates the ways in which law and narratives are related. Various critical writers have focused on particular senses in which legal processes and values can be illuminated by reference to literary analogies, or through the use of literary devices.

Some writers have studied representations of law, lawyers, judges, and clients in literature. Others have used literary texts, such as novels, plays or poetry, to address issues of justice and ethics. Another use of literary materials is to compare the practices and understandings of literary criticism with legal criticism. Similarly, some critical writers have tried to show the relevance to legal theory of contemporary debates in literary or cultural theory. For example, the use of deconstructive techniques in unearthing alternative readings for standard literary productions has been applied to legal texts. The apparent anti-authoritarianism of deconstruction has made it an appealing method for radical legal critics.

Critical writers have also intervened in current debates about the "interpretive" nature of legal understanding. Their contribution highlights the political nature of the choice of readings by the person empowered to arrive at an authoritative declaration of the meaning of a statutory or constitutional provision or a precedent. These debates have contested the value of seeing law as essentially a matter of interpretation. Efforts by jurisprudential writers such as Richard Posner to differentiate law from literature (and, in his case, to assimilate law to economic analysis) have been criticized by, among others, Robin West. She has used a literary source, Kafka's fiction, to illustrate the problematic vision of personality and inner life that underlies Posner's economic view of the purpose of law. In addition, West has doubted whether legal decision-making is best conceived primarily as a process of interpretation. She concedes that some aspects of legal interpretation resemble literary interpretation, but she emphasizes the "imperative" nature of adjudication. That is, decision-making is an act of political power, and interpretivism has the unfortunate consequence of constraining criticism of the law.

One of the more recent contributions of critical writers has been in regard to "narrative" jurisprudence. According to some authors, especially those who study law from the perspective of gender or race, legal scholarship would benefit from exposure to narratives or stories in the form of first-hand experiential accounts, autobiographies and biographies, or fiction that give an account not reflected in mainstream legal thinking. So, for example, by hearing or reading the story of a woman of color, in her encounters with prejudice, poverty, or sexual oppression, one's understanding of the cultural framework in which actual lives are lived would be enriched. The concrete details of such stories would be an antidote to the ordinarily abstract and objective tones of legal discourse. These accounts may not follow the usual conventions of factual accounts found in legal materials: they may be highly emotional, nonlinear representations. They may serve to sharpen the moral sensibilities of readers. By compiling composite stories, come critical authors have tried to reveal the distinctive insights that members of minority groups can articulate, preferably in "their own voice." On this approach, experience itself is treated as a valuable mode of knowledge: it does not have to be filtered through a legal grid before it is validated.

Not all critical writers accept that narratives themselves accomplish the task of providing alternative visions of social justice. These critics still require that normative arguments be presented (with, perhaps, the stories as an illuminating background). The complaint here is that stories are open to competing interpretations and that it is not clear what prescriptions necessarily follow from a narrative.

* * * *

ABRAMS, Kathryn, "Hearing the Call of Stories" (1991) 79 Cal. L. Rev. 971-1052

ALLEN, Anita L., "The Jurisprudence of *Jane Eyre*" (1992) 15 Harv. Wom. L. J. 173-238

AYER, John D., "Not So Fast on the Crits: A Grudging Tribute (or Concession) to Crit Style" (1990) 1 Scribes J. Legal Writing 45-54

BALL, Milner S., "Confessions" (1989) 1(2) Cardozo Stud. L. & Lit. 185-97

BALL, Milner S., *The Word and the Law* (Chicago: University of Chicago Press, 1993)

BATEY, Robert, "Alienation By Contract in Paris Trout" (1994) 35 S. Tex. L. Rev. 289-329

COFFINO, Michael, "Genre, Narrative and Judgment: Legal and Protest Song Stories in Two Criminal Cases" [1994] Wis. L. Rev. 679-718

DELGADO, Richard, "Storytelling for Oppositionists and Others: A Plea for Narrative" (1989) 87 Mich. L. Rev. 2411-41 [reprinted in David Ray Papke (ed.), *Narrative and the Legal Discourse: A Reader in Storytelling and the Law* (Liverpool: Deborah Charles, 1991) 289-312]

DELGADO, Richard and **STEFANCIC**, Jean, "Imposition" (1994) 35 Wm. & Mary L. Rev. 1025-59

DELGADO, Richard and **STEFANCIC**, Jean, "Norms and Narratives: Can Judges Avoid Serious Moral Error?" (1991) 69 Tex. L. Rev. 1929-83

DELGADO, Richard and **STEFANCIC**, Jean, "Scorn" (1994) 35 Wm. & Mary L. Rev. 1061-99

DENVIR, John, "'Deep Dialogue' — James Joyce's Contribution to American Constitutional Theory" (1991) 3(1) Cardozo Stud. L. & Lit. 1-19

DENVIR, John, "William Shakespeare and the Jurisprudence of Comedy" (1987) 39 Stan. L. Rev. 825-49

FREEMAN, Jody, "Constitutive Rhetoric: Law as a Literary Activity" (1991) 14 Harv. Wom. L. J. 305-25

FRIEDRICHS, David O., "Narrative Jurisprudence and Other Heresies: Legal Education at the Margin" (1990) 40 J. Legal Educ. 3-18 [reprinted in

David Ray Papke (ed.), *Narrative and the Legal Discourse: A Reader in Storytelling and the Law* (Liverpool: Deborah Charles, 1991) 43-59]

GOODRICH, Peter, "Antirrhesis: The Polemical Structures of Common Law Thought" in Austin Sarat and Thomas R. Kearns (eds.), *The Rhetoric of Law* (Ann Arbor: University of Michigan Press, 1994) 57-102

GOODRICH, Peter, "The Continuance of the Antirrhetoric" (1992) 4(2) Cardozo Stud. L. & Lit. 207-22

GOODRICH, Peter, "We Orators" [review of Brian Vickers, *In Defence of Rhetoric*] (1990) 53 Mod. L. Rev. 546-63

HAMILTON, K. Scott, "Prolegomenon to Myth and Fiction in Legal Reasoning: Common Law Adjudication and Critical Legal Studies" (1989) 35 Wayne L. Rev. 1449-80

HARRISON, Melissa, "A Time of Passionate Learning: Using Feminism, Law, and Literature to Create a Learning Community" (1993) 60 Tenn. L. Rev. 393-429

HASIAN, Marouf, Jr., "Myth and Ideology in Legal Discourse: Moving From Critical Legal Studies Toward Rhetorical Consciousness" (1994) 17 Legal Stud. F. 347-65

HEILBRUN, Carolyn and RESNIK, Judith A., "Convergences: Law, Literature, and Feminism" (1990) 99 Yale L. J. 1913-56

HIBBITTS, Bernard J., "Making Sense of Metaphors: Visuality, Aurality, and the Reconfiguration of American Legal Discourse" (1994) 16 Cardozo L. Rev. 229-356

JOHNSON, Barbara, "The Alchemy of Style and Law" in Austin Sarat and Thomas R. Kearns (eds.), *The Rhetoric of Law* (Ann Arbor: University of Michigan Press, 1994) 261-74

KOFFLER, Judith, "The Assimilation of Law and Literature: An Approach to Metanoia" (May, 1978) 3(1) A.L.S.A. Forum 5-11

KOFFLER, Judith Schenck, "The Feminine Presence in *Billy Budd*" (1989) 1(1) Carodozo Stud. L. & Lit. 1-14

KOFFLER, Judith Schenck, "Forged Alliance: Law and Literature" [review of Richard A. Posner, *Law and Literature: A Misunderstood Relation* and Sanford Levinson and Steven Mailloux (eds.), *Interpreting Law and Literature: A Hermeneutic Reader*] (1989) 89 Colum. L. Rev. 1374-93

KOFFLER, Judith S., "Reflections on Detente: Law and Literature" (1984) 62 Tex. L. Rev. 1157-70

LaRUE, L. H., "The Portrayal of Law in Literature: Weisberg's *Failure of the Word*" [1986] Am. Bar Fdn. Res. J. 313-20

LaRUE, L. H., "Posner and Literature" (1986) 85 Mich. L. Rev. 325-28

MARTIKAN, Owen Peter, "Unmasking Jargon as Substance: How the Crits Have Made a Dialect Out of Dialectic" (1990) 1 Scribes J. Legal Writing 111-23

MASSARO, Toni M., "Empathy, Legal Storytelling, and the Rule of Law: New Words, Old Wounds" (1989) 87 Mich. L. Rev. 2099-127

MATSUDA, Mari J., "Public Response to Racist Speech: Considering the Victim's Story" (1989) 87 Mich. L. Rev. 2320-81

MINDA, Gary, *Postmodern Legal Movements: Law and Jurisprudence at Century's End* (New York: New York University Press, 1995) 149-66

MINKKINEN, Panu, "The Law-Giver's Place: On the Unethical Quality of Legal Wisdom" (1993) 2 Social & Legal Stud. 445-59

MINKKINEN, Panu, "The Radiance of Justice: On the Minor Jurisprudence of Franz Kafka" (1994) 3 Social & Legal Stud. 349-63

MONTOYA, Margaret E., "*Mascaras, Trenzas, y Grenas*: Un/masking the Self While Un/braiding Latina Stories and Legal Discourse" (1994) 17 Harv. Wom. L. J. 185-220

MORSE, Anita L., "Pandora's Box: An Essay Review of American Law and Literature on Prostitution" (1988) 4 Wis. Wom. L. J. 21-62

PAPKE, David Ray, "Discharge as Denouement: Appreciating the Storytelling of Appellate Opinions" (1990) 40 J. Legal Educ. 145-59 [reprinted in David Ray Papke (ed.), *Narrative and the Legal Discourse: A*

Reader in Storytelling and the Law (Liverpool: Deborah Charles, 1991) 206-21]

PAPKE, David Ray, "Neo-Marxists, Nietzscheans, and New Critics: The Voices of the Contemporary Law and Literature Discourse" [1985] Am. Bar Fdn. Res. J. 883-97

SANDMAN, Warren, "Critical Legal Studies and Critical Rhetoric: Toward a Reconceptualization of the Acting Human Agent" (1994) 17 Legal Stud. F. 367-85

SARAT, Austin, "Speaking of Death: Narratives of Violence in Capital Trials" in Austin Sarat and Thomas R. Kearns (eds.), *The Rhetoric of Law* (Ann Arbor: University of Michigan Press, 1994) 135-83

SCALES-TRENT, Judy, "Using Literature in Law School: The Importance of Reading and Telling Stories" (1992) 7 Berk. Wom. L. J. 90-124

SHERRY, Suzanna and **FARBER**, Daniel A., "Telling Stories Out of School: An Essay on Legal Narratives" (1993) 45 Stan. L. Rev. 807-55

SINGER, Joseph William, "Persuasion" (1989) 87 Mich. L. Rev. 2442-58

SOIFER, Aviam, "Assaying Communities: Notes for *The Tempest*" (1989) 21 Conn. L. Rev. 871-97

STEFANCIC, Jean and **DELGADO**, Richard, "Panthers and Pinstripes: The Case of Ezra Pound and Archibald MacLeish" (1990) 63 S. Cal. L. Rev. 907-36

SUGGS, Jon Christian, "Epistemology and the Law in Four African American Fictions" (1990) 14 Legal Stud. Forum 141-62

TEUBNER, Gunther, "Regulatory Law: Chronicle of a Death Foretold" (1992) 1 Social & Legal Stud. 451-75

THURSCHWELL, Adam, "Reading the Law" in Austin Sarat and Thomas R. Kearns (eds.), *The Rhetoric of Law* (Ann Arbor: University of Michigan Press, 1994) 275-32

WEST, Robin L., "Adjudication is Not Interpretation: Some Reservations About the Law-as-Literature Movement" (1987) 54 Tenn. L. Rev. 203-78 [reprinted in Robin L. West, *Narrative, Authority, and Law* (Ann Arbor: University of Michigan Press, 1993) 89-176]

WEST, Robin L., "Communities, Texts, and Law: Reflections on the Law and Literature Movement" (1988) 1 Yale J. L. & Hum. 129-56

WEST, Robin L., "Economic Man and Literary Woman: One Contrast" (1988) 39 Mercer L. Rev. 867-78

WEST, Robin, "Jurisprudence as Narrative: An Aesthetic Analysis of Modern Legal Theory" (1985) 60 N.Y.U. L. Rev. 145-211 [reprinted in Robin L. West, *Narrative, Authority, and Law* (Ann Arbor: University of Michigan Press, 1993) 345-418

WEST, Robin, "Law, Literature, and the Celebration of Authority" [review of Richard A. Posner, *Law and Literature: A Misunderstood Relation*] (1989) 83 Nw. U. L. Rev. 977-1011

WEST, Robin L., "Narrative, Responsibility, and Death" in *Narrative, Authority, and Law* (Ann Arbor: University of Michigan Press, 1993) 419-39

WEST, Robin L., "The Word in the Law" [review of Milner S. Ball, *The Word and the Law*] (1994) 35 Wm. & Mary L. Rev. 1101-34

WHITE, Lucie, "Ordering Voice: Rhetoric and Democracy in Project Head Start" in Austin Sarat and Thomas R. Kearns (eds.), *The Rhetoric of Law* (Ann Arbor: University of Michigan Press, 1994) 185-223

WHITE, Lucie E., "Subordination, Rhetorical Survival Skills, and Sunday Shoes: Notes on the Hearing of Mrs. G." (1990) 38 Buffalo L. Rev. 1-58

WINTER, Steven L., "The Cognitive Dimension of the Agon Between Legal Power and Narrative Meaning" (1989) 87 Mich. L. Rev. 2225-79

31

Legal Scholarship

According to critical legal writers such as Mark Tushnet, legal scholarship in the last two-thirds of the twentieth century has been peripheral to intellectual life in Western societies. This situation contrasts with the period in the U.S. from Holmes to the legal realists, when the invention and application of new ideas spilled over from the law into social and political life generally. Several causes contribute to this more recent marginality. First, legal education in the universities has been largely structured around an ideology of "professionalism." Students and lawyers tend to use legal research for highly practical purposes. Legal academics have responded by engaging in narrow "advocacy" studies that do not venture much beyond case analysis. A great deal of energy and space is devoted to identifying, defining, organizing, and criticizing legal rules. This process of "rationalization" takes place internally (that is, with the aim of contrusting a coherent system of doctrine) or externally (by reference to external social or economic goals). There is a minor element within this type of unambitious research for policy presciptions or for moderate and modest reform recommendations. On Tushnet's survey of U.S. law reviews, conventional research designed to satisfy these pragmatic needs constitutes the majority of the work published.

Where legal scholars have augmented their scholarly methods with concepts or techniques drawn from other disciplines, the point has been to try to show the normative foundations of legal rules. Arguably, legal reasoning becomes parasitic on some other form of rationality, such as economic analysis or moral philosophy. This approach denies the autonomy of law as a peculiar field of knowledge, and to that extent makes legal scholarship appear secondary, since the guiding principles are found in non-legal materials.

A third cause for the marginal status of legal scholarship has been its relative lack of controversy over the liberal premises that form the foundation to legal doctrine and legal theory. The liberal conception of the rule of law disguises legal rules as objective or neutral. Even though legal realists had long before exposed the partiality of legal reasoning, the overwhelming preponderance of legal scholarship (at least, before critical legal studies came along) operated as if legal rules had a determinative content, cases could be correctly decided, and judges were neutral arbiters, more or less.

Critical legal writing has self-consciously departed from these assumptions. Various critiques have challenged the "formalistic" understanding of law as a neutral enterprise (or even an alleged science), pointed out the incoherence and indeterminacy of legal doctrine, and the naturalness of traditional legal categories. The division of human experience into legal categories such as contract, tort, or criminal behavior is, according to some critics, a social construction which, because of its contingency, can be broken down, examined, and rearranged.

Various critics have offered new methodologies for practising legal scholarship. Indeed, the issue of how theory relates to practice has been a topic itself subjected to critical scrutiny. Some critical scholarship seems to have been inspired by continental forms of critical theory, in which the analysis aimed at exposing the antinomies of liberal and Enlightenment thought, especially as these are manifest in the law. There has been little explicit writing about the precise relationship between critical legal studies and Frankfurt School thinking, whether in its historical or contemporary phases. At best, some writers such as David Kennedy have alluded to some features that might usefully be compared in studying the relationship between dialectical projects of various types. His discussion falls short of genetically linking critical legal studies with other forms of dialectical critique. Not much notice has been taken either, at least in U.S. critical writing, of the contemporary legal theories of such figures as Gunther Teubner or Niklas Luhmann. Critical legal discussion in the U.K. has been more in tune with other European intellectual developments.

Other writers, especially in samples of critical legal work from the 1970s and 80s, followed a structuralist trend. Under this inspiration, for example, Duncan Kennedy's work on the structured consciousness or typical belief systems associated with various historical periods or contexts has been an influential model of critique. Among the tasks of critical writers has been to expose these configurations of consciousness in legal assumptions and argument. By showing the modes in which these structures frame our understanding and rigidify our thinking, the first step in achieving some relief from these structures has been made. Genuine liberation requires keeping a self-critical stance towards even these ideological insights.

Critical legal scholarship appears to have been aimed largely at an audience composed of other legal scholars or students. Some of it is framed in complex and technical language, though it is arguable whether it is really any less accessible to the lay reader than more conventional legal writing. Many of the political purposes of critical legal authors seems to have been displaced onto the law schools themselves. There are suggestions that a readership for critical work exists among progressive lawyers of the left, though some radical critics dispute even this characterization of which audience critical scholarship is supposed to serve.

Partly because so much early critical writing seemed to deal on an abstract plane about ideology and consciousness, there has been a noticeable (and possibly countervailing) shift in later scholarship toward "contextualizing" the ways in which law sustains oppression and injustice. Critical writing in an experiential mode, that speaks personally or autobiographically about how the law actually affects individual lives and communities, has become common, due in part no doubt to the influence of feminism and critical race discourse. There are continuing debates among legal scholars over what counts as authenticity in this context and how these new forms of scholarship fit in with traditional views about what constitutes legal research. The very idea of treating novel forms of scholarship as "alternative" (that is, outside the mainstream) raises its own problems, especially from the perspective of those scholars belonging to a group that traditionally has been excluded from power and from the legal academy.

Finally, critical legal approaches to legal scholarship have used methods and perspectives derived from poststructuralism and postmodernism. Under this influence, the very characerization of law as a form of knowledge that can be subject to its own discipline has been challenged. Poststructuralists also criticize legal theories that depend on assumptions about authorial intention or authoritative meaning. Deconstruction, as one form of these contemporary methods, leads to doubts about the usefulness of traditional theoretical projects. Instead, there has been a good deal of deconstuctive energy devoted to uncovering the construction and reproduction of law through texts. The point here is not to resolve traditional questions, but to query the form in which those issues are framed and also to uncover what is excluded from attempts to provide answers. This kind of analysis reads texts "at the margins." With deconstructive goals in mind, there is less interest than in earlier critical writing in building a definitive social theory or arriving at a correct textual interpretation. Instead, the analysis relies on a close reading of texts (comparing them minutely with other texts), in an effort to unsettle the "privileged" interpretations that have been inherited or imposed.

* * * *

AUSTIN, Arthur, "Deconstructing Voice Scholarship" (1993) 30 Hous. L. Rev. 1671-84

BARKAN, Steven M., "Deconstructing Legal Research: A Law Librarian's Commentary on Critical Legal Studies" (1987) 79 L. Libr. J. 617-37

BARKAN, Steven M., "Response to Schanck: On the Need for Critical Law Librarianship, Or Are We All Legal Realists Now?" (1990) 82 L. Libr. J. 23-35

BARNES, Robin D., "Scholarly Discourse" (1992) 16 Vt. L. Rev. 933-42

CARRASCO, Gilbert Paul, "Effecting Social Change Through Legal Scholarship" (1992) 10 St. Louis U. Pub. L. Rev. 161-67

CHASE, Anthony, "The Legal Scholar as Producer" (1988) 13 Nova L. Rev. 57-67

COHEN, Lloyd, "A Different Black Voice in Legal Scholarship" (1992) 37 N.Y. L. Sch. L. Rev. 301-23

CULP, Jerome M., Jr., "Autobiography and Legal Scholarship and Teaching: Finding the Me in Legal Academy" (1991) 77 Va. L. Rev. 539-59

CULP, Jerome M., Jr., "Firing Legal Canons and Shooting Blanks: Finding a Neutral Way in the Law" (1991) 10 St. Louis U. Pub. L. Rev. 185-95

DELGADO, Richard and **STEFANCIC**, Jean, "Why Do We All Tell the Same Stories? Law Reform, Critical Librarianship, and the Triple Helix Dilemma" (1989) 42 Stan. L. Rev. 207-35

ESPINOZA, Leslie, "Labeling Scholarship: Recognition or Barrier to Legitimacy" (1991) 10 St. Louis U. Pub. L. Rev. 197-206

ESPINOZA, Leslie G., "Masks and Other Disguises: Exposing Legal Academia" (1992) 103 Harv. L. Rev. 1878-86

FREEMAN, Alan, "Truth and Mystification in Legal Scholarship" (1981) 90 Yale L. J. 1229-37

GABEL, Peter and **KENNEDY**, Duncan, "Roll Over Beethoven" (1984) 36 Stan. L. Rev. 1-55

GORDON, Robert W., "Historicism in Legal Scholarship" (1981) 90 Yale L. J. 1017-56

JOHNSON, Alex M., Jr., "Scholarly Paradigms: A New Tradition Based on Context and Color" (1992) 16 Vt. L. Rev. 913-32

KELMAN, Mark, "The Past and Future of Legal Scholarship" (1983) 33 J. Legal Educ. 432-36

KELMAN, Mark, "Trashing" (1984) 36 Stan. L. Rev. 293-348

KENNEDY, David, "Critical Theory, Structuralism, and Contemporary Legal Scholarship" (1985-86) 21 New Eng. L. Rev. 209-89

KENNEDY, David, "Primitive Legal Scholarship" (1986) 27 Harv. Int'l L. J. 1-98

MATSUDA, Mari J., "Affirmative Action and Legal Knowledge: Planting Seeds in Plowed-Up Ground" (1988) 11 Harv. Wom. L. J. 1-17

SCHANCK, Peter C., "Taking Up Barkan's Challenge: Looking at the Judicial Process and Legal Research" (1990) 82 L. Libr. J. 1-22

SCHLEGEL, John Henry, "American Legal Realism and Empirical Social Science: From the Yale Experience" (1979) 28 Buffalo L. Rev. 459-586

SCHLEGEL, John Henry, "American Legal Realism and Empirical Social Science: The Singular Case of Underhill Moore" (1980) 29 Buffalo L. Rev. 195-328

SMITH, J. Clay, Jr., "Exceptional Differences in Scholarly Paradigms and Scholarly Trends" (1992) 10 St. Louis U. Pub. L. Rev. 207-29

SOIFER, Aviam, "MuSings" (1987) 37 J. Legal Educ. 20-27

STRICKLAND, Rennard, "Scholarship in the Academic Circus or the Balancing Act at the Minority Side Show" (1986) 20 U.S.F. L. Rev. 491-502

TRUBEK, David and **GALANTER**, Marc, "Scholars in Self-Estrangement" [1974] Wis. L. Rev. 1062-1102

TUSHNET, Mark, "Legal Scholarship in the United States: An Overview" (1987) 50 Mod. L. Rev. 804-17

TUSHNET, Mark, "Legal Scholarship: Its Causes and Cure" (1981) 90 Yale L. J. 1205-23

TUSHNET, Mark, "Political Correctness, the Law, and the Legal Academy" (1992) 4 Yale J. L. & Hum. 127-63

TUSHNET, Mark, "Post-Realist Legal Scholarship" [1980] Wis. L. Rev. 1383-1401

WISE, Virginia, "Of Lizards, Intersubjective Zap, and Trashing: Critical Legal Studies and the Librarian" (1988) 8 Legal References Services Q. 7-27

32

Critiques of Critical Legal Studies

The agitational character of much critical legal writing has provoked a significant body of agitated responses. A number of critiques have assessed the assumptions, the methods, and the aims of the radical project itself. Some of the responses have sought to defend or redeem legal liberalism against the charges brought by its critics. The debates have sometimes turned polemical, especially where the opponents of a critical legal approach have denounced it as a "mechanical polemic" in its own right.

Among the issues over which the radical movment has been challenged are the following. Opponents have argued that critical legal writers generally miscast liberalism as involving commitments to philosophical premises to which no modern, sophisticated liberal theorists actually adhere. So, for example, the simplistic idea that liberalism relies on the values of individualism and egoism fails to do justice to the social and historical contexts in which liberal theorists have made claims about self-interest and the role of the state. There are, according to detractors of critical legal studies such as Don Herzog, richer versions of liberal political philosophy which critical legal writers ignore. Instead, they tend too often to offer a caricature of liberal commitments. In Herzog's view, critical legal writing is deficient in that it attacks liberalism against a background of metaphysical, psychological, epistemological, and ethical philosophizing. But it signally fails to engage liberal thinking directly on the matter of its political principles and practices. Any discussion of this type is second-best, since it is filtered through the critique of legal doctrine, where traces of liberalism are allegedly embedded.

Another ground on which critical legal analysis has been disputed is the relationship between liberalism and the contingency of social and economic life. Radical critiques have tended to attribute to liberalism the view that capitalistic structures such as the market and the commodification of goods are inherently liberal constructions. This has been challenged as a misunderstanding of the theoretical and historical connections between liberal theories and the evolution of economic ideas. Not all liberals are committed to one or other version of capitalism.

Opponents have also questioned critical representations of the ideal of law as an autonomous and coherent system. The critical legal attacks on "formalism" have not convinced other legal scholars who claim to have recognized the subtle political context in which judicial decisionmaking takes place. In Ronald Dworkin's view, this theme has been "emphasized more quietly" for many decades in U.S. jurisprudence.

One strand of critical thinking that has invited strong reactions, not only from outside the movement, but from within critical legal studies itself, is the tendency towards "irrationalism" or "nihilism." Several critical legal authors have made sweeping, skeptical claims about the lack of shared standards of rationality or about the impossibility of deriving an authoritative meaning from standard legal texts such as statutes or precedents. This nihilist tag has occasionally been self-avowed, as well as applied scathingly by the movement's opponents. Among those objecting to this tendency has been Roberto Unger, who dismisses the total skepticism offered by some fellow critics, in part because his positive program requires some degree of legal determinacy in order to make social change effective. Other critiques of nihilism originate from opponents of critical legal studies who doubt whether radical critics have succeeded in justifying this skeptical perspective. Donald Brosnan, for example, has claimed that critical theorists have had to borrow their perspectives from outside the law. In his estimation, critical treatments have often "misused" much of the philosophy, such as Richard Rorty's pragmatism, which they have tried to apply in their own scholarship.

Another issue that commonly sparks challenges to critical legal analysis is the significance of "indeterminacy" in the law. Opponents have drawn different inferences from the presence of some contradictory (often dualistic) rules within legal doctrine. First, these are not necessarily entailed by legal liberalism: some opponents of critical legal thinking view these inconsistencies as arising from the predicament of individuals living in a society, regardless of whether that society frames its legal order according to a liberal model. Second, some opponents deny that many of the contradictions raised by critical analysis actually inform legal reasoning to the extent claimed in the critiques. Third, critical authors have been challenged for failing to show how mere exposure of these contradictions is supposed to lead to a better social order. The invocations by critical legal authors of "participatory democracy," "conversation," or "equality" have struck some of the movement's opponents as unsatisfyingly threadbare proposals for social change. A few opponents have gone so far as to see in the radical strategy threatening and ominous political consequences, involving a license to substitute possibly new and worse forms of domination. This specter seems to worry those opponents most who feel that the self-proclaimed virtue of political disarray within the critical legal studies movement is really a defect and a refusal to engage in concrete political action. On this view, critical writing is politically passive and inordinately devoted to metaphysical abstraction.

One aspect of critical legal work that is a frequent cause for complaint among its opponents is the lack of clear, practical lessons that derive from the critique. After the legal doctrine in question has been deconstructed and demystified, several commentators on critical analysis have registered their dissatisfaction with the relatively small amount of space given over to the implications of the critique in terms of altering or improving decisionmaking or larger institutional redesign.

* * * *

ADDIS, Adeno, "Critical Legal Studies and the Issue of Constructive Alternatives" (1988) 34 Loy. L. Rev. 277-86

ALTMAN, Andrew, *Critical Legal Studies: A Liberal Critique* (Princeton: Princeton University Press, 1990)

BALKIN, J. M., Review of Andrew Altman, *Critical Legal Studies: A Liberal Critique* (1991) 43 Stan. L. Rev. 1133-69

BATOR, Paul, "Legal Methodology and the Academy" (1985) 8 Harv. J. L. & Pub. Pol'y 335-39

BAUMAN, Richard W., "The Communitarian Vision of Critical Legal Studies" (1988) 33 McGill L. J. 295-356

BECK, Randy, "The Faith of the 'Crits': Critical Legal Studies and Human Nature" (1988) 11 Harv. J. L. & Pub. Pol'y 433-59

BELLIOTTI, Raymond A., "Critical Legal Studies — The Paradoxes of Indeterminacy and Critique" (1987) 13(2) Phil. & Soc. Criticism 145-55

BELLIOTTI, Raymond A., "Is Law a Sham?" (1987) 48 Phil. & Phenom. Res. 25-44

BEYLEVELD, Derek and **BROWNSWORD**, Roger, "Critical Legal Studies" (1984) 47 Mod. L. Rev. 359-69

BICKENBACH, Jerome E., "CLS and CLS-ers" (1984) 9 Queen's L. J. 263-72

BINDER, Guyora, "Beyond Criticism" (1988) 55 U. Chi. L. Rev. 888-915

BINDER, Guyora, "On Critical Legal Studies as Guerrilla Warfare" (1987) 76 Geo. L. J. 1-36

BINDER, Guyora, "What's Left?" (1991) 69 Tex. L. Rev. 1985-2041

BORK, Robert, "Battle for the Law Schools" (Sept. 26, 1986) The National Rev. 44

BORK, Robert H., *The Tempting of America: The Political Seduction of the Law* (New York: Free Press, 1990)

BROSNAN, Donald F., "Serious But Not Critical" (1987) 60 S. Cal. L. Rev. 259-396

BURTON, Stephen J., "Reaffirming Legal Reasoning: The Challenge from the Left" (1986) 36 J. Legal Educ. 358-70

CARRINGTON, Paul, "Of Law and the River" (1984) 34 J. Legal Educ. 222-28

CHOW, Daniel C. K., "Trashing Nihilism" (1990) 65 Tul. L. Rev. 221-98

CLARK, Robert C., "The Return of Langdell" (1985) 8 Harv. J. L. & Pub. Pol'y 299-308

COLEMAN, Jules L. and **LEITER**, Brian, "Determinacy, Objectivity, and Authority" (1993) 142 U. Pa. L. Rev. 549-637

COOMBE, Rosemary J., "Room for Manoeuver: Toward a Theory of Practice in Critical Legal Studies" (1989) 14 L. & Soc. Inquiry 69-121

D'AMATO, Anthony, "Aspects of Deconstruction: Refuting Indeterminacy With One Bold Thought" (1990) 85 Nw. U. L. Rev. 113-18

DWORKIN, Ronald, *Law's Empire* (Cambridge, Mass.: Harvard University Press, 1986) 271-75

FAIRLEY, H. Scott, "Is Critique All There Is?" (1989) 11 Sup. Ct. L. Rev. 481-95

FARBER, Daniel, "Down By Law" [review of Mark Kelman, *A Guide to Critical Legal Studies*] (January 4 & 11, 1988) New Republic 36-40

FARBER, Daniel, "The Outmoded Debate Over Affirmative Action" (1994) 82 Cal. L. Rev. 893-934

FINNIS, John, "On 'The Critical Legal Studies Movement'" (1985) 30 Am. J. Juris. 21-42

FISCHL, Richard Michael, "The Question That Killed Critical Legal Studies" [review of Mark Kelman, *A Guide to Critical Legal Studies*] (1992) 17 L. & Soc. Inquiry 779-820

FISCHL, Richard Michael, "Some Realism About Critical Legal Studies" (1987) U. Mia. L. Rev. 505-32

FISH, Stanley, "Anti-Professionalism" (1986) 7 Cardozo L. Rev. 645-77 [reprinted in *Doing What Comes Naturally: Change, Rhetoric, and the Practice of Theory in Literary and Legal Studies* (Durham: Duke University Press, 1989) 215-46]

FISH, Stanley, "Dennis Martinez and the Uses of Theory" (1987) 96 Yale L. J. 1773-800 [reprinted in *Doing What Comes Naturally: Change, Rhetoric, and the Practice of Theory in Literary and Legal Studies* (Durham: Duke University Press, 1989) 372-98

FISS, Owen, "The Death of the Law?" (1986) 72 Cornell L. Rev. 1-16

FORBATH, William, "Taking Lefts Seriously" [review of David Kairys (ed.), *The Politics of Law: A Progressive Critique*] (1983) 92 Yale L. J. 1041-64

FRAZER, Elizabeth and **LACEY**, Nicola, *The Politics of Community: A Feminist Critique of the Liberal-Communitarian Debate* (Hemel Hempstead: Harvester, 1993)

GALLOWAY, Donald, "Critical Mistakes" in Richard F. Devlin (ed.), *Canadian Perspectives on Legal Theory* (Toronto: Emond Montgomery, 1991) 255-68

GALLOWAY, Donald, "No Guru, No Method . . . (A Critique of Allan Hutchinson's *Dwelling on the Threshold*)" (1988) 8 Windsor Y.B. Acc. Just. 304-17

GENOVESE, Eugene D., "Critical Legal Studies as Radical Politics and World View" [review of Mark Kelman, *A Guide to Critical Legal Studies*] (1991) 3 Yale J. L. & Hum. 131-56

GEORGE, Lawrence C., "Asking the Right Questions" (1987) 15 Fla. St. U. L. Rev. 447-75

GEY, Steven G., "The Unfortunate Revival of Civic Republicanism" (1993) 141 U. Pa. L. Rev. 801-98

GOEBEL, John P., "Rules and Standards: A Critique of Two Critical Theorists" (1992) 31 Duquesne L. Rev. 51-86

HEGLAND, Kenney, "Goodbye to Deconstruction" (1985) S. Cal. L. Rev. 1203-21

HERZOG, Don, "As Many as Six Impossible Things Before Breakfast" (1987) 75 Cal. L. Rev. 609-30

HOLLAND, Maurice J., "A Hurried Perspective on the Critical Studies Movement: The Marx Brothers Assault the Citadel" (1985) 8 Harv. J. L. & Pub. Pol'y 239-47

HUNT, Alan, "The Theory of Critical Legal Studies" (1986) 6 Oxford J. Legal Stud. 1-45

JOHNSON, Phillip E., "Do You Sincerely Want To Be Radical?" (1984) 36 Stan. L. Rev. 247-91

KRISTOL, William, "On the Utility of Critical Legal Studies" (1985) 8 Harv. J. L. & Pub. Pol'y 327-34

KRYGIER, Martin, "Critical Legal Studies and Social Theory — A Response to Alan Hunt" (1987) 7 Oxford J. Legal Stud. 26-39

LANGILLE, Brian, "Political World" (1990) 2 Can. J. L. & Juris. 139-53

LANGILLE, Brian, "Revolution Without Foundation: The Grammar of Skepticism and Law" (1988) 33 McGill L. J. 451-505

LEITER, Brian, "Intellectual Voyeurism in Legal Scholarship" (1992) 4 Yale J. L. & Hum. 79-104

LEWIS, Harold S., Jr., "The Unbalanced Critical Legal Scholars and Their Overbalanced Critics" (1989) 40 Mercer L. Rev. 913-35

LICHTERMAN, Andrew M., "Social Movements and Legal Elites: Some Notes from the Margin on The Politics of Law: A Progressive Critique" [1984] Wis. L. Rev. 1035-67

MacCORMICK, Neil, "Reconstruction After Deconstruction: A Response to Critical Legal Studies" (1990) 10 Oxford J. Legal Stud. 539-58

MACKLEM, Patrick, "Of Texts and Democratic Narratives" [review of Allan C. Hutchinson, *Dwelling on the Threshold*] (1991) 41 U. Toronto L. J. 114-45

MARKOVITS, Richard S., "Duncan's Do Nots: Cost-Benefit Analysis and the Determination of Legal Entitlements" (1984) 36 Stan. L. Rev. 1169-98

MASNER, Charles, "Understanding Postmodern Thought and the Deconstruction and Reconstruction of Freedom" (1992) 23 Rutgers L. J. 475-518

MASSEY, Calvin R., "Law's Inferno" [review of Mark Kelman, *A Guide to Critical Legal Studies*] (1988) 39 Hast. L. J. 1269-95

MEYERSON, Denise, "Fundamental Contradictions in Critical Legal Studies" (1991) 11 Oxford J. Legal Stud. 439-51

MORAWETZ, Thomas, "Understanding Disagreement, the Root Issue of Jurisprudence: Applying Wittgenstein to Positivism, Critical Theory, and Judging" (1992) 141 U. Pa. L. Rev. 371-456

MUNGER, Frank and **SERON**, Carroll, "Critical Legal Studies versus Critical Legal Theory: A Comment on Method" (1984) 6 L. & Policy 257-97

O'BYRNE, Shannon, "Legal Criticism as Storytelling" (1991) 23 Ottawa L. Rev. 487-503

POSNER, Richard A., "Duncan Kennedy on Affirmative Action" [1990] Duke L. J. 1157-62

POSNER, Richard A., "Jurisprudence and Skepticism" (1988) 86 Mich. L. Rev. 827-91

POSNER, Richard A., "The Present Situation in Legal Scholarship" (1981) 90 Yale L. J. 1113-30

PRICE, David Andrew, "Taking Rights Cynically: A Review of Critical Legal Studies" (1989) 48 Cambridge L. J. 271-301

RUBIN, Alvin, "Does Law Matter? A Judge's Response to the Critical Legal Studies Movement" (1987) 37 J. Legal Educ. 307-14

RUBIN, Alvin J., "Judges and the Critical Legal Studies Movement" (1987) 18 Syllabus 6(1)

SCHWARTZ, Bernard, "Critical Legal Studies: Academic Nihilism" in *Main Currents in American Legal Thought* (Durham: Carolina Academic Press, 1993) 604-13

SCHWARTZ, Gary T., "Tort Law and the Economy in Nineteenth-Century America: A Reinterpretation" (1981) 90 Yale L. J. 1717-75

SCHWARTZ, Louis B., "With Gun and Camera Through Darkest CLS-Land" (1984) 36 Stan. L. Rev. 413-64

SELZNICK, Philip, "The Idea of a Communitarian Morality" (1987) 75 Cal. L. Rev. 445-63

SHUPACK, Paul M., "Rules and Standards in Kennedy's *Form and Substance*" (1985) 6 Cardozo L. Rev. 947-69

SIMPSON, A. W. B., "The Horwitz Thesis and the History of Contracts" (1979) 46 U. Chi. L. Rev. 533-601

SOLUM, Lawrence B., "On the Indeterminacy Crisis: Critiquing Critical Dogma" (1987) 54 U. Chi. L. Rev. 462-503

SPARER, Edward, "Fundamental Human Rights, Legal Entitlements, and the Social Struggle: A Friendly Critique of the Critical Legal Studies Movement" (1984) 36 Stan. L. Rev. 509-74

STEIN, Alex, "Defending Liberal Law: A Review Essay" (1993) 22 Anglo-Am. L. Rev. 194-220

STICK, John, "Can Nihilism Be Pragmatic?" (1986) 100 Harv. L. Rev. 332-401

STICK, John, "Charting the Development of Critical Legal Studies" [review of Mark Kelman, *A Guide to Critical Legal Studies*] (1988) 88 Colum. L. Rev. 407-32

WALZER, Michael, "The Communitarian Critique of Liberalism" (1990) 18 Pol. Theory 6-23

WEST, Cornel, *Keeping Faith: Philosophy and Race in America* (New York: Routledge, 1993) 195-247

WEST, Cornel, "Reassessing the Critical Legal Studies Movement" (1988) 34 Loy. L. Rev. 265-75

WHITE, G. Edward, "The Inevitability of Critical Legal Studies" (1984) 36 Stan. L. Rev. 649-72

WHITE, G. Edward, "Reflections on the 'Republican Revival': Interdisplinary Scholarship in the Legal Academy" (1994) 6 Yale J. L. & Hum. 1-35

WHITE, G. Edward, "The Studied Ambiguity of Horwitz's Legal History" (1987) 29 Wm. & Mary L. Rev. 101-12

WILLIAMS, Daniel, "Law, Deconstruction and Resistance: The Critical Stances of Derrida and Foucault" (1988) 6 Cardozo Arts & Entertainment L. J. 359-410

WILLIAMS, Joan C., "Critical Legal Studies: The Death of Transcendence and the Rise of the New Langdells" (1987) 62 N.Y.U. L. Rev. 429-96

WILLIAMS, Stephen F., "Transforming American Law: Doubtful Economics Make Doubtful History" (1978) 25 U.C.L.A. L. Rev. 1187-218

WINTER, Steven L., "Bull Durham and the Uses of Theory" (1990) 42 Stan. L. Rev. 639-93

WOLFE, Christopher, "Grand Theories and Ambiguous Republican Critique: Tushnet on Constitutional Law" [review of Mark Tushnet, *Red, White and Blue*] (1990) 15 L. & Soc. Inquiry 831-76

WONNELL, Christopher T., "Problems in the Application of Political Philosophy to Law" (1987) 86 Mich. L. Rev. 123-55

YABLON, Charles M., "The Indeterminacy of the Law: Critical Legal Studies and the Problem of Legal Explanation" (1985) 6 Cardozo L. Rev. 917-45

Index

About the Book and Author

Contemporary legal thought has been powerfully influenced by critical legal studies, a school of legal scholars whose work has sustained a continuing radical critique of established legal doctrines. In this essential reference work, Richard Bauman presents the most thorough, up-to-date guide available for this essential literature.

In addition to providing the basic bibliographic information, Bauman offers a set of effective introductions to contextualize and explain the work being surveyed. He has created a fundamental handbook not only for the law but also for politics and radical thought.

Richard W. Bauman is associate professor of law at the University of Alberta.